Completing Your
Qualitative
Dissertation

Julia Esther Lippert (1906–1997)
Carmella Volpe (1908–1977)
Two remarkable women,
who at different times and in different places,
through their wisdom,
impacted our lives and instilled in us a love of learning.
Their spirits live on.

Completing Your Qualitative Dissertation

A Roadmap From Beginning to End

Linda Dale Bloomberg
Marie Volpe
Teachers College, Columbia University

SAGE Publications
Los Angeles • London • New Delhi • Singapore

For information:

Sage Publications, Inc.
2455 Teller Road
Thousand Oaks, California 91320
E-mail: order@sagepub.com

Sage Publications Ltd.
1 Oliver's Yard
55 City Road
London EC1Y 1SP
United Kingdom

Sage Publications India Pvt. Ltd.
B 1/I 1 Mohan Cooperative Industrial Area
Mathura Road, New Delhi 110 044
India

Sage Publications Asia-Pacific Pte. Ltd.
33 Pekin Street #02-01
Far East Square
Singapore 048763

Printed in the United States of America

Library of Congress Cataloging-in-Publication Data

Bloomberg, Linda Dale.
Completing your qualitative dissertation : a roadmap from beginning to end / Linda Dale Bloomberg, Marie Volpe.
p. cm.
Includes bibliographical references and index.
ISBN 978-1-4129-5650-5 (cloth)
ISBN 978-1-4129-5651-2 (pbk.)

1. Qualitative research. 2. Dissertations, Academic. I. Volpe, Marie. II. Title.

H62.B58555 2008
808'.02—dc22   2007036404

This book is printed on acid-free paper.

09   10   11   12   10   9   8   7   6   5   4   3   2

Acquisitions Editor:	Vicki Knight
Associate Editor:	Sean Connelly
Editorial Assistant:	Lauren Habib
Production Editor:	Kristen Gibson
Copy Editor:	Heather Jefferson
Typesetter:	C&M Digitals (P) Ltd.
Proofreader:	Sally Scott
Indexer:	Jean Casalegno
Cover Designer:	Janet Foulger
Marketing Manager:	Stephanie Adams

Contents

List of Tables

List of Figures

List of Appendices

Foreword

This book was created from and through the experiences of the authors and the many doctoral students who have taken the journey of qualitative research with them that earned students both a degree and the confidence that comes from knowing one can successfully conduct a high-quality research project. Included in this book are also the voices of 20 students from doctoral programs at eight universities—Columbia University, Wayne State University, University of Massachusetts, University of Georgia, University of Southern California, University of Michigan, Rutgers University, and Northwestern University—who participated in a research study designed to ground the advice provided in this book.

The insights and guidance contained herein have further been honed and tested through many combined years of dissertation advisement and successful doctoral defenses. As a result, the authors—who have walked in the shoes of the readers—offer reality-based advice about how to organize one's work and life to master the completion of a qualitative research project that leads to a doctoral degree.

Other books have been written to reach this goal. Many of them are complementary to this guide. Each differs based on the authors' background and experience with qualitative research and on the purpose for reaching out to students on this journey. The advice provided here is unique to the strengths of the authors, but it also speaks to general principles and ways of working with qualitative data. Everyone might not approach the research project in exactly this way . . . and that does not mean that either this way or other ways is right or wrong. There are many paths in qualitative research. As the authors emphasize throughout, one size does not fit all. Qualitative research projects are organic and vary in design and execution based on their underlying research philosophy—although they share some principles in common.

Some readers will follow this guide closely, step by step. Others may use some ideas, but not others. All, I am sure, will find help that makes their research easier or more effective. What will the reader gain from using this book? There are benefits for both the head and the heart.

First, there is sound step-by-step advice about the process. The authors' goal is not to lead the reader unthinkingly through a recipe or "quick fix." Instead, the authors offer templates that demystify the process of undertaking qualitative research. Dissertation sponsors may not see what novice researchers need or may not understand because the sponsor's advice grows out of a complete picture of what good research looks like that has been shaped over the years. Their advice is intended as a series of dots that, once connected, are meant to represent that picture of good research. But the advice provided by the sponsor may not convey the same meaning to the novice researcher, who could see many unconnected dots on a page, rather than the completed picture to which the dots are meant to lead.

This book makes explicit the thinking behind the dissertation process that may not be readily apparent to novice researchers because they have not yet "been there, done that." This trip is likely the novice researcher's first, whereas the journey has been taken many times by the sponsor. To help the novice researcher, years of collective experience have been encoded into roadmaps that will help the neophyte travel the research road with greater ease and speed, and thus learn—through support for doing—why and how each research step should be undertaken. The authors focus on what is common about finding and articulating a clear research problem, purpose, and questions; laying out a research design that will lead to gathering the right kind of data and support the right kind of analysis to answer the research questions; and writing up and defending the study.

These topics are covered in other books as well. A differentiating feature is that this book is based, in part, on interviews with doctoral students about what helped and hindered them in carrying out their own studies. This research is used to illustrate each chapter that explains the research process, from proposal writing (including literature review) through presentation and analysis of findings, drawing of conclusions, and providing recommendations. Students can relate to this example because it will tap into their own experiences—whether alike or different—and thus make it easier to follow the example throughout all phases of the research.

Unlike some books that focus primarily on research design and execution, the authors also offer valuable insights into what goes on before and after preparing and defending the study. For example, they offer advice for thinking about how to choose the right dissertation sponsor, how to avoid morale traps such as isolation and getting stuck, how to organize one's work practices and processes from the beginning to support dissertation work, how to prepare for the defense, and how to make changes and finish up after the defense has taken place.

In writing this book, the authors provide for the heart as well as the head. The authors take the reader by the hand, and they also offer a shoulder for support and empathy at every step of the way. Writing a dissertation can feel like climbing a mountain while wearing blinders. Throughout this book, they offer practical advice to guide one up the mountain without fatal flaws and time-consuming setbacks. They suggest ways to mitigate and handle the stress that dissertation writing can entail. Their advice is intended to make the study rigorous and to help students complete the study in a timely manner, with as little unnecessary trauma as possible.

So I invite readers to savor this book and use what helps them among the gold nuggets offered to support the dissertation journey. One's dissertation sponsor is always one's primary guide. But this book—and supplemental readings annotated in each chapter—can add insight couched in the voice of others who have trod this path before. The resource material in the appendices offers additional rich examples, many drawing on the data from the study the authors conducted with students traveling this same research path.

In closing, I add a personal note. I have worked for many years in partnership with Dr. Volpe to support the dissertation journey of students in our doctoral programs. We have served together as a team, sometimes in the role of sponsor and sometimes as second or third reader. I have recently begun a similar partnership with Dr. Bloomberg. Countless students have told me how they value the advice and support that both of these authors give to them. Fewer tell me directly that they rely on these authors to "translate" what they learn through conversations with me and other faculty who teach their research courses, but I know for a fact they do. Students value the soundness of their advice, offered in language and terms the students can understand. They value the morale-boosting energy and tips for how to make the journey easier, shorter, less painful, and more fun. I lift my hat to these two authors . . . and imagine that you will too after reading and using ideas from this book in your own journey.

—Victoria J. Marsick, PhD
Professor of Adult and Organizational Learning
Teachers College, Columbia University

Preface

WHO SHOULD READ THIS BOOK?

This book is a dissertation in action; an explanation and illustration of content and process. It is geared primarily for doctoral students in the social sciences (education, psychology, sociology, social work, nursing, community development, management, etc.) who are about to embark on or who are already conducting a qualitative research study. This book is for you if:

- You are contemplating entering a doctoral program and want to know more about what lies ahead in terms of conducting research and writing a dissertation.
- You are enrolled in a doctoral program; having difficulty identifying a sound, researchable topic; and hence are unable to develop your dissertation proposal.
- You have completed all the course requirements and are about to begin the research but are unsure of how and where to get started.
- You are stuck in some part of the research process and are unable to make progress toward completion of your dissertation.
- You have just about abandoned the idea of ever completing your dissertation for whatever reason.

During most doctoral programs, there is a heavy emphasis on the theoretical concepts that form the basis of research. Having completed all the required research courses, as well as having passed a certification examination, there is an expectation that doctoral students have mastered the various aspects of research design and methodology. However, once students are "out on their own" to complete their dissertations, they are often unclear about appropriate style, content, and/or procedures and are uncertain as to how to proceed. As a result, every university and college has a significant number of what are commonly referred to as All-But-Dissertation (ABD) students, those who never manage to complete the dissertation—the culminating product needed to fulfill the requirements to graduate with a doctorate. If you suspect that you might fall into this category, then read on.

We have witnessed and experienced many of the frustrations voiced by students confronted with the academic challenge of writing a dissertation. How do I select a suitable topic? How do I narrow and focus an idea? What exactly is a research problem? How do I go about formulating a research purpose? How and in what ways do the research questions relate to the study's overall purpose? How do I conduct a literature review? How do I manage and analyze my data? In response to these and other challenges, we have developed what we call "roadmaps" for understanding the content of the dissertation and navigating through the iterative, recursive, and often messy dissertation process, from its inception to its ultimate successful completion.

Completing a dissertation is fraught with many challenges, both personal and professional. These challenges often lead to a sense of confusion and feelings of inadequacy, incompetence, and frustration. Overwhelming feelings such as these can often spiral to despondency and apathy. It is at this level that many of the students with whom we spoke find themselves. Faced with life's demands and compounded with the stresses of academic rigor, students often bow out, putting aside their dissertations, sometimes forever.

This book represents our combined efforts to facilitate an understanding of the dissertation process so that the student feels confident and competent in successfully pursuing its completion. Our experience has been shaped by our work with our own students through the dissertation advisement process. We have been fortunate to draw on and benefit from the feedback and insight of colleagues and students who saw the value of a book such as this.

One challenge in compiling a book of this nature is to acknowledge that institutional requirements vary. There is no universally agreed-on format, and each school has its unique structural regulations regarding the dissertation. Moreover, each academic program differs, and in fact even each advisor or sponsor usually has her or his own requirements as well. Although dissertations can vary in form and length, depending on the institution, they do share basic components. All dissertations must have an introduction, review of the relevant literature, review of methodology, presentation of findings, presentation of analysis and interpretation, and presentation of conclusions and recommendations. In this book, although we address each of these components comprehensively as separate chapters, we are aware that in some institutions or programs some of these components might be combined in the same chapter. As such, readers should always adhere to the guidelines set by their own institutions and be mindful of the preferences of their own advisors.

THE PURPOSE OF THIS BOOK

Logical and systematic thinking is necessary to successfully complete a qualitative dissertation. Completing the dissertation will depend on your ability to successfully master both the content and the process. Aside from offering clear guidelines as to the necessary content, the intent of this book is to shed light on structure and style, thereby making the dissertation process organized and manageable. The purpose of the book is to assist you at whatever stage you find yourself. You might be right at the beginning of the process, unable to select a topic that is interesting and/or researchable. You might already have a topic but are unsure of how to focus it narrowly and articulate a researchable problem. You might have covered a lot of ground already, even having collected and analyzed some of your data, but are feeling stuck, lost, or adrift. Writing a dissertation is a process, but not one that is neat and linear. Our intent is to help you better understand the various elements involved in the qualitative dissertation process and be able to address these elements appropriately and effectively.

Our hope, and the motivation behind this book, is that we make the process of conducting research and writing a dissertation more understandable and, hence, manageable. Moreover, our hope is that the process is a meaningful one for you. A dissertation is intended to be an academically rigorous process, the completion of which demonstrates that you are qualified to join a research community whose members carry the title "Dr." As we see it, a dissertation should not be viewed as a punishment. Rather, it is a unique opportunity to choose a topic of your own interest, to learn more about it, and to make a contribution to existing bodies of knowledge in your field. We understand the frustrations and difficulties involved in taking on a project of this magnitude. We understand the level of commitment required and the sacrifices that you have made to get to this point. We also understand how important it is for you to complete your dissertation so that you do not remain an ABD forever. Therefore, the goal of this book is that you are able to produce a dissertation, and so we offer this step-by-step guide from inception to completion. Our sincere hope is that this book helps you understand the process, embrace it, and succeed!

HOW THIS BOOK WORKS

In this book, we offer a series of roadmaps that are designed to help you steer your way through the various activities that constitute the process of writing a qualitative dissertation. At each juncture of the process, the roadmaps allow you to clarify your objectives, understand and tackle the task at hand, and check on what you have accomplished before you proceed to the next step.

In this book, we use an actual research problem, which is the problem that confronts you, the reader. You are reading this book because you have not yet managed to complete your dissertation. This same problem is the example that will be addressed as the basis of discussion throughout this book. This problem is referred to insofar as it relates to each step of the dissertation process, and as such you will see a common thread running throughout each of the chapters. We proceed from laying out and articulating the problem statement, through developing a research purpose and associated research questions. Based on the problem, we formulate appropriate data-collection methods, analyze and synthesize data, and present conclusions and recommendations. In effect, the problem that is used in this book provides a model for you in conducting and writing up your own dissertation.

Our approach throughout is to emphasize conceptual understanding as it relates to the practical aspects involved in navigating the dissertation process. As such, this approach bears some caution as it may be seen as an attempt to reduce the complexity and "messiness" of qualitative research by way of a series of simplified "how-to" offerings. Although our intent is to demystify the dissertation process, we do not sacrifice intellectual rigor for the sake of simplification. This book is not intended to be a quick-fix, nor do we offer an easy recipe for success. In our experience, completing a dissertation is a rigorous and demanding process. It is iterative, unpredictable, and nonlinear. However, with the development of a clearer understanding, sharpened competencies, and a set of resources to guide you, the dissertation is, in fact, doable.

As a second caveat, we remind the reader throughout that there are various institutional differences and requirements regarding the structure of a dissertation. As such, this book is meant to be a guide rather than a prescriptive one-fits-all approach. Although we do offer a general structure regarding the writing of a dissertation, we do not believe this structure will stifle students' creativity. Creativity comes into play through your own initiative in how you design your instruments, develop your conceptual frameworks and related coding schemes, present your findings, and analyze, interpret, and synthesize your data. Essentially, however, qualitative research must not be viewed as an exercise in creative writing when it is, in fact, an exercise in conducting a research project that is integrative and intellectually rigorous. Rigor and structure are necessary to account for subjectivity and keep creative speculation in check.

Readers of this book are at different stages of the dissertation process. Our advice is that you start off by finding your own entry point and, depending on where you are in the dissertation process, begin at the chapter that is most relevant to you. If you are just starting out on your research study, with no as yet clearly defined topic, you should start reading this book from the beginning. If you are further along in the research process, choose to focus on those chapters that are most relevant to your unfolding experience. We readily acknowledge that researchers never move in a linear fashion. Conducting research and writing a dissertation is not like strolling along a clearly marked path. Rather, it is a process that is iterative and recursive, looping back and forth, with many unanticipated events along the way. This book is intended, through its roadmaps, to walk you through that process and through the confusion.

ORGANIZATION OF THIS BOOK

This book is organized in three parts. We use Part I as the point of entry. Part I constitutes a broad introduction to the complex task of writing a dissertation and offers an overview of the steps involved in thinking about and preparing for the dissertation process. Included are discussions around becoming reenergized and surmounting self-doubt, getting organized, identifying and developing a researchable topic, choosing a research approach, selecting advisers, and developing the dissertation proposal. We also offer guidelines for good writing and identifying resources.

The chapters of Part II narrow and focus the scope of the discussion and direct the reader's attention to the discrete aspects involved in conceptualizing and addressing the research and writing process. Each of the chapters of Part II provides comprehensive instructions with respect to the content of a specific dissertation chapter. These instructions are accompanied by illustrations of what a completed chapter should look like by applying the specific research problem addressed in this book. Although the application section of each chapter represents a model of application, in a real dissertation, the discussion would need to be elaborated as required. Part II is organized in such a way as to reflect and describe the actual chapters of a dissertation.

Chapter 1 explores the foundational elements that are necessary in the first chapter of a dissertation. This includes how to formulate a researchable problem statement and the related purpose and research questions. Also covered are the additional components of the first chapter of a dissertation, such as researcher assumptions, anticipated outcomes, overview of approach, and clarification of terminology used.

Chapter 2 provides an outline of a dissertation literature review. Included is how to approach the literature review, rationale for selection of topics, what resources to utilize, and preparation of summaries based on review. This chapter concludes with a description of a conceptual framework, that is, a working tool that guides the entire research study.

Chapter 3 offers a guide for tackling chapter 3 of the dissertation, that is, the methodology chapter. Included are an overview of information needed, research design, proposed use of selected methods, literature on methods, ethical issues, reliability and validity, and identification of the limitations of the research.

Chapter 4 demonstrates how to write and present the findings of a research study. This chapter begins with a description of the various approaches to and the elements involved in the processes of organizing and analyzing data.

Chapter 5 explains how to analyze and interpret findings of the research. This chapter demonstrates how to integrate and synthesize the findings with the literature, and to present the meaning behind those findings, which is the essence of the research.

Chapter 6, the final chapter of Part II, presents the ways in which to address the last chapter of a dissertation: conclusions and recommendations. Included is an explanation of what conclusions are as distinct from findings and interpretations, as well as suggestions for developing sound conclusions and practical and research-based recommendations.

Part III addresses the final stage of the dissertation process. Here we offer advice and suggestions regarding checking the alignment among all the key elements of the dissertation, selecting an appropriate title, assembling the manuscript, proofreading and editing, choosing a committee, and preparing for a successful defense, as well as thinking about possible avenues for the presentation and publication of your work.

DEFINING FEATURES OF THIS BOOK

Some books on writing a dissertation explain the process in overcomplicated language—the classic textbook scholarly writing style that tends to mystify and overwhelm the reader. Other books on the subject make assumptions that by following a set of instructions the reader will somehow know how to conduct the process and do not take into account the inherent messiness of qualitative research. Still others offer way too many unrelated examples and fail to provide sufficient detail and strong examples of the various elements involved. All these versions are difficult to learn from. Included in *Completing Your Qualitative Dissertation: A Roadmap From Beginning to End* are a number of useful and reader-friendly features that set this book apart:

- A real researchable problem is illustrated up front and is carried through in each chapter to demonstrate each step of the dissertation process. By using a real problem, we model what a real dissertation should look like. Carrying one research problem throughout the chapters allows you to follow the same idea as it threads through all the different sections required in a dissertation.
- The focus throughout is on conceptual understanding as it relates to the practical aspects involved in navigating the dissertation process.
- Chapter objectives are outlined at the start of each chapter.
- The purpose of each chapter is twofold: to provide instruction and demonstrate application. In this way, the chapters are, in effect, a dissertation in action.

- Roadmaps in the form of tables, figures, and checklists are provided throughout the book. These afford the reader, at a glance, overviews at each stage of the research-writing process. These roadmaps are our own creation and have not been previously published.
- Based on the idea of roadmaps, we emphasize the use of working tools to clarify your thinking and organize and present your data. Within each chapter, we include templates for how to go about creating these working tools. In the appendices, we include various completed examples that offer the reader some idea of what the finished products might look like.
- There is an emphasis throughout on how to store and manage information.
- We acknowledge and reinforce throughout the book that there are often institutional and/or program-related differences vis-à-vis the dissertation process. The processes described do not apply universally. This is particularly pertinent with respect to the nature of advisement, committee structure, and proposal requirements.
- Where appropriate, we flag possible instances of differences in the content and structure of the dissertation so that students are aware of these.
- Where appropriate, we point out qualitative language and terminology that allows for differences among doctoral programs and higher education institutions.
- Where appropriate, we point out instances where qualitative traditions or genres might differ in application among themselves. This is particularly pertinent with respect to literature review and analysis of data.
- Each chapter concludes with an integrative summary discussion. These discussions highlight key concepts and issues raised in the chapter, as well as providing segues or transitions from one chapter to the next.
- A checklist is provided at the end of each chapter. This checklist is a supplement to the narrative and serves to review what needs to be accomplished before proceeding to the subsequent chapter.
- A final comprehensive checklist of all the activities in the dissertation process is provided on the inside of the back cover. This is a useful tool intended to help the reader get started on the process and keep him or herself in check at every stage along the way.
- Each chapter includes an annotated bibliography for easy referral to additional relevant sources. In preparing this book, we have done extensive research and share sources that we have found to be most useful. In many cases, this includes seminal works in the field, but we also include works that are less well known.

Acknowledgments

This book is meant as a tribute to the resolve of the countless doctoral students with whom we have worked and continue to work and from whom we have learned so much. We could not have begun to conceptualize this book without being a part of their experiences. Of special importance to the completion of this work were the doctoral students we interviewed, who generously gave of their time, and who candidly shared their insights. We owe much as well to our colleagues and friends who encouraged and supported us on our journey. We thank Sage Publications for recognizing the value of this book, especially our editorial team, who worked with us tirelessly to prepare this book for publication in record time. Finally, great appreciation and love goes to our families, whose patience and support knew no bounds.

—LDB and MV

About the Authors

Linda Dale Bloomberg is adjunct faculty at Teachers College Columbia University, where she focuses primarily on qualitative research and dissertation advisement. She is also an adjunct professor in various distance education master's degree programs in which she teaches qualitative research, academic writing skills, and leadership development. She received her doctorate in adult education from Columbia University. She has master's degrees in Counseling Psychology and Organizational Psychology from the University of the Witwatersrand, Johannesburg, South Africa, and in Jewish Education from the Siegal College of Judaic Studies, Cleveland, Ohio. Over the past 25 years, Dr. Bloomberg has practiced as a psychologist, career counselor, and educational and business consultant, and has held research and teaching positions at various institutes in the United States as well as abroad. She is the author and editor of numerous publications in the fields of counseling psychology, organizational evaluation, qualitative research, leadership development, adult education, Jewish education, and distance education.

Marie Volpe is adjunct assistant professor of adult and organizational learning at Teachers College Columbia University, where she teaches dissertation seminars and serves as advisor to doctoral candidates. She received her doctorate in adult education and master's in organizational psychology from Columbia University and has done postdoctoral work at Harvard University. She regularly conducts workshops for teachers in Mongolia and lectures on qualitative research methods at Suzho University, China. After a career spanning 35 years with Exxon Corporation, where she held the position of manager of education and development, Dr. Volpe embarked on a second career in higher education, where she has practiced for the past 15 years. She is the author of numerous publications in the areas of staff development, training and education, and informal learning in the workplace.

PART I

Taking Charge of
Yourself and Your Work

OVERVIEW

Part I presents a broad introduction to the complex task of conducting and writing a dissertation. Figure I.1 depicts the cyclical qualitative dissertation process in its entirety. As you will no doubt experience it, the

process is not linear, but rather iterative and recursive, sometimes unpredictable, and more often than not very "messy."

Although the process appears complex, if viewed incrementally, it is one you can master. Thus, we encourage you to recognize that you can do this work if you have the

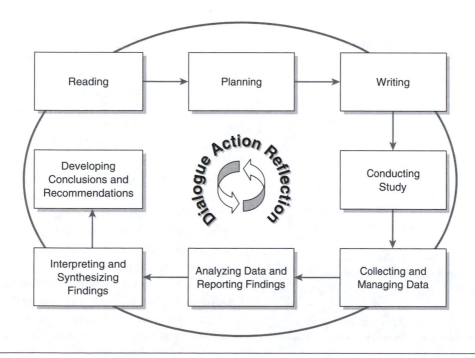

Figure I.1   The Dissertation Process

1

right attitude, understand the content and process involved in conducting a research project, and are willing to develop and/or sharpen the skills required to carry out the research. Although this work is intellectually rigorous, requiring a lot of thinking, preparation, and planning, it is not so much a matter of having superior intellect as it is a matter of having tenacity, perseverance, and patience. It is, in fact, a process of continuous learning because, for most people, conducting research and writing a dissertation is a first-time endeavor, an undertaking for which there is little experience. By the end of the process, you will have learned as much about yourself and how to do research as you will have learned about the subject of your inquiry. This section presents the initial steps involved in thinking about and preparing for the dissertation process. However, we don't want to get you bogged down here. Part II is where the real work and learning occur. If you feel what you are reading is not relevant, skip it and go on to Part II.

OBJECTIVES

Part I Objectives

The objectives that follow address the knowledge, skills, and attitudes required to successfully complete a dissertation:

- Provide *information* that will broaden student understanding of what comprises a sound research study.
- Demonstrate the *skills* needed to conduct and write up the study.
- Recognize, appreciate, and adopt the *attitudes* that will contribute to the success of the research project.

GETTING REENERGIZED

Undoubtedly, if you are reading this book, you are a continuous learner; it is the reason you decided to pursue a doctoral degree in the first place. It takes a certain amount of courage to take on this work because in many ways it is fraught with uncertainty. For those of you who are just starting out and for those who need to restart and continue, it can seem an overwhelming process. If the truth be told, for everyone who has ever embarked on this journey, most likely they have experienced a certain amount of anxiety, if not downright fear. Will I know how to do this work? Will I be up to the task? What if I fail? Ah, what if I succeed? Will it meet my expectations? These are some of the cobwebs that cloud our vision and stand in our way. It is okay to feel anxiety and fear. As a matter of fact, these feelings are natural as long as they do not debilitate us.

One way not to become overwhelmed is to look at the entire process of completing a dissertation as an incremental one. It is like the novice skier, who recognizes that a good way not to be overwhelmed by the sheer size of the mountain is to traverse it—going from side to side, conquering it, bit by bit. It is a matter of taking one step at a time and finding out what is needed at each step along the way. That is what this book is all about—giving you the information you need and helping you to develop the skills required along the way to complete this work.

So let us take up our journey and begin by getting ourselves organized mentally and physically. Begin by taking a reflective stance—think about those things, personal and professional, that have caused you to procrastinate, get stuck, or even abandon the work. Come to terms with those obstacles. Develop a plan to deal with the real challenges you face and determine to move beyond your own self-imposed obstacles by taking action. Commit to acting despite your apprehensions and commit to developing an "I can do this" attitude; become your best friend and not your own worst enemy. This is of paramount importance. Once you have the right mindset, you can begin to get organized.

ORGANIZING AND MANAGING YOUR PROJECT

Your dissertation is a project that will extend over a period of time. Therefore, successful completion requires careful organization and planning. To begin the process of getting organized, you need to create a "workspace" for your dissertation—a physical as well as a mental/intellectual space. One of the first steps in beginning to create a system for organizing and managing your work on this project is to start keeping records—of information as well as of your thinking.

As you begin your research and as you live with your study, you will begin to gather and accumulate a diverse array of material that has potential relevance. As you become immersed in your work, you will continue to be inundated with large amounts of information, including formal documents, correspondence, photocopies of articles, pieces of reflective writing, class notes, reading notes, discussion notes, handouts, memos, as well as other miscellaneous scraps of paper. All of this information is the precursor to the final data. It is the raw material of the inquiry that will be of use later. You certainly do not want to lose any of your material, nor do you want to drown in it. Organizing and managing dissertation-related "stuff" right from the beginning is essential to getting on track and staying focused. In this regard, you will need to make sure that it is sorted systematically and stored safely and securely, and that it will be easily retrievable when you need to access it.

In addition to storing various forms of information, you also should make sure that you keep the various drafts of your dissertation. During the process of writing your dissertation, drafts will need to be edited and refined. As you make revisions and update earlier versions, you will find yourself continually writing and rewriting. These drafts are important and should not be discarded. It is possible that you may want to revisit some text of an earlier version to check on something you have written. In addition, as your research and writing progress, by comparing drafts you can keep a check on your progress, as well as note any developments in your understanding of certain issues and phenomena. Therefore, before making revisions, original drafts should be kept intact, and each revised version should be labeled, dated, and stored in a designated file or folder for easy retrieval.

There are various systems for handling information at a practical level and, based on your learning style preference, different methods will seem more appealing. Those of us who are more visual and tactile like to print hard copies of everything and have the physical "evidence" in our hands. Some people "file" material in stacks—some of which are neatly piled and precisely ordered and others are strewn across every surface of their workspace. Some people do better with neatly labeled file drawers. Still others are less inclined to file manually and more inclined toward a computer-based system. They prefer to set up electronic folders in which to store information by way of emerging topics or chapters, rather than actual files or folders.

In our experience, it seems that an effective way to organize and sort information would involve a blend of approaches—manual and computerized. One of the ways to start collecting and managing the material that you are accumulating—and something we have found extremely useful—is to set up a three-ring dissertation binder with tabs for each chapter. This binder becomes a place to save information and notes on each chapter of your forthcoming dissertation. As you progress, print out completed chapters and insert them in your binder. The binder not only helps control notes and information, but it also gives you a sense of your progress. When the binder is complete, you are just about at the end of the process and can see the light at the end of the tunnel.

Whatever methods work best for you and whatever strategy of information management you choose, your computer will become your best friend throughout the dissertation process. Using your computer, you can catalogue, record, and manage multiple forms of information. Becoming familiar with your computer and technological resources before you start your research will save you much time and frustration. Developing computer literacy and mastering the software does add another layer of learning to an already intensive experience, but one that is well worth the effort. If you feel overwhelmed in this regard, you might want to seek technical assistance.

In addition, no matter what kind of computer system or software package you are working with, a necessary and, in fact, absolutely essential consideration is that you are—right from the beginning—vigilant in saving information. This goal can be accomplished by regularly and frequently backing up your files by way of copying them to your hard drive, as well as to a disc or flash drive. You can never back up too much. Many people recommend printing out hard copies of completed sections in addition to saving electronic copies. As useful as they are, computers are not infallible. They can and do crash. Losing chunks or even all of your work can be a devastating setback in the dissertation process.

Up to this point, much of the discussion has focused on the practical details of the organization and management of dissertation-related material. Aside from keeping track of information, you need to keep track of your thinking. Just as it is important to have the relevant material on file, so it is important to keep a record of your changing thoughts about the research process. One way to ensure that you preserve your reasoning and are able to spell out the development of your ideas is to keep a research journal. Recording your thinking means that you will accumulate material that can be revisited and drawn on and that can form a substantial part of the methodology and analysis chapters of your dissertation. Keeping careful records also implies an open-minded and critical approach and can contribute to what Lincoln and Guba (1985) refer to as an "audit trail," which provides useful material for making validity claims for your study.

Journaling allows you to be meticulous about keeping an orderly record of your research activities. Journaling also engenders a reflective stance, which offers the opportunity to create a record of your experiences— your insights, speculations, hunches, questions, methodological and analytical concerns, tentative interpretations, and so on. In the qualitative inquiry process, you as the researcher/ writer are the main instrument of data collection and data analysis. It is your task to provide personal insight into the experience under study. Integral to the notion of *self as instrument* is a capacity for reflection. The act of reflection, as Dewey (1916) suggests, affords the potential for reconstructing the meaning of experience that actually yields learning. In effect, a journal provides a solid link to and keeps track of the many levels of experience that are involved in the dissertation process. In the qualitative dissertation, what you bring to the inquiry is as important as what you discover as you live with your project. The quality and credibility of the dissertation indeed rests on your capacity for insightful conceptual reflection.

Creating your new workspace means that you also should begin identifying writing resources. In addition to purchasing the relevant textbooks, online library databases will become invaluable as well. Your computer, in connection with your university library system, is a literature searching and bibliographic management tool. An ongoing literature review begins right from the beginning stages of topic identification; continues with reviews of research methodologies, specific methods of data collection, and issues of trustworthiness; and carries through to the final stages of analysis and synthesis. In addition, you have to produce a bibliography or reference list that is formatted correctly and in perfect synchronization with the materials referenced in the body of your dissertation. This ongoing literature review can indeed be one of the most time consuming of all the dissertation challenges. It is certainly worth taking the time to become familiar with using your library's computerized search capability, as well as with the variety of software programs that allow you to efficiently perform the tasks of referencing your materials. We just briefly mention this now so that you can start adding these thoughts to your new mental workspace. Further details pertaining to some of the more commonly used online library databases for the social sciences are presented as Appendix A.

Although much of the work involved in the dissertation process—in both the researching and writing phases—is done independently, you need not feel you must "go this alone"; you should not isolate yourself. As a resourceful doctoral candidate, you need to create a support system that contributes to your success. There are many people who have the potential to promote your progress. In our experience, we have found the graduate student network to be a particularly valuable resource. It is to your advantage to reach out to graduates and other professionals and colleagues whom you believe might be helpful to you.

Once you have gotten your mental and physical house in order, and with strong personal commitment and the will to succeed in completing your dissertation, you are ready to take the first step or resume wherever you left off in the process.

IDENTIFYING AND DEVELOPING A RESEARCHABLE TOPIC

The starting point for any research project, and indeed the first major challenge in conducting research, involves coming to some decision about a sound, doable topic. The topic is the subject of inquiry around a particular research problem that your study will address. For some, choosing a topic can be an exciting process; finally, you have the opportunity to pursue an area in which you have long been interested. For others, generating and selecting a topic can be a frustrating and somewhat overwhelming experience; you are torn between several topics—all of which are seemingly interesting and fascinating—with each piece of reading that you do adding further ideas and fueling your desire to explore everything. A real dilemma! Still there are others who are exasperated by the process and are unable to find a workable topic. For them this step is a painful experience. Commonly, students consider a few potential topics before finally settling on one.

In selecting a topic, most students focus on trying to be original and exhibiting the desire to contribute to the existing knowledge base. Most universities and doctoral faculties agree that a dissertation should be an original piece of research and should make a significant contribution to the field. At the outset, it is important to remember, however, that making an original contribution does not imply that there need be an enormous "breakthrough." In social science research, the discovery of new facts is rarely an important or even challenging criterion. Rather, research is a process of searching or re-searching for new insights; it is about advancing knowledge or understanding of a practice or phenomenon. In fact, it is perfectly acceptable to model your research on a previous study and develop some aspect of it or even replicate it. Replicating a previous study or aspects of a previous study is appropriate because knowledge accumulates through studies that build on each other over time.

In seeking a topic, you should remember that the objective of doing a dissertation is to obtain the credentials by demonstrating that you understand and can therefore conduct good research. The dissertation should not be centered on any grandiose ideas that you want to pursue—that can come later at another point in your life. For the purpose of successfully completing your dissertation, the focus should be on a sound topic—one that is crystal clear and concise.

For the most part, identification of what to study evolves slowly as you become immersed in a variety of concepts, philosophies, and theories. The way to begin developing a researchable topic is to look around you at the activities in which you are involved and to draw on your own personal and professional experiences. Most students find that they can best access areas in which they already have substantial expertise or familiarity with practice in the field or existing research. Once you have identified an area of interest, begin to examine and become familiar with the available literature related to your topic. Especially useful are reviews of literature found in journals specifically committed to publishing extensive review articles, as well as policy-oriented publications that discuss current and emerging issues. In addition, all discipline areas have their own encyclopedias, yearbooks, and handbooks, most of which can be accessed on the Internet. You also might take time to look over earlier dissertations and seek previous studies that in some respects mirror your own interests and topic.

In addition to seeking out relevant literature, engage in conversation with colleagues and peers to hear different perspectives about pertinent issues, and so begin to sharpen your topical focus. Generating and selecting a viable topic is a complex process that involves various competing factors. As you may notice throughout this book, our predisposition toward research and writing is that both are highly interactive processes. Seeking the feedback and critique of academic advisors, faculty committee members, and colleagues is, in our experience, an integral part of the dissertation process.

Once you have identified a general area of interest, you need to begin narrowing your topic. The process of developing a researchable topic is a process of idea generation; the movement from a general interest "out there" toward a more clearly refined idea around a researchable problem. It is important that the problem becomes specific and narrow enough to let you master a reasonable amount of information. If your problem is too broad—that is, if you try to take on too many aspects of one problem—you will encounter a data glut, which makes the reporting of findings and analysis of your data extremely difficult and tedious.

Refining the problem to be addressed calls for reflecting on whether that problem *can* and *should* be researched in the first place. First, whether the problem can or cannot be researched involves giving some thought to the practical feasibility or *doability* involved. Important judgments will have to be made regarding the possibility of access to potential sites and potential research populations, availability of sources of information, the researcher's knowledge and skills, and the availability of time and resources at your disposal to collect and analyze data over a sustained period of time. Second is the question of *should*. This question is complex and brings various factors into play. Considering the *should-doability* of a study calls into consideration the practical as well as the theoretical implications of pursuing a research problem. You therefore need to take the following into account:

1. The potential audience. Who would appreciate the worth of my study? Who would care enough to read it? Who would be interested?

2. The intellectual value and worth of the study. What, if any, is the wider significance of this research? Who would benefit by this study? Would a study in this area contribute to the ongoing conversation in a particular social science discipline or applied field? Would the study generate theoretical and/or conceptual understanding? What, if anything, would be the significance for policy? Will the study contribute to the development of professional practice?

3. Personal and professional goals. Will this study further my personal and professional interests? Will it enhance my career and/or career change? Will the research problem sustain my interest over the ensuing months and years?

4. Ethical considerations. Does the research involve practices or strategies that might embarrass or harm participants? Are there any political risks to others or me in reporting fairly and accurately the findings and outcomes of the potential study?

Undertaking a dissertation is a rigorous and long-term engagement, in terms of both conducting the fieldwork and working with the data. Although the dissertation need not necessarily be one's "life's work," caring about the topic at hand and having a compelling interest to learn what is not yet known are critical to sustaining motivation and commitment and, hence, momentum. The sooner you can begin to narrow your research interests and identify and develop

a topical focus, the better. Having a fairly good idea of the area in which you will be situated, you will most productively be able to utilize your time to refine your research problem and so further the dissertation objectives.

Students often labor over coming up with a dissertation title at the early stages of dissertation work. It is a good idea to create what is, in effect, a "working title," as you think about your topic and hone your problem, and to refine this title as your study proceeds. A title generally captures the major thrust of your research. A working title becomes a guiding focus as you move through your study. Keeping notes about how and why your title changes over time is a useful exercise because it tracks developments in your thinking as your study progresses. A more extensive discussion regarding selecting a final dissertation title is included in Part III of this book.

CHOOSING A QUALITATIVE RESEARCH APPROACH

Choice of research approach is directly tied to research problem and purpose. As the researcher, you actively create the link among problem, purpose, and approach through a process of reflecting on problem and purpose, focusing on researchable questions, and considering how to best address these questions. Thinking along these lines affords a research study methodological congruence (Morse & Richards, 2002). A research problem should not be modified to fit a particular research approach. You cannot assume a particular qualitative approach regardless of your research problem. In other words, research approach follows research problem; the appropriate research approach is the one that best fits with your research problem.

Qualitative research is suited to promoting a deep understanding of a social setting or activity as viewed from the perspective of the research participants. This approach implies an emphasis on exploration, discovery, and description. Quantitative research, in contrast, is applied to describe current conditions, investigate relationships, and study cause–effect phenomena. Both research approaches involve complex processes in which particular data-collection and data analysis methods assume meaning and significance in relation to the assumptions underlying the larger intellectual traditions within which these methods are applied.

In recent years, the fierce debate between quantitative and qualitative methodologists—often referred to in the literature as "the paradigm wars"—has softened (Denzin & Lincoln, 1998, 2003; Ercikan & Roth, 2006; Reichardt & Rallis, 1994). A consensus gradually emerged among researchers that, rather than universally advocate any single methodological approach for all research, the challenge is to appropriately match the research approach to purposes, questions, and issues. Thus, as a researcher, you are obliged to understand those theoretical principles that shape the logic of your inquiry. Understanding the logic behind research approach allows your study to be appropriately positioned within an inquiry tradition and also lays the foundation for supporting your study's findings. Preliminary steps in formulating a research approach include (a) assessing the knowledge claims that the researcher brings to the study based on her or his theoretical perspectives, and (b) identifying the strategy or tradition of inquiry that informs the procedures of the research.

Knowledge Claims

A knowledge claim implies certain assumptions about what the researcher will learn during the inquiry and how she or he will learn. These claims might be called *research paradigms*. Philosophically, researchers make claims about what knowledge is (ontology), how we know what we know (epistemology), what values go into knowing what we know (axiology), and the processes for studying knowledge (methodology). There are essentially four schools of thought or paradigms.

Postpositivism

Postpositivism is referred to frequently as "the scientific method," "quantitative research," or "empirical science." It refers to the thinking that developed from logical positivism, a school of thought that maintains that all knowledge can be derived from direct observation and logical inferences based on that observation (Phillips & Burbules, 2000). Postpositivism reflects a deterministic philosophy, and the problems studied by postpositivists typically examine causes that influence or affect outcomes. Thinking within this paradigm is reductionistic. The belief is that there are laws or theories that govern the world, and that these can be tested and verified. Thus, research typically begins with a theory and a set of hypotheses, and the intent is to test ideas. Research is concerned with causal relationships, and the aim is to advance the relationship between variables. The knowledge that develops through a postpositivist lens is based on careful observation and measurement. Results of a study either support or refute the theory. Being objective is an integral component of inquiry, and standards of reliability and validity are important.

Social Constructivism, Interpretivism, or Naturalistic Inquiry

Social constructivism challenges the scientific-realist assumption of postpositivism that reality can be reduced to its component parts. The basic tenet of constructivism is that reality is socially, culturally, and historically constructed (Lincoln & Guba, 1985, 2000; Neuman, 2000; Schwandt, 2000). Therefore, research attempts to understand social phenomena from a context-specific perspective. Social constructivists view inquiry as value-bound rather than value-free, meaning that the process of inquiry is influenced by the researcher and the context under study (Lincoln & Guba, 1985).

The central assumption of this paradigm is that reality is socially constructed, that individuals develop subjective meanings of their own personal experience, and that this gives way to multiple meanings. Therefore, it is the researcher's role to understand the multiple realities from the perspectives of participants. The only way to achieve this understanding is for the researcher to become involved in the reality of the participants and to interact with them in meaningful ways. Thus, constructivist researchers often address the "process" of interaction among individuals. They also focus on the specific contexts in which people live and work to understand particular cultural and historical settings. The constructivist researcher's role is essentially that of "passionate participant," as the facilitator of multivoice reconstruction (Guba & Lincoln, 1998; Lincoln & Guba, 2000). Constructivist researchers recognize and acknowledge that their own background shapes their interpretation, and they thus "position" themselves in the research to acknowledge their own cultural, social, and historical experiences. Rather than starting with a theory (as in postpositivism), researchers pose research questions and generate or inductively develop meaning from the data collected in the field.

Critical Theory/Advocacy

The critical theory paradigm, which also is referred to as an advocacy or liberatory framework, includes feminist perspectives, racialized discourses, queer theory, and disability inquiry. It has a clear focus on social justice (Creswell, 2003). This framework arose during the late 1980s from the critique that postpositivist assumptions imposed unfair structural laws and theories that did not fit marginalized or disenfranchised individuals or groups. In addition, the critique of constructivism is that it did not go far enough in advocating for an action agenda to address the injustice and inequality inflicted on those who have become the passive object of inquiry.

Critical theorists view research as intertwined with politics, and therefore advocate that research contain an integral action agenda that will bring about reform that will change the lives of the research participants, the institutions and communities in which individuals live and work, as well as the researcher's life (Brookfield, 2005). Critical perspectives involve research strategies (e.g., action research, participatory action research, and narrative analysis) that are openly ideological and have empowering and democratizing goals. It is assumed that the researcher will engage participants as active collaborators in the inquiry so as not to further marginalize them as a result of the inquiry. To achieve this, participants are typically involved in designing questions, collecting data, and analyzing and interpreting information. Advocacy means providing a platform for research participants so that their voice can be heard and their consciousness can be raised. The goal of research is to create political debate and discussion to empower people to take action, to bring about change in existing social structures and processes, and to reconceptualize the entire research process.

Pragmatism

Pragmatism arises from the work of Pierce, James, Mead, and Dewey. Pragmatism is not committed to any one research philosophy or paradigm. For the many forms of pragmatism, knowledge claims arise out of situations, actions, and consequences, rather than from antecedent conditions (as in postpositivism). There is a concern with practical application and workable solutions to research problems (Patton, 1990). Instead of methods being important, the problem is primary. Researchers posit that research is contextually based and typically employs both quantitative and qualitative approaches to understand the problem. Pragmatic researchers propose that, within the same study, methods can be combined in creative ways to more fully or completely understand a research problem. It is contended that researchers should be free to choose the methods and procedures that best meet their needs and purposes, and that the research questions should determine the methods used (Krathwohl, 1998). Pragmatists thus adopt multiple data-collection and data analysis methods.

Strategies or Traditions of Inquiry

In addition to assumptions about knowledge and operating at a more applied level are strategies or traditions of inquiry that provide specific direction for procedures in a research design. These strategies or traditions, in turn, contribute to decisions regarding research methods.

Strategies of inquiry associated with quantitative research invoke postpositivist perspectives. Such strategies include descriptive research (involves collecting data to test hypotheses or answer questions about the current status of the subject of inquiry), correlational studies (involves collecting data to determine whether and to what degree a relationship exists between two or more quantifiable variables), causal-comparative research (attempts to determine the cause or reason for existing differences in the behavior or status of groups of individuals),

and experimental research (this includes true experiments as well as the less rigorous experiments or quasiexperiments). In both strategies, at least one independent variable is manipulated, other relevant variables are controlled, and the effect on one or more dependent variables is observed. Although there are variations among these strategies regarding their goals and their data-collection procedures, what is common among them is that all quantitative strategies collect and analyze numerical data to explain, predict, and/or control phenomena of interest.

Qualitative research is a broad approach to the study of social phenomena and is based essentially on a constructivist and/or critical perspective (Lincoln & Denzin, 2003). Within the qualitative approach, there are a variety of traditions or genres (the word *strategy* is more suited to quantitative research), each distinguished by specific form, terms, focus, and assumptions regarding what constitutes inquiry within the qualitative paradigm. Creswell (1998) identifies five main traditions: case study, ethnography, phenomenology, grounded theory, and narrative research. To that list, we add a sixth tradition—namely, hermeneutics. There are others, but they are more content-specific. There are many types of textual analysis, including conversation analysis and discourse analysis. There also are many forms of action research and feminist pedagogies. Traditions are not always wholly separate and may overlap. Moreover, to complicate matters, each tradition is not necessarily an agreed-upon whole, and distinctions and divisions have come to characterize some traditions.

Although all of qualitative research holds a number of characteristics and assumptions in common, there are variations in how a qualitative study might be designed and what the intent of the study might be. Just as the choice of research approach is directly tied to and fits with the research problem, purpose, and research questions, so is the choice of qualitative research tradition. In other words, choice of research tradition follows research problem and purpose. Following is a brief description of some of the primary qualitative traditions. As you read on, you will notice that the primary difference among these traditions lies in the particulars of the social context examined.

- *Case Study:* As a form of research methodology, case study is an intensive description and analysis of a phenomenon, social unit, or system bounded by time or place (Berg, 2004; Creswell, 1998; Merriam, 1998; Merriam & Associates, 2002; Stake, 1995; Yin, 2003). Case study involves a detailed description of a setting and its participants, accompanied by an analysis of the data for themes, patterns, and issues (Merriam, 1998; Stake, 1995; Wolcott, 1995). There might be one or more cases involved in the study.

- *Ethnography:* The researcher studies a cultural or social group in its natural setting, closely examining customs and ways of life, with the aim of describing and interpreting cultural patterns of behavior, values, and practices (Van Maanen, 1988, 1995). Rooted in cultural anthropology, the researcher's role is that of a participant observer, with the researcher becoming immersed in the day-to-day lives of the participants. To produce a holistic "cultural portrait," the researcher gains access to the group through "gatekeepers" and "key informants."

- *Phenomenology:* The purpose of phenomenological research is to investigate the meaning of the *lived experience* of people to identify the core essence of human experience as described by research participants. Rooted in the philosophical perspectives of Edmund Husserl (1859–1938) and subsequent philosophical discussions by Heidegger (1889–1976) and Merleau-Ponty (1908–1961), phenomenological research involves studying

a small number of subjects through extensive and prolonged engagement to develop patterns and relationships of meaning (Moustakas, 1994). In this process, the researcher "brackets" her or his own experiences to understand the participants' experiences (Van Manen, 1990).

- *Grounded Theory:* The researcher attempts to generate or discover a theory of a process, action, or interaction grounded in the views of the research participants. To examine changing experiences over time and to describe the dimensions of experience, research involves multiple stages of data collection and the refinement of abstract categories of information (Charmaz, 2000; Strauss & Corbin, 1990, 1998). Two primary characteristics of grounded theory are the constant comparative method of data analysis (i.e., the ongoing comparison of data with emerging categories) and theoretical sampling of different groups to maximize the similarities and differences of information. The objective is to generate theory from the data or modify or extend existing theory. The researcher integrates categories into a theoretical framework that specifies causes, conditions, and consequences of the studied process.

- *Narrative Inquiry/Biography:* In this form of research, the researcher studies the lives of one or more individuals through the telling of stories. The information gleaned from the story or stories is then retold or "restoried" by the researcher into a "narrative chronology" (Creswell, 2003). Ultimately, the narrative combines views from the participants' lives with those of the researcher's life, culminating in a collaborative narrative (Clandinin & Connelly, 2000).

- *Hermeneutics:* Developed by Dilthy (1833–1911), the German philosopher, this highly specialized form of research has been described as the interpretation of texts or transcribed meanings (Polkinghorne, 1983). Pioneered by biblical scholars who made use of textual analysis, this research method has been applied to secular texts to derive a richer understanding of the context that gives it meaning. This method involves an openly dialogical process of returning again and again to the object of inquiry (the text), each time with an increased understanding. Gadamer (1960) explains the *Hermeneutic Circle*, whereby a text is understood by reference to the context in which it was generated; the text, in turn, produces an understanding of the originator and context. Parts of the text are understood by reference to the whole, and the whole is understood in terms of its parts.

Having decided on a qualitative research approach, you will proceed to design your study within the framework of one of the traditions or genres of qualitative inquiry. Thus, the components of the design process (e.g., the theoretical framework, research purpose, and methods of data collection and data analysis) reflect the principles and features that characterize that tradition. However, one need not be so rigid as to not mix traditions, employing, for example, a grounded theory analysis procedure within a case study design or conducting a hermeneutic phenomenological inquiry (Van Manen, 1990). We recommend that you have some knowledge of the available traditions before making a choice, and that you understand each one as rigorous in its own right before combining them.

Qualitative research can be construed metaphorically as "an intricate fabric composed of minute threads, many colors, different textures, and various blends of material" (Creswell, 1998). Because of the complexity of qualitative research, this fabric is not explained easily or simply. There are, however, some common core elements that characterize qualitative research.

In summary, qualitative research involves the collection, analysis, and interpretation of narrative and visual (nonnumerical) data to gain insight into a particular phenomenon of interest. Because understanding is the primary goal of qualitative research, the researcher is the primary instrument for data collection and analysis. The researcher strives to describe the meaning of the findings from the perspective of the research participants; to achieve this goal, data are gathered directly from the participants. Taking place within natural or nonmanipulated settings, qualitative research allows for complex social phenomena to be viewed holistically.

An important assumption that underlies qualitative research is that the world is neither stable nor uniform, and, therefore, there are many truths. Qualitative data are analyzed inductively, requiring flexibility in the research design—one of the hallmarks of qualitative research. Data analysis often occurs concurrently with data collection. As the data are analyzed, the researcher seeks patterns and common themes. Qualitative research is iterative. That is, there is a continuous movement between data and ideas. Qualitative research reports include detailed descriptions of the study and clearly express the participants' voices. Qualitative research seeks to establish credibility and dependability and is concerned with the issue of transferability; that is, how and in what ways the findings of a particular study might apply or be useful in other similar contexts.

Table I.1 provides a summary overview of qualitative research, illustrating its primary characteristics and indicating how these compare and contrast with the characteristics of quantitative and mixed-methods approaches.

With a researchable problem in mind and with a clear idea of what qualitative research involves, you are in a position to think about carrying your ideas further and consolidating these ideas in terms of developing a dissertation proposal. You also need to begin thinking about selecting advisors.

Table I.1   Choosing a Qualitative Research Approach[1]

	Quantitative Research	Qualitative Research	Mixed Methods
Research paradigm	Postpositivist	Constructivist, Critical Theory/Advocacy	Pragmatic
Strategy/tradition/ genre of inquiry	Descriptive, correlational, causal/comparative, and experimental research	Case study, Grounded Theory, Ethnography, Hermeneutics, Narrative Inquiry, Phenomenology	*Sequential design can be exploratory or explanatory *Concurrent design triangulates methods
Research purpose	*Seek consensus (the norm) *Examine topic in order to quantify results *Investigate relationships and cause–effect phenomena	*Seek variation in findings *Delves into the "essence" of the topic	*Combination of quantitative and qualitative methods are needed to fully understand a problem
Researcher role	*Adopts an *etic* (outsider) point of view *Seeks to test or verify theory *Identifies variables, makes predictions, and seeks specific evidence that will support or disconfirm hypothesis *Believes that research can be value-free *Attempts to remain unbiased, objective, and impartial	*Adopts an *emic* (insider) point of view *Seeks to discover and understand meaning of experience *Adopts a flexible stance and is open to change *Is reflective about own voice and perspective *Acknowledges personal values, and brings own experience to bear on the study *Is active and involved	*Appreciates how quantitative and qualitative data might complement each other *Develops a rationale for integrating aspects of qualitative and quantitative research *Decides whether to prioritize one or other type of approach or to consider them equally important
Research design	*Hypothetic-deductive: Research is about "idea testing" *Design is determined up front and follows systematic procedures *Large samples are selected randomly *Study is conducted under controlled conditions	*Inductive: Research is about "idea generation" *Design is proposed up front, but is open and emergent, rather than rigid and fixed to permit exploration *Small samples are selected purposefully	*Design combines quantitative structure and qualitative flexibility *Borrows distinct elements from both quantitative and qualitative approaches *Purposeful or random sample selection *Researcher-designed framework allows for innovation or creativity

(Continued)

13

Table I.1 (Continued)

	Quantitative Research	Qualitative Research	Mixed Methods
	*Usually involves some form of pre- and posttest *Little opportunity for creativity outside prestructured research design	*Research takes place within natural contexts *Real-world situations are studied as they naturally unfold *Researcher-designed framework allows for flexibility and creativity	
Methods of data collection	*Uses existing instrumentation *Experimentation follows rigid guidelines *Survey includes closed-ended questions, scales, and ranking order checklists *Instruments yield performance data, observational data, attitude data, and census data	*Researcher as instrument *Methods are emergent and flexible *Instruments include observation, survey, interviews, documents, focus group, and critical incidents *Questions are generally open ended *Multiple methods are combined to achieve triangulation	*Research questions determine the methods *Instruments yield multiple forms of information that can be triangulated
Methods of data analysis	*Deductive design reduces data to precise numerical indices *Statistical analysis occurs after all data have been collected *Researcher offers causal explanations *Analytic process is linear and unidirectional	*Inductive design leads to holistic, richly descriptive findings *Analysis is based on identifying themes and patterns *Phenomena are understood as holistic and complex systems and are viewed within particular social and/or historical contexts	*Research employs both quantitative and qualitative practices *Statistical as well as textual analysis are used

	Quantitative Research	Qualitative Research	Mixed Methods
		*Researcher tries to authentically depict the voices of participants while remaining reflexive and politically aware *Context sensitivity and understanding allows for interpretation *Analysis is iterative, cyclical, and ongoing	
Issues of trustworthiness	*Seeks to uphold scientific standards of validity and reliability *Seeks to generalize results from research sample to the larger population	*Seeks to establish credibility and dependability by way of triangulation and other strategies *Seeks to explain transferability of findings to other similar contexts	*Decisions are made according to methods used
Presentation of findings	*Charts, graphs, and diagrams are used to display results *Discussion explains and augments visual displays	*Thick, rich description is the primary mode of data presentation *Visual displays are used to augment the narrative discussion	*Both quantitative and qualitative modes of presentation are used to illustrate the research design and to portray and describe findings

SOURCE: This table first appeared in Bloomberg, L. D. (2007). Revisiting research approaches. Unpublished manuscript.

[1]Note: Although qualitative research is presented here as one broad approach, it must be remembered that each tradition or genre has its own peculiarities and nuances. Moreover, although qualitative research as an overall approach is based on certain central assumptions, it also is characterized by an ongoing discourse regarding the appropriate and acceptable use of terminology. Current thinking over the years has caused some qualitative researchers to develop their own terminology to better reflect the nature and distinction of qualitative research, whereas others still borrow terminology from quantitative research.

FINDING THE RIGHT ADVISORS

One of the most important tasks of a doctoral candidate is finding a suitable advisement team. Each university has a different system in this regard, and you need to make sure of your institution and/or program's policies and procedures. At some universities, the doctoral committee structure is based on an apprenticeship model and is used as a vehicle to guide the student from coursework through the dissertation defense. The dissertation committee in effect becomes the group of faculty responsible for your progress right from the beginning of the process, with all members contributing to the development of an acceptable dissertation. The committee is a hierarchical organization, with each member of the committee having a different responsibility vis-à-vis your research. At some universities, you work with an advisor (sponsor) and second reader from the proposal stage onward; when you have almost completed your dissertation, a dissertation committee needs to be formed.

Ideally, the doctoral committee is composed of faculty with different areas of expertise and whose resources you will be able to tap in the process of working on your dissertation. Again, this is a matter of institutional difference. In some instances (but not always), you can select your committee from among those in your department and related departments, those whose courses you have taken and/or those whose work bears some relation to the focus of your dissertation. Some faculty may be members of other programs or other schools within your university. In other instances, choice of committee may be more tightly constrained. In some cases (but not always), experts beyond your university are chosen. It is strongly advised that you be clear about your own institutional requirements so you can follow the necessary protocol and take into account acceptable policy and procedures. Bear in mind, too, that in most instances a faculty member has the choice to accept or decline to serve on a doctoral committee, so be prepared to make alternative choices should the need arise.

In most cases, a dissertation committee comprises four members. Working in collaboration with your sponsor and second reader, you typically need to select two additional committee members who will be your third and fourth readers. Most frequently (but not always), the third reader is someone known to the student as someone with whom she or the has previously worked. The third reader is, in most instances, the dissertation chairperson. Her or his role is to direct and moderate the discussion. The fourth committee member is usually assigned through the Office of Doctoral Studies because this person usually comes from outside the department. In some cases, a dissertation committee consists of three faculty members who guide the development and completion of the dissertation. A final oral panel is convened consisting of the dissertation committee plus two outside readers selected by the graduate office.

Because you have known from the beginning of the program that faculty members will eventually have to be selected, rather than wait for the time close to the dissertation defense, you should start thinking early on about who might best serve on your committee. The more information you have about potential committee members, the easier it is for you to make decisions regarding which individuals may agree to work with you and help you achieve your goals. You certainly want your committee to enhance the quality of your academic work and to be supportive of your progress. Therefore, you need to identify the best match between your learning style and the faculty who are available to work with you. In addition, because progress, to a large extent, is the function of a collaborative team effort, you also need to give careful consideration as to how faculty members get along with each other.

Remember that your advisor will hopefully be your mentor, principle guide, and primary resource throughout the dissertation process. Therefore, you need to spend time looking for the kind of authentic educator you feel confident can help you. Take the time to do some research, ask others about their experiences, and find out as much as you can about the faculty at your institution and their areas of interest. Considerations in looking for the right advisor include:

- *Expertise*—Your advisor/sponsor need not be a content expert with regard to your particular topic, but should be a process expert. In this case, you may select a second reader who is a content expert, and in this way you would have a strong combination of resources.
- *Chemistry*—You need to feel comfortable with a prospective advisor and confident that you will be able to develop a good working rapport with him or her. There also need to be good lines of communication between your sponsor and your second reader so that you are never caught in the middle trying to resolve different perspectives.
- *Access and availability*—You may find the kind of expertise you are looking for in a prospective sponsor and feel comfortable with that faculty person, but he or she may be so busy that it makes getting advisement time and feedback difficult and even frustrating.
- *Other characteristics*—Ideally, you need to find a person who will really listen to your concerns and help you deal with them. All too often, work is interrupted by life issues; you need to find someone who is willing to give you understanding and encouragement from the sidelines and who knows when to push you to start moving again. Above all, this person must have a genuine interest in helping you succeed.

Once you select an advisor, be proactive in establishing and maintaining a good working relationship. Keep your advisor apprised of your status along the way by regularly sending progress reports. This communication serves to maintain contact throughout and is a strategy for gaining the necessary support and feedback as you proceed to tackle your dissertation.

Finding just the right advisor is a tall order, and you might be wondering what happens if you do not make the right selection or if you are appointed an advisor who is not the right fit for you. Many students are afraid to change advisors because they view it from a political perspective. Yet in all institutions, it is okay and even appropriate to make changes by going through the correct channels, seeking out the most appropriate person within your department, and asking for their help and advice. Most important, if you make changes, give your existing advisor the respect and courtesy of informing him or her of your desire to change.

DEVELOPING YOUR PROPOSAL

A completed proposal is the point at which you present and justify your research ideas to gain approval from a faculty committee to proceed with your study. Once your proposal has been approved, you are ready to embark on the research. Holding the proposal meeting represents a vital step in the dissertation process. At this meeting, you and your committee will discuss your proposed study relative to its scope, significance, design, and instrumentation. You also agree on expectations and procedures for the study's duration.

The proposal is a well-thought-out written action plan that identifies (a) a narrowly defined and clearly written problem statement; (b) a purpose statement that describes how the problem will be addressed; (c) research questions that are tied to the purpose and, when answered will shed light on the problem; (d) a review of the literature and relevant research to determine what is already known about the topic; and (e) data-collection and data analysis methods. Rather than merely descriptive specifications of what you will do, a qualitative proposal should present a clear argument that explains and justifies the logic of your study. In effect, a dissertation proposal is a "working document on the way to the production of a dissertation" (Kilbourn, 2006, p. 530).

A proposal is not an end in itself. Although a proposal is mandatory, it also is the means to obtain feedback from advisors before implementing your study, and this feedback is usually useful in improving the proposed study. Typically, you will write multiple drafts of your proposal. Based on the feedback you receive, you will continue work toward an increasingly more integrated presentation of the different components guiding the proposed study.

A completed proposal approved for execution and signed by all members of the sponsoring committee constitutes a bond of agreement between you and your advisors. The approved proposal describes a study that, if conducted competently and completely, should provide the basis for an extensive research report (the dissertation) that will meet all the standards of acceptability. However, that design flexibility is one of the hallmarks of qualitative research. Although the proposal is a contractual document, it is also a working document. Therefore, as the research progresses, some changes or modifications will, in all likelihood, have to be made along the way.

Some universities make specific demands regarding the format of proposals, whereas others provide more general guidelines for form and content. You will no doubt have to attend carefully to the variations that reflect the expectations and requirements of your particular institution. Several writers (Berg, 2004; Creswell, 2003; Marshall & Rossman, 2006; Maxwell, 2005; Schram, 2003) describe the proposal as representing the first three chapters of a dissertation. This notion might apply to some institutions, but not all. Therefore, it is highly advisable that you make inquiries as to your own institution's requirements regarding the content and structure of the proposal.

Following is a brief explanation of each of the sections that constitute a three-part proposal. Chapters 1 through 3 of this book provide more elaboration on each of these sections. Proposals are written in the future tense because they are proposing research that has not yet taken place. Once you have carried out your study and proceed to write up your dissertation, be sure to change your writing to the past tense.

Introduction to the Study

The introduction includes the context or background for your study, the problem statement, the purpose of the study, your research questions, the research approach, researcher assumptions and expertise, significance of and rationale for the study, and explanation of key terminology. The introductory section serves three major purposes. First, it orients your readers by providing them with the context leading to the problem that you are addressing and the overall purpose of your inquiry. Second, it identifies your research questions and the research approach you are adopting. Third, it begins to frame the study by explaining what has led you to focus on your topic, conveying a personal orientation as well as a more general sense of the rationale and significance of the study. In summary, the introduction sets the stage for explaining and justifying the research. It should draw readers into your inquiry while orienting them to its nature and purpose.

Literature Review

The literature review identifies what is already known about your topic/problem and what consensus or lack there is around your topic/problem under study. Literature is reviewed to identify other relevant research so that you can situate your work in the literature, as well as draw from the literature to inform your study. The literature review helps develop the argument for your study by showing how your study is part of a larger conversation and/or part of a broader theoretical scheme. Following the review, it is recommended that you present a conceptual framework, which is designed to guide your study. The categories of the conceptual framework are tied directly to the research questions. These are the same categories under which your data are sorted. The conceptual framework is not some abstract model. It is, in fact, a working tool. These categories continue to evolve and become further refined as data emerge. The conceptual framework is, in our experience, one of the most misunderstood pieces in the dissertation puzzle. Hence, more about developing the conceptual framework is explained in chapter 2.

Methodology

The methodology section includes an overview of the research design, information needed and sources of data, proposed research sample, plans and methods for data collection and data analysis, and a rationale for the methods to be used. The strategies you intend to employ for both collecting and analyzing data are determined by the particular qualitative tradition that you have adopted for the study; thus, in your discussion, you need to demonstrate these connections. In addition, there should be some mention of how you intend to deal with issues of trustworthiness (validity/credibility and reliability/dependability), anticipated ethical issues and your plans for dealing with these issues, as well as limitations and some plans for addressing these limitations.

The methodology section of the proposal helps further develop the argument for your study by showing how you are going to go about conducting your study. Although research proposals do not always necessitate the collection of data, it is often recommended that you include in your proposal reports of pilot studies, which present the findings of actual preliminary work. In our view, conducting pilot studies and presenting the findings thereof certainly serve to strengthen a proposal. By doing the "spadework" and by saying, "I tried it, and here is how it worked," you demonstrate the availability of participants, the practicality of procedures, as well as your skills and capabilities as a researcher. Moreover, pilot studies have additional benefits. As Locke et al. (2000) point out, "the modest pilot study is the best possible basis for making wise decisions in designing research" (p. 74).

In addition to the three parts of the proposal outlined previously, we recommend the inclusion of a tentative chapter outline for the dissertation, as well as a detailed projected timetable for your research. Both of these illustrate that you are able to plan and think ahead. This timeline will convince the reader that you have given serious thought to the tasks involved and your estimation of the time needed to complete each task. The timeline will help the reader (and you) judge the feasibility of the proposed study and may suggest implications for logistics and practicality that might not be immediately apparent in the body of the proposal. Additionally, you need to attach as appendices all necessary information, such as a copy of Institutional Review Board ([IRB] or similar body) approval for your proposed study, tailored consent forms with a clear outline of the steps you will take to protect research participants, projected instruments and forms used in pilot studies, projected coding schemes and projected matrices, and any other appropriate forms and letters. Of course, a bibliography and proper use of references and citations are absolutely necessary.

A proposal requires a logical structure. The conceptual and methodological parts of the proposal need to make sense in relation to one another, and the writing must be clear and concise. You need to think carefully about the interrelationship between the various parts of your proposal and how the various parts are aligned with each other. This sense of interrelatedness will not only provide your readers with a cohesive picture of the proposed project, but will help you, as the researcher/writer, to conceptualize the entire process involved.

It is important to point out that this understanding of structural interrelationship, while implying clear definition and cohesiveness, does not necessitate a rigid framework. It is vital that your proposal preserves the design flexibility that is characteristic of qualitative research. In this regard, you should expect that, before it evolves toward its final form, your proposal will most likely undergo many drafts as you refine your thinking. The thinking, writing, and rewriting involved in developing a sound proposal will help you to develop a logic and a plan that will guide and direct your research. As such, the time and energy spent in writing a proposal that is carefully explained, theoretically sound, and methodologically thoughtful will reap rewards throughout the dissertation endeavor.

ESTABLISHING A TIMELINE

One of the major challenges of completing the dissertation is developing and honing the habit of thinking critically. Another challenge is the practical application of ideas, including the need to systematically plan the study, collect and analyze the data, and write up the dissertation. The ability to focus, problem solve, and make informed decisions

at every step of the way will bring your study to completion. Time is part of the equation.

Clearly, the more time you devote to carefully thinking about, planning, and completing your study, the more effective your discipline will be. Because the time commitment required of an individual doing qualitative research is substantial, you need to pace yourself from the beginning. Be sure to keep your goals realistic or you will set yourself up for failure. As such, be honest about the time that particular tasks might take to complete and what other life demands are competing with the dissertation demands. Aside from time constraints, you also need to plan carefully for what can be achieved given your available resources (e.g., personnel and financial support). Finally, you must consider developing realistic deadlines with regard to institutional constraints. For example, many university departments are typically understaffed during the summer months and over winter vacation. Expecting feedback from advisors, gaining approval from review boards, or even attempting to set meeting times with research participants at these particular times of the year would be somewhat unrealistic.

In line with the ski metaphor mentioned earlier, it is important that you set yourself a time frame within which to complete each section of the dissertation. Just as the experienced skier traverses the terrain, bench marking is fundamental to success in the dissertation process, too. In developing realistic deadlines, we recommend that students "chunk" the tasks in conjunction with a multiyear calendar. Create a system whereby you work on parts that contribute to the whole—chapter by chapter or even one part of a chapter at a time. The dissertation journey is essentially about achieving milestones one step at a time.

A useful guiding principle is to always have a sense of your next step. Identifying the various stages in the process, pacing yourself, and documenting your achievement of goals and subgoals along the way are important and will contribute to keeping you task-oriented and focused. Having some sense of how your progress is moving you closer and closer to completion will help to keep you motivated. In this regard, we recommend marking your progress on a checklist that you create for yourself. A sample checklist appears on the inside back cover.

It is especially critical that you not lose momentum once formal coursework has ended. At this moment of being out there on their own, many students experience over-whelming feelings and are unsure of how to proceed. The longer they remain fixed and unmoving, the more their inclination to start on the dissertation wanes; the longer this continues, the more difficult it becomes to get going again.

You also should bear in mind that, in most institutions, once a student is certified and becomes a doctoral "candidate," he or she usually has a designated number of years in which to complete the dissertation or else he or she will have to be recertified (which involves retaking the "certification" or "candidacy" exam—a most unappealing thought). In any event, although extensions may be granted for extenuating circumstances, to get an extension, a student usually has to demonstrate that she or he has been making significant progress. This is all the more reason to take the time to develop a timeline, stay on task, and set realistic, appropriate, and reasonable goals. After all, this doctoral program is a once-in-a-lifetime venture and you surely want to succeed.

In following up with our students as to their progress, we often hear, "I'm still reading." Reading widely indeed allows you to become knowledgeable and proficient in a specific domain. Although reading is essential, it can sometimes be an avoidance mechanism when it is time to write. It is now time to start *writing* your dissertation. The sooner you begin writing, the easier it is to continue writing and the more rapidly your dissertation is likely to progress. Adopt a do-it-now attitude and get started.

GUIDELINES FOR GOOD WRITING

A dissertation is the combination of performing research and writing about your research to describe and explain it. As a researcher/writer, knowing how to best express your ideas in written form to convey them to the reader becomes an essential skill. The impact of any research is likely to be enhanced if you are able to write well about your work. The dissertation requires a high level of scholarly writing. Although not everyone enjoys scholarly writing nor is everyone good at it, you have to get into the mode of writing for a particular audience— the academic community. Academic or scholarly writing is, in essence, writing that is clear, concise, precise, and bold. Above all, good writing is a function of good thinking.

Clarity, Coherence, and Cohesiveness

Whatever chapter of your dissertation you are busy with, it is important that you spend time planning not only *what* you will write, but also *how* you will write. Creating an outline or "mind map" that traces the path of your argument is one way to begin thinking about this. Creating outlines is an effective way to organize your thinking and sequentially guide your writing. In writing your dissertation, your intention is not only to demonstrate your knowledge of the topic. You also want to capture the interest of and guide the reader throughout so that she or he understands and can follow your train of thought. To ensure that your paper is user-friendly, aim for clarity and logic:

- In your introductory section, write a paragraph that describes your outline. This paragraph lets readers know where you will take them. A strong introduction as well as a strong conclusion (described further on) will help readers to see the significance of your work.

- Make use of headings and subheadings to provide structure to your writing. These are useful in communicating the key ideas to the reader. Crowding makes reading difficult and unpleasant.
- Resist jargon. Jargon excludes and mystifies the reader. Do not assume that all readers understand specialized language. If you must use a specialized term, be sure to explain it.
- Build coherence through connecting sentences. Every sentence should be a logical sequel to the one that preceded it.
- Use transitions or segues to trace the path of your argument and to guide the reader. Transitions are "bridge sentences" between paragraphs and help make your discussion easy to follow.
- Organize your thoughts in a coherent, well-constructed paragraph. Create paragraphs that contain one main idea only. Begin each paragraph with a topic sentence, followed by supporting sentences that illustrate, elaborate, explain, and clarify your main idea.
- Each paragraph should logically and sequentially lead to the next. Remember to pay particular attention to the last sentence of each paragraph because this is the springboard to the subsequent paragraph.
- Paragraphs should not be overly long because this overwhelms the reader. If a paragraph is one page or more, break it into two or more paragraphs.
- Make sure that each section and/or chapter ends by summarizing and integrating the main points/themes. The summary allows the reader to come away with a clear understanding of what you have written and what will follow.

After writing each paragraph, it is helpful to read it aloud. In this way, you can check for syntax, as well as for coherence and flow. In academic writing, it is essential that you are clear and precise. In reviewing your work, ask yourself: Is what I am reading really what I intended to write? Does it say what I mean it to say? If a written passage sounds awkward, you might need to add new words, phrases, or sentences to establish clearer connections. You also should watch out for sharp breaks where the reader is left "hanging"; in these cases, you should consider restructuring the sentence or phrase.

In reading aloud, watch for any assumptions and unsupported statements. In these cases, the reader might ask, "Who says so?" You must provide evidence to support what you say. In dissertation writing, you have to get in the habit of writing defensively. In other words, you need to stop after each paragraph and ask yourself: "Have I provoked any questions in the reader's mind?" This step is important because the process in the defense of a qualitative dissertation is one of questioning and challenging any assumptions you may have made. As soon as you provoke questions in the reader's mind, she or he begins to lose confidence in your argument and may even go looking for more questions. That is the last thing you want to happen.

Reading aloud also allows you to check for grammatical errors:

- Make sure that you use complete sentences, not fragmented ones.
- Do not use unwieldy, run-on sentences. Long, complicated sentences force the reader to decide which of the points you are making should be emphasized. Each sentence should contain one thought only. Aim for short, clear, and crisp sentences.
- Check for incorrect use of punctuation, which can affect meaning.
- Be consistent in your tenses.
- Place descriptive words and phrases as close as possible to the words they describe or they may inadvertently describe the wrong word.
- Be careful not to end a sentence with a preposition (*to*, *from*, *with*, etc.).

- Whenever possible, use the active rather than the passive voice. The active voice reduces wordiness and is more direct, giving vitality and force to your writing.
- Look for unnecessary adjectives and delete vague qualifications such as *very*.
- Remember that academic writing is formal writing. As such, slang expressions, colloquialisms, and idioms are not appropriate.

Format and Style Requirements

A research report must consistently follow a selected system for format and style. Format refers to the general pattern of organization and arrangement of the report. Style refers to appropriate writing conventions and includes rules of grammar, spelling, capitalization, and punctuation to be followed in preparing the report. Most colleges and universities require the use of a specific style—either their own or that in a published style manual. You need to make inquiries regarding your particular department's recommended style preference.

A note regarding use of first-person "I" in your writing: In qualitative research, the researcher is the main research tool or instrument. The unique style and narration of the researcher is an integral part of the study, and, as such, the first-person "I" is sometimes used. According to some (but not all) views, this usage can be justified in a qualitative research report, as opposed to "the researcher" or "the author," which tends to sound distant and uninvolved. Because there may be different preferences regarding the use of the first person, we strongly advise that you check with your advisor before proceeding to write.

The most frequently used style manuals in the social sciences are APA (American Psychological Association), MLA (Modern Language Association), CMS (Chicago Manual of Style), and Turabian. Although different style manuals emphasize different rules of writing, several rules are common to most. Regardless of which manual you use, you are expected to adhere to its rules meticulously. Early on in the dissertation process, you should become familiar with your required manual and use it consistently throughout. Mastering the manual's technical nuances early on (such as the use of headings, footnotes, tables, and figures) will save you considerable time and effort in the long run. Be especially careful to follow the manual's guidelines regarding citation of references. Citations must be accurate; from the beginning, you should remain vigilant in updating your reference list each time you add a citation. Do not imagine that you will remember to do so later. Searching for "lost" references is time-consuming and very frustrating.

Tables and figures are often included in a dissertation to augment the narrative, thereby enabling the reader to more clearly understand the issues being discussed. These graphic organizers are somewhat distinguished from one another:

- Tables are typeset, rather than photographed, from artwork supplied by the author. Tables consist of text only and are frequently used to present quantitative data. Tables offer precise details, including percentages and whole numbers, and should always include group size (i.e., $N = . . .$).
- Figures are typically used to convey structural or pictorial concepts. Figures can be line graphs, bar graphs, pie graphs, maps, drawings, and photographs. Choose a figure if you want to reinforce the point you are making by way of a strong image.

Tables and figures are used to present material in summary form and should add clarity to the overall presentation of the report. These follow their related textual discussion and are referred to by number. Readers of dissertations are drawn to graphic displays of information. If you choose to use displays of any sort, make sure that they are appropriately included and do not unnecessarily disrupt the flow of the text. The potential usefulness and importance of visual displays suggest a need to dedicate time and care in creating them. Tables and figures should be uncluttered and self-explanatory; it is better to use two tables (or figures) than a single overcrowded one. If you choose to include tables and figures, be sure to contact your style manual for correct format and usage.

In addition to general format requirements, there are books that deal specifically with the rules and principles of writing. These offer useful suggestions regarding sentence construction and word choice. Although writers tend to have their favorites, we have found Strunk and White's (2000) *The Elements of Style* and Hacker's (2003) *A Writer's Reference* to be extremely helpful guides.

Integrity Matters

The strength of your writing rests on your ability to refer to and incorporate the work of others. It is imperative, however, that you attribute recognition to all and any sources of information that you use. Plagiarism and other forms of academic dishonesty are matters that have serious consequences. Types of plagiarism include:

1. Using another writer's words without proper citation

2. Using another writer's ideas without proper citation

3. Using the exact words of a source without quotation marks or indentation

4. Borrowing all or part of another student's paper or having somebody else write your paper or parts of your paper

5. Falsifying data

For proper use of quotations, refer to your style manual. There is no fixed rule regarding when and how much to quote and paraphrase. If you quote and cite too often, you may seem to offer too little of your own thinking. If you quote too little, readers may think that your claims lack support, or they may not be able to see how your work relates to that of others. However, there are some general rules of thumb, as outlined by Booth, Colomb, and Williams (2003): Use direct quotations when you are using the work of others as primary data or when the specific words of your source are of particular significance. Paraphrase sources when you can say the same thing more clearly or when you are more interested in conveying the general idea, rather than how it is expressed by a particular source. Do not quote because you think it is easier or you think you lack the authority to speak for your sources. Make your own argument with your own claims, reasons, and evidence.

Proofreading and Editing

Always proofread your work. The goal of proofreading is to enable you to find and correct your own errors in thought and organization. After writing each section, examine your sentences for clarity and grammar. In an effort to present an organized, logical, and coherent argument, be prepared to spend time editing and reediting as you "polish" your narrative, correct sentence structure, and trim excess wordiness and redundancy. You will find yourself writing and rewriting throughout the process of doing your dissertation. Writing multiple drafts of a manuscript is part of the writing process and is standard practice for most writers.

If you feel that you need assistance with writing, be sure to contact your instructor for additional resources and guidance. It should be obvious that the expectations for correctness and accuracy in academic writing are high. If you feel that you are unable to meet these demands at your current level of writing proficiency, you may need to seek outside assistance. It is quite acceptable to hire an editor or proofreader to help meet academic writing expectations. In addition, most universities offer writing classes and/or workshops.

A dissertation is indeed a "creation" or "construction" that takes effort and time. Constructing a dissertation is both an art and a science and takes thoughtful and careful planning. A good dissertation is built on solid outlines and is constructed logically and sequentially, paragraph by paragraph. This process includes paying close attention to style, format, and precise language. Most important, your writing should flow logically and smoothly. You do not want to lose the reader.

SUMMARY AND DISCUSSION

Taking Charge of Yourself and Your Work

- Overcome your anxieties and frustrations by acting and seeing your work in increments—piece by piece, step by step. Action leads to progress, and progress leads to increasing levels of confidence.
- Develop your own system to organize and manage the ongoing accumulation of data. This will help you feel in control and less overwhelmed.
- Maintain a journal to capture your thoughts, ideas, and strategies; a journal can also become an important audit trail.
- Familiarize yourself with data sources that you will need throughout the process (e.g., library resources, computer databases, and relevant textbooks).
- Determine what you want to research and what you want to learn. To identify a researchable topic, begin by looking at a broad area—one you know something about or in which you have a general interest. Although you do not necessarily have to be passionate about your topic, you should like the subject matter because your

interest will sustain you and keep you going.
- Fashion a narrowly defined problem statement from your topic to control the scope of your research.
- Develop a working title that can serve as a guide and focus. The working title should remain flexible so that it can be refined and re-refined as your study progresses. Keeping notes about how and why your title changes over time is a useful exercise.
- Select a research approach based on the nature of your research problem and your study's purpose and research questions. There are six primary approaches in designing a qualitative study: case study, ethnography, phenomenology, grounded theory, narrative inquiry/biography, and hermeneutics. In choosing sponsors and advisors, important considerations include expertise, chemistry, access and availability, and ability to listen. If you make an inappropriate selection, you can and should seek an advisor who fits your needs.
- Check on institutional and/or program-related requirements with regard to the process of choosing advisors and forming your dissertation committee.
- Make multiple drafts of a proposal as you refine your ideas and become more precise about what will happen in your study. The proposal consists of the first three chapters of what will become your dissertation—introduction, literature review, and methodology.
- In effect, your proposal is your proposed plan to carry out a particular piece of research. It is brought forth to a hearing by a committee for endorsement and approval to proceed. The proposal also requires a review by your university's institutional review board. As such, completing your proposal and holding the proposal meeting is a major step on the road to completing your dissertation.
- Check on institutional and/or program-related requirements with regard to dissertation proposal requirements.
- Plan your time carefully. The time commitment involved in doing your dissertation is substantial given the volume of work.

- Considering that your audience is primarily the academic community, use formal, scholarly writing. Such writing requires command of basic writing skills, such as good sentence and paragraph construction, logical organization, and appropriate transitions.
- Use outlines to plan and present your writing.
- Read your work aloud to check syntax, flow, and any unwarranted assumptions and unsupported statements that you may have made.
- Get in the habit of writing defensively. This approach not only ensures clarity, but also helps to ensure that what you are writing does not provoke questions in the mind of the readers. Questions can unnecessarily bring into suspect the totality of your argument.
- Ensure that format and style adhere to your specific institution and program's requirements.
- Avoid plagiarism and other forms of academic dishonesty, which are serious matters with serious consequences.
- Proofread and edit your work. The quality of your work is a reflection of your respect for the reader.

ANNOTATED BIBLIOGRAPHY

Creswell, J. W. (1998). *Qualitative inquiry and research design: Choosing among five traditions.* Thousand Oaks, CA: Sage.

This book summarizes the distinctive features and guiding assumptions of the five major qualitative research traditions—biography, phenomenology, grounded theory, ethnography, and case study—along philosophical, theoretical, and practical lines. Chapters 1 through 5 compare the various phases of research design inherent in each of the five traditions, from conceptualization to analysis and interpretation. The emphasis throughout is on the variation among the five traditions, offering the reader insights into and understanding of the inherent philosophical underpinnings, theories, assumptions, and practices of each tradition. Especially useful is Creswell's comprehensive list of additional readings regarding each of the five traditions, as well as the glossary of definitions of terminology presented by tradition.

Denzin, N. K., & Lincoln, Y. S. (Eds.). (2000). *Handbook of qualitative research* (2nd ed.). Thousand Oaks, CA: Sage.

Built on the foundation of the landmark first edition, published in 1994, this handbook represents a comprehensive overview of the state of the art for the theory and practice of qualitative inquiry. Included are useful examples of qualitative research studies and their application, with the contributors examining the relevant histories, controversies, and current practices associated with the various qualitative traditions and their associated strategies and methods.

Hacker, D. (2003). *A writer's reference* (5th ed.). Boston: Bedford/St. Martin's.

Rather than providing a set of grammar lessons, this book should be consulted as needed to master the academic style of scholarly writing. The author provides details pertaining to word choice, grammar, sentence style, and punctuation. The author also discusses the most commonly used academic writing styles (APA, MLA, and CMS/Chicago), as well as various online resources (search engines and databases) that can be accessed through library portals.

Holloway, I. (1997). *Basic concepts for qualitative research.* Oxford, UK: Blackwell.

A complex and interconnected family of concepts, constructs, and assumptions surround the term *qualitative research.* Although it was published a decade ago, it is still a highly accessible reference book that provides descriptions and explanations of the "language" and processes used in qualitative research. The first section includes an overview of the historical evolution of qualitative research, its characteristics and aims, and the key methodological issues involved. The second section identifies and describes a comprehensive range of the most commonly used terms, concepts, and methods within qualitative research. This section is ordered alphabetically for ease of access to the information.

Marshall, C., & Rossman, G. B. (2006). *Designing qualitative research* (4th ed.). Thousand Oaks, CA: Sage.

This book offers a detailed overview of the process of designing a qualitative study, providing details of the various steps involved in conducting and reporting research. In addition, the authors expand on the methodological challenges involved. This work is an excellent introduction to qualitative research and provides clear and comprehensive guidance for preparing a research proposal.

Pellegrino, V. C. (2003). *A writer's guide to powerful paragraphs*. Wailuku, HI: Maui'ar Thoughts Company.

Writing is best when it is concise, meaningful, and easily understood, and this book is written with these objectives in mind. The book is designed for writers who seek to improve their writing by providing everything one needs to know about structuring and writing effective paragraphs—the essential element of good writing. As the author points out, a paragraph should be considered "a unit of thought, expressing a single idea, communicated through related sentences." The author provides clear and concise explanations of different types of paragraphs and offers practical examples and suggestions. This book can assist writers in learning how to plan their writing by breaking down their ideas into understandable segments and then organizing and combining these segments to produce a logical, flowing, coherent whole.

Rossman, G. B., & Rallis, S. F. (2003). *Learning in the field: An introduction to qualitative research* (2nd ed.). Thousand Oaks, CA: Sage.

This book is a clearly written and straightforward introduction to qualitative research. The authors creatively integrate the scientific and artistic dimensions of qualitative research, explaining how the research process unfolds from planning and design, through fieldwork and data gathering, to the presentation of findings, analysis, and interpretation. The underlying theme cutting across all the chapters is that research is a process of learning and the utility of research requires clarity of purpose. This book is excellent for novice researchers and introduces the puzzles and tensions that one faces in embarking on a qualitative study, offering some assistance in grasping the core concepts, issues, and complexities involved.

Strunk, W., & White, E. B. (2000). *The elements of style* (4th ed.). New York: Longman.

This timeless book is a wonderful companion as you proceed to write your dissertation. It clarifies the rules and principles of grammar and composition, emphasizing the power of words and the clear expression of thoughts and feelings. Published for the first time in 1919 and then again in 1972, this book is a gem and is small enough and important enough to carry around in your pocket!

Content and Process:
A Chapter-by-Chapter Roadmap

OVERVIEW

Part II is about writing up your study. Each of the chapters in Part II mirrors the respective chapters of an actual dissertation. Chapters 1 through 3 set up the study and constitute the study's framework. As pointed out in Part I, these three chapters form your proposal. Chapters 4 through 6 discuss how you actually deal with the data that you collect. Chapter 4 presents the research findings. Chapter 5 is the analysis and synthesis of those findings. Chapter 6 presents conclusions and recommendations based on the findings.

The problem identified in Part I, which addresses the issue of why people who have completed all the coursework do not go on to complete the research and write their dissertations, is used throughout each of the chapters in Part II. In this way, you can follow the same idea as it threads through all the different sections that constitute a dissertation. Each chapter in Part II is presented in two sections. Section I provides instructions on the specific content of each chapter and how that content is developed. Section II is the application that demonstrates what a written-up chapter would look like based on the content developed. In the "Instruction" section of each chapter of Part II, we offer various roadmaps—in the form of tables and figures—to guide and plan your thinking. In the appendices, we include completed examples of such roadmaps based on the "Application" section in each of the chapters.

Although the objective in each "Application" section is to illustrate the content of an actual dissertation, it is beyond the scope of this book to present a complete dissertation. Therefore, what we present in each "Application" section is not a full-blown dissertation chapter, but a representation or model of what the chapter should look like. As such, bear in mind that in a real dissertation the discussion would need to be somewhat elaborated and extended. The intent is that you will have a clear grasp of the content, as well as understand the process, and thereby be able to apply this to your own dissertation.

OBJECTIVES

Part II Objectives

The objectives that follow address the knowledge and skills required to conduct a qualitative research study and write the dissertation.

Section I: Instruction

- Provide guidelines as to the required content of each dissertation chapter and how to develop that content.
- Offer an understanding of the processes involved in setting up each dissertation chapter.

Section II: Application

Demonstrate what each chapter of a dissertation should look like by way of a consistent research example that is carried throughout all the chapters.

The following table provides an overview of the contents of an entire dissertation. It is a prelude to the steps involved in each of the chapters that are described and demonstrated in Part II.

Table 1.1   Overview of Dissertation Content

Chapter 1: Introduction to Research Problem	Chapter 2: Literature Review	Chapter 3: Research Methodology	Chapter 4: Presentation of Findings	Chapter 5: Analysis & Interpretation of Findings	Chapter 6: Conclusions and Recommendations
Context • Problem • Purpose • Research Questions • Research Approach • Anticipated Outcomes • Researcher Assumptions • Rationale & Significance • Researcher Perspectives • Definitions of Terminology	• Purpose • Rationale for Topics • Description: Topic I • Description: Topic II • Description Topic III • Summary • Conceptual Framework a. Narrative description b. Graphic depiction	• Purpose • Introduction • Overview of Information Needed • Overview of Methodology • Demographic Data • Analysis & Synthesis of Data • Issues of Trustworthiness • Limitations • Summary	• Purpose • Description of findings must be *objective.* • Findings are not subject to interpretation by researcher	• Purpose • Description of meaning tied to each finding—is *subjective* • Analysis relates to research questions and is synthesized with data from other methods and literature	• Conclusions • Typically each conclusion drawn should be tied to the respective finding and interpretations • Recommendations • Typically there are recommendations for (a) the organization or institution, (b) people in the particular discipline under study, and (c) for further research
			Matrix of Findings Through Recommendations: "If/Then/Therefore/Thus"		
			"If I find this . . ."	*"then I think this means . . ."*	*"therefore I conclude, or what I now know to be true is . . ."* / *"thus I recommend that . . ."*

Introduction to Your Study

OVERVIEW

The first chapter of your dissertation is the most critical, and everything that follows hinges on how well this first chapter is constructed. Chapter 1 begins with the *Context*, which introduces the research by providing the background that sets the stage for the *Problem* to be investigated. Once you have identified a sound, researchable problem, the next step is to describe the *Purpose* of the research—that is, *how* you will go about addressing the problem. To carry out the Purpose, three to five *Research Questions* are developed that, when answered, will shed light on the problem you have identified. Therefore, the Problem, Purpose, and Research Questions are the building blocks—the very core—of your study; they are intrinsically tied together and from which everything else develops.

Our objective in this chapter is twofold: to provide you with an understanding of how to think through and identify the critical elements in setting up and carrying out a research study, and to provide you with an illustration of what a well-constructed introductory chapter looks like. In this chapter, we introduce the research problem on which this book is based, and we continue to use this same problem throughout the succeeding chapters to illustrate each step of the dissertation process.

CHAPTER OBJECTIVES

Chapter 1 Objectives

Section I: Instruction

- Narrow and refine the problem statement.
- Develop a purpose statement that addresses the problem.
- Identify the research questions that are tied to the purpose and, when answered, shed light on the problem.
- Understand and develop the context that sets up the problem.
- Describe and define content for subcategories: research approach, anticipated outcomes, researcher's assumptions, rationale and significance, researcher perspectives, and definitions of key terminology.

Section II: Application

- Presentation of a completed dissertation chapter 1 based on the content as described earlier.

The first chapter of a dissertation is about defining what is to be studied and why it is worth studying. We begin this chapter by reviewing the key elements involved in setting up a sound qualitative study. Although the requirements vary among programs and/or institutions, some common core elements need to be included in a dissertation's first chapter—namely, problem, purpose, and research questions. Each of these elements is described and illustrated in greater detail in the following section.

SECTION I: INSTRUCTION

The Problem

Beginning researchers often confuse a topic with a research problem. A *topic* refers to a general area of interest. For example, we may be interested in the issue of change because we are living in a time when rapid and increasing changes are taking place all around us. A *research problem* is more specific. It seeks to understand some aspect of the general topic. For example, given our interest in change, we want to better understand how people learn to master or adapt to change. Thus, our problem focuses on the participants' perceptions with respect to some specific change event. In qualitative research, the problem should be open ended and exploratory in nature.

The problem indicates the need for the study. In writing up your problem statement, be sure that it refers to an important authentic, genuine problem that we know little about, but that is significant and therefore worthy of investigation. Ask yourself: So why is this a problem? The fact that there may be little in the literature on the subject is *not* a problem. For every problem there has to be a worthwhile reason for the study to be conducted. We do not do research because we are interested in a certain topic or because

we have a hunch about something and we want to go and *prove* it, as would be the case with quantitative research.

All qualitative research emerges from a perceived problem, some unsatisfactory situation, condition, or phenomenon that we want to confront. Sometimes the source of research is around a particular scholarly debate, a pressing social issue, or some workplace phenomena we want to better understand. Basically, the problem statement is the discrepancy between what we already know and what we want to know. A research problem is driven by what Booth, Colomb, and Williams (2003) state is ". . . incomplete knowledge or flawed understanding. You solve it not by changing the world but by understanding it better" (p. 59). The problem statement also illustrates why we care—why this study should be conducted.

Identifying a good topic/research problem is one of the most often cited stumbling blocks for students who are just beginning the dissertation journey. All too often, students have grand ideas about conducting big and important research in a particular area of interest to them. And, all too often, we remind students that, although every topic should have the potential to make a contribution to a particular field, this should not be the overriding objective. Rather, what is most important is that a topic be so narrowly defined and discrete that it is specific enough to be carried out to its conclusion. In other words, if you have too many aspects associated with your problem statement, which is often the case, you will not be able to properly manage and account for all of those aspects.

The first thing to keep in mind in searching for a problem area to investigate is that the problem must be narrowly focused. Second, a logical place to begin looking for an appropriate research topic/problem is within your own personal and/or professional environment. In this way, you may be able to identify a problem/topic that: (a) can sustain your interest—this is important since you will be living with your topic for a while, (b) will enable you to demonstrate to the university that you can conduct and carry out a logical and well-developed research project, and (c) will enable you to make recommendations that may benefit you personally, or benefit a particular situation or some aspect of your workplace. These are the considerations we took into account in selecting a topic/problem we could use as an example to illustrate each of the steps in the dissertation process.

The problem we work with here is: *Why do some doctoral candidates complete all the course work and yet do not go on to complete the research and write their dissertations?* This problem is narrowly defined and focuses on a specific segment of the population; it is relevant to the reader and, hopefully, will contribute to the reader's ability to complete the research and write the dissertation. Once you have identified your own narrowly defined topic and clear, concise problem statement, you are ready to formulate your purpose statement and research questions that must be addressed and answered to shed light on the problem.

The Purpose Statement and Research Questions

The purpose statement is the major objective or intent of the study; it enables the reader to understand the central thrust of the research. Specifically, the purpose refers to *how* you will go about addressing the problem; that is, who will be involved and what perceptions they have that are germane to your problem. Given the importance of the purpose, it is helpful to frame it as a short, crisp, almost "bite-sized" statement that can be retained by the reader and researcher alike. Because the purpose is a critical piece of the entire study, it needs to be given careful attention and must be written in clear and concise language.

Henceforth, we recommend that each succeeding chapter of the dissertation should include the purpose statement in the introductory paragraph. This notion is demonstrated in each Application Section. Please note, however, that inclusion of the purpose statement in this way is a requirement that applies to some programs, but not all. If you choose to include the purpose statement in the opening section of all your chapters, be sure that you word this statement exactly the same throughout so that it can be easily identified. Even if you do not include the purpose statement in each chapter's introductory paragraph, in every instance that you mention your study's purpose, be sure to adhere to the same wording throughout. Accuracy and precision in this respect allow for clarity and help avoid potential confusion. This stage is not the time to be creative, but rather to remain practical!

There is a close relationship between the research tradition and purpose statement. In all traditions, you are trying to *discover* something. With a case study, ethnography, or phenomenology, you are trying to understand, describe, or explore a phenomenon. In grounded theory studies, you are trying to develop or generate theory. Therefore, you need to be specific about the words that you use to define your purpose statement. In addition, the purpose statement should include terms that refer to the specific tradition of inquiry, the research site, and the research participants.

You will see from Fig. 1.1 that the purpose is directly related to and flows from the research problem, and that the research questions in turn are related to and flow from the purpose. A good strategy for testing the interconnectedness and logic of your problem, purpose, and research questions is to lay all three of these elements out on one page as illustrated in the following example. It is vital to complete this step before you begin writing chapter 1 because these three elements are the heart of your study and you must get them right. This simple exercise helps you achieve clarity around the problem in its simplest form, and it identifies how you will go about shedding light on the problem. This step forces you to implode for clarity before you explode and fully develop the subject matter. In other words, to keep your problem in focus, you need to reduce it to simple terms before you can present it in more scholarly and elegant ways. When you do this, you are less likely to lose sight of exactly what aspects of a particularly phenomenon you seek to explore. If you take the time to produce this simple one page, it will greatly facilitate the writing of a well-developed first chapter.

Chapter 1 is the shortest chapter in a dissertation, averaging between 12 and 16 pages at the most. Although short, this chapter is arguably the most important because everything that follows is a result of how well the critical elements—problem, purpose, and research questions—have been developed.

As you can see from Fig. 1.1, the research questions are directly tied to the purpose. This underscores that you must ask the right questions to shed light on the problem. Drafting good research questions is a process that requires mind work. Research questions are often developed at the start of a project, but in qualitative research, there is an ongoing process of formulating and modifying them. Research questions are general questions about

Problem: Research indicates that significant numbers of people in doctoral programs complete all the course requirements, yet do not go on to complete the research or produce their dissertations. Hence, despite their significant investment in time and money, these people never receive the doctoral degree that they set out to obtain and thus remain ABD. There is little information as to why this phenomenon occurs.

Purpose: The purpose of this multicase study is to explore a sample of doctoral candidates' perceptions of why they have not managed to complete their dissertations.

Research Questions:

(1) On completion of their coursework, to what extent did participants perceive they were prepared to conduct research and write their dissertations?

(2) What did participants perceive they needed to learn to complete their dissertations?

(3) How did participants attempt to develop the knowledge, skills, and attitudes they perceived are necessary to complete their dissertations?

(4) What factors did participants perceive might help them to complete their dissertations?

(5) What factors did participants perceive have impeded and/or continue to impede their progress in working toward completing their dissertations?

Figure 1.1   Roadmap for Developing the Dissertation's First Chapter: Necessary Elements

the phenomenon under study—what the researcher wishes to learn or understand about it. Research questions are quite different from the more specific questions asked in interviews: The former provides a framework for understanding a phenomenon, whereas the latter are intended to produce the data for the answers to the research questions.

Good research questions should be clear, specific, and unambiguously stated. They should also be interconnected; that is, related to each other in some meaningful way. As such, the questions should be displayed in a logical order. Mostly, the research questions must be substantively relevant; they must be worthy of the research effort to be expended. Therefore, you need to consider carefully the nature of your research questions and the kind of understanding they may generate. Maxwell (2005) offers a useful categorization of the kinds of understanding that qualitative inquiry can generate by way of the following types of questions:

1. Descriptive—these ask what is going on in terms of actual observable (or potentially observable) events and behavior;

2. Interpretive—these seek to explore the meaning of things, situations, and conditions for the people involved; and

3. Theoretical—these are aimed at examining why certain things happen and how they can be explained.

Qualitative research questions usually start with "*how*" or "*in what ways*" and "*what,*" thus conveying an open and emerging design. In developing your research questions, it is important that the questions be open ended to foster exploration and discovery. Therefore, avoid wording your questions in ways that solicit yes or no answers. Your research questions should be nondirectional. They should not imply cause and effect or in any way suggest measurement. Do not use terminology that suggests or infers quantitative

research, such as *affect, influence, cause,* or *amount.* Also, be sure that your questions remind the reader, and yourself, that you are focusing essentially on perceptions.

Once you have developed your research questions, it is a good idea to step back and test them. You do this by looking at each and asking yourself: "What kind of information will I likely get in response to this question?" As a matter of fact, your cumulative answers form the story line of your study. Let us explain. If the data collection methods are implemented correctly, we should know why people enrolled, what they thought they needed to be successful, what means they took to get what they needed, and what helped or hindered them along the way. Thus, the responses to the questions should tell us why a certain group of people has been unable to achieve what they set out to do in enrolling in a doctoral program.

It should be obvious that if you are going to ask people questions, you have to be able to categorize their responses in some way. The "conceptual framework," which is used to categorize participants' responses, is described more fully at the end of chapter 2. It is mentioned now because the design of the conceptual framework also is tied directly to the research questions; that is, each research question is identified by an appropriate category and set of subcategories. For example, Research Question 1 would be categorized as motivation and will have subcategories such as the various kinds of intrinsic and extrinsic motivations that emanate from theories of motivation in the literature.

Additional Elements for Chapter 1

In addition to the problem, purpose, and research questions, there are other associated elements or subsections that appear in a fully developed chapter 1. It should be noted, however, that, aside from Problem, Purpose, and Research Questions, there may be some variations in required subheadings depending on individual programs and/or universities. Begin this section with one or two brief introductory paragraphs in which you tell the reader what research methodology you have used and mention the site and research sample. In this introduction, you also should lay out the organization of the remainder of the chapter so that the reader has a clear idea of this up front. After this brief introduction, you are ready to discuss the context. Following is an outline of typical subheadings that comprise chapter 1. These headings appear in sequential order:

Context—This is the beginning of the dissertation; it is the stage setting leading up to and introducing the problem to be addressed in the study. The context provides the history, background, and issues germane to the problem. It gives the reader an understanding of circumstances that may have precipitated the problem, the current state of the situation surrounding the problem, and the primary reasons that an exploration of the problem is warranted. It is important to embed your discussion of the context in the ongoing dialogue in the literature. This is not a formal review of the literature, as is done in chapter 2 of the dissertation; rather it helps you build the case for why your research should be undertaken and to convince the reader of the study's need and value. It is in this way that you set up the legitimacy of the problem. The context can usually be covered effectively in five to seven pages.

Problem—as described above

Purpose—as described above

Research Questions—as described above

Research Design Overview—This section briefly describes the kind of study you are conducting, identifying which among the different qualitative traditions you will be choosing. In this section, you also describe the site and research participants, data-collection methods that you use, type of data that you are collecting, as well as the strategies you use for data analysis. This discussion should not be more than a page or two because more explicit information regarding your research approach is provided in chapter 3.

Assumptions—These statements reflect what you hold to be true as you go into the study and from which you believe you will be able to draw some conclusions. Your assumptions are based on certain premises that may either hold up or be shown to be unwarranted. There are usually four or five assumptions identified by the researcher. These are the important issues around your topic that you believe to be true as you begin your research. Later on, at end of your research (in the analysis chapter), you will revisit and reflect on your initial assumptions.

Rationale and Significance—This discussion is presented in two well-thought-out paragraphs that provide the rationale for the study and its significance. The rationale is the justification for the study presented as a logical argument. It describes the genesis of the study and why it is important to carry it out. This is distinct from the significance of the study, which addresses the benefits that may be derived from doing the study. The significance addresses questions regarding your study such as "So what?" or "What difference does it make?" Therefore, the issue of significance reaffirms the research purpose and is a more detailed explanation of the implications of your study—that is, what benefits will be derived from the study. In other words, in attempting to establish the significance of your research, you should think about the various ways in which your study is likely to contribute to: (a) theory (by adding to research and literature), (b) potential practical application, and/or (c) ways in which the study might improve policy.

The Researcher—This section informs the reader what you—as the researcher—bring to the study. Begin by describing your background, education, and professional experience that lends itself to your interest in and knowledge about the subject of your inquiry. You also can share your unique perspectives and interests as they relate to and inform the study. In this way, the reader develops some idea as to why you are prepared (*qualified* is too strong a word) to carry out your research.

Definitions—This section provides the definitions of terminology used in the study that do not have a common meaning or those terms that have the possibility of being misunderstood. These terms should be operationally defined or explained; that is, they clarify how these terms are used in *your* study. If you use the definitions of others, be sure to include the authoritative sources to support these definitions. Which terms to define and clarify is a matter of judgment. Generally these are the terms that are central to your study and that are used throughout. Making terms explicit adds precision and ensures clarity of understanding.

Now that we have reviewed and explained all the essential elements required to construct a research study and introduce it in chapter 1, we are ready to see what an actual written-up chapter 1 would look like using the problem previously identified.

SECTION II: APPLICATION

CHAPTER I
Introduction

This study seeks to explore the phenomenon of why some people who enter doctoral programs complete all the course work, but do not go on to complete their dissertations. The purpose of this multicase study is to explore with a sample of doctoral candidates their perceptions of why they have not managed to complete their dissertations. It was anticipated that the knowledge generated from this inquiry would afford new insights and so inform higher education practice. This research employed qualitative multicase study methodology to illustrate the phenomenon under examination. Participants of this study included a purposefully selected group consisting of 20 doctoral candidates who had completed the course work but not yet completed their dissertations.

This chapter begins with an overview of the context and background that frames the study.

Following this is the problem statement, the statement of purpose, and accompanying research questions. Also included in this chapter is discussion around research approach, researcher's perspectives, and researcher's assumptions. The chapter concludes with a discussion of the proposed rationale and significance of this research study and definitions of some of the key terminology used.

Background and Context

Although there has been a proliferation in the number of doctoral degrees granted in the last two decades, there also has been an increase in attrition rates in doctoral programs. The status of "All-But-Dissertation" (ABD) has been a critical one in American graduate education since the 1960s, and its poignancy—and its permanency—has been growing (Sternberg, 1981). That doctoral candidates struggle, stall, and ultimately fail to complete their doctorates remains one of the central issues in doctoral education in the United States today (Chronicle of Higher Education, January 16, 2004).

It is estimated that around 50% or more of students who enter doctoral programs leave without graduating (Bair & Haworth, 1999; Berg, 2007; Bowen & Rudenstein, 1992; Lovitts, 1996, 2001; Lovitts & Nelson, 2000). As Bowen and Rudenstein (1992) state, "The percentage of students who never earn PhDs inspite of having achieved ABD status has risen . . . the absolute numbers are high enough to be grounds for serious concern" (p. 253). These authors further report that, for many of those who eventually receive the degree, it has taken between 6 and 12 years to do so. Failure to complete doctoral programs represents not only a personal setback to the individual in pursuit of the degree, but also is wasteful in terms of resources, time, and money for institutions and academic departments (Katz, 1995; Lenz, 1995).

The completion of a doctoral dissertation is usually the most taxing and difficult academic requirement a student will face during her or his term of graduate education (Brause, 2004; Meloy, 1992,

1994; Rudestam & Newton, 2001; Sternberg, 1981). The journey through the required research and writing processes is a challenging one, pushing the student intellectually, philosophically, emotionally, and financially. Many studies have been conducted to understand the reasons for students' attrition in doctoral programs (Bair & Haworth, 1999; Green & Kluever, 1996, 1997; Heinrich, 1991; Lovitts, 1996; Meloy, 1994; Miller, 1995). The studies of Heinrich (1991) and Meloy (1992), for example, indicate the significant role played by the advisement relationship. Lovitts (1996) identifies lack of institutional support as a major contributing factor; this support could be in the form of information about the program or in relationships between students and faculty.

It appears that many students in doctoral programs proceed through the steps with only a vague understanding of the process of writing a dissertation. They are not fully prepared for the complexity and intensity inherent in the doctoral process. They lack the necessary knowledge and skills, and hence find themselves floundering. Although one can speculate as to what knowledge, skills, and attitudes are needed to successfully complete a dissertation, and although existing literature provides a multitude of perspectives regarding what it takes to successfully complete a dissertation, there seems to be little conclusive agreement. Therefore, this study seeks to shed light on why some people who enroll in doctoral programs complete all the course requirements, but do not complete their dissertations and obtain the degree they sought. It is this problem that this study seeks to address.

Problem Statement

Research indicates that significant numbers of people in doctoral programs complete all the course requirements, yet they do not go on to complete the research and produce the dissertation. Hence, despite their significant investment in time and money, these people never receive the doctoral degree that they set out to obtain and, thus, remain ABD. There is little information as to why this phenomenon occurs.

Statement of Purpose and Research Questions

The purpose of this multicase study was to explore with 20 doctoral candidates their perceptions of why they have not completed their dissertations. It is anticipated that, through a better understanding of the motivation and needs of doctoral candidates, the issues and challenges they face, and the availability of academic resources, more informed decisions can be made by both prospective and current doctoral candidates as well as academic institutions. To shed light on the problem, the following research questions are addressed:

1. On completion of their course work, to what extent did participants perceive they were prepared to conduct research and write the dissertation?

2. What did participants perceive they needed to learn to complete their dissertation?

3. How did participants attempt to develop the knowledge, skills, and attitudes they perceived are necessary to complete the dissertation?

4. What factors did participants perceive might help them to complete the dissertation?

5. What factors did participants perceive have impeded and/or continue to impede their progress in working toward completing their dissertation?

Research Approach

With the approval of the University's Institutional Review Board, the researcher studied the experiences and perceptions of 20 doctoral candidates. These participants had completed all the required course work, yet had not been able to complete their dissertations. This investigation represented a multicase study using qualitative research methods.

In-depth interviews were the primary method of data collection. The interview process began with the researcher conducting two pilot interviews. The information obtained through 20 individual interviews subsequently formed the basis for the overall findings of this study. Each interviewee was identified by a pseudonym, and all interviews were tape recorded and transcribed verbatim. To support the findings emanating from the in-depth interviews, participants completed critical incident reports.

Although the nature of this study prevented the researcher from achieving triangulation of data, a comprehensive review of the relevant literature and pilot tests shaped and refined the two data-collection methods used. Coding categories were thus developed and refined on an ongoing basis, guided by the study's conceptual framework. In addition, various strategies were employed, including the search for discrepant evidence, inter-rater reliability in the coding process, and peer review at different stages as the study progressed.

Assumptions

Based on the researchers' experience and background as academic advisers, three primary assumptions were made regarding this study. First, coursework does not prepare doctoral candidates to conduct research and write their dissertations. This assumption is based on the premise that the attrition rate in doctoral programs is so high—estimated at 50%. Second, because doctoral students are mature adults, they will be sufficiently self-reliant and self-directed, and that will enable them to conduct research and write the dissertation. This assumption is guided by a predominant adult learning principle that says adults have a preference for planning and directing their own learning. Third, because students have successfully completed all their course requirements, they should be able to carry out a research project and write a dissertation. This assumption is based on the premise that past success is likely to be a predictor of future success. Fourth, doctoral candidates do not always receive the direction and guidance they need from their advisors, and hence will learn informally to obtain what they need to successfully complete their work. This assumption is based on the experience that we have had as dissertation advisors. Fifth and finally, people who enroll in doctoral programs are strongly motivated to obtain the doctoral degree. This

assumption is premised on the notion that people would not make the significant investment in time and money to enroll in a doctoral program without a strong desire to achieve the goal of obtaining the degree.

The Researcher

At the time of conducting this study, both researchers were employed as faculty members in a doctoral program; both as teachers and academic advisors. Thus, the researchers bring to the inquiry process practical experience as working professionals in a doctoral program, with both having knowledge and understanding of the environmental context.

The researchers acknowledge that the same experiences that are so valuable in providing insight could serve as a liability, biasing their judgment regarding research design and the interpretation of findings. In addition to their assumptions and theoretical orientation being made explicit at the outset of the study, the researchers remained committed to engage in ongoing critical self-reflection by way of journaling and dialogue with professional colleagues and advisors. Moreover, to address their subjectivity and strengthen the credibility of the research, various procedural safeguards were taken, such as triangulation of data sources, triangulation of methods, and inter-rater reliability checks with professional colleagues.

Rationale and Significance

The rationale for this study emanates from the researchers' desire to uncover ways to encourage and help students complete their dissertations. These students may be prospective doctoral students, candidates stalled at some stage of the process, as well as those who may have decided to abandon their work altogether.

Increased understanding of the research process and development of the skills needed to write and complete the dissertation may not only reduce the numbers of ABDs, but also increase the potential for greater numbers of students to attain a doctoral degree. A terminal degree may not only afford the recipients more career options and personal gratification, but also has the potential to be of benefit to society at large.

Definitions of Key Terminology Used in This Study

ABD—An acronym that refers to those people who have enrolled in a doctoral program and have completed all the course work, but who did not go on to complete their dissertations and graduate with a doctoral degree.

Dissertation—A major research project that presents a problem for investigation, employs methods to collect data on the problem, reports and analyzes findings emanating from the data collection, draws conclusions, and makes recommendations based on the findings.

Doctoral Student—A student enrolled in a doctoral program who has not yet taken the mandated certification exam, but who is active in some phase of the required course work.

Doctoral Candidate—A student who has completed all the coursework and passed the certification exam and either is working on the proposal development or involved in some stage of dissertation research.

Proposal—The point at which you present and justify your research ideas in order to gain approval from a faculty committee to proceed with your study. Only when your proposal has been approved can you embark on the research. The proposal consists of the first three chapters of a student's dissertation.

SUMMARY DISCUSSION FOR CHAPTER 1

This chapter described the critical components that set in place a research study: problem, purpose, and research questions. It stressed the interconnectedness of each of these components and underscored that they are at the core of the research and that everything that follows hinges on how well these components are constructed and aligned. In addition to these major components, the chapter also described and illustrated all the other elements that comprise a well-developed introductory chapter, including research approach, researcher assumptions and perspectives, rationale and significance, and definitions of key terminology.

Chapter Checklist

✓ Is the problem appropriate for qualitative inquiry?
✓ Is the problem situated within the literature? That is, is the literature used to place the problem within a context?
✓ Is the problem clearly and unambiguously stated?
✓ Is the problem narrow in scope?
✓ Is the purpose clearly stated?
✓ Are the research questions clearly focused or too broad?
✓ Are the research questions answerable and able to shed light on the problem?
✓ Is there strong alignment among problem, purpose, and research questions?
✓ Is the research approach appropriate and feasible?
✓ Is the researcher's perspective and relationship to the problem discussed?
✓ Are the researcher's assumptions and biases revealed and explained?
✓ Is there a well-thought-out rationale and justification for the study?

✓ Is a convincing argument explicitly or implicitly made for the importance or significance of this research? Is it clear how it will contribute to the knowledge base and/or practice?

✓ Does the chapter conclude with definitions and/or explanations of the key terms used in the study that do not have a commonly understood meaning? If these are definitions, have you included authoritative sources to support these definitions?

✓ Have you checked for institutional and/or program-related differences regarding the content and structure of chapter 1?

✓ Have you checked for institutional and/or program-related differences regarding the appropriate use of qualitative language and terminology?

ANNOTATED BIBLIOGRAPHY

Booth, W. C., Colomb, G. G., & Williams, J. M. (2003). *The craft of research* (2nd ed.). Chicago: University of Chicago Press.

This book offers clear, helpful, and systematic guidelines on how to conduct qualitative research and report it effectively. Especially helpful are chapters 3 and 4, which offer informed instruction on how to move from an interest to a topic and then how to shape the topic into a more clearly defined and researchable problem replete with purpose and associated research questions. Chapter 15 offers useful suggestions for how to communicate and present evidence visually. Throughout the book, the authors emphasize the importance of clarity and precision in designing a viable, cogent study.

Creswell, J. W. (1998). *Qualitative inquiry and research design: Choosing among five traditions*. Thousand Oaks, CA: Sage.

A classic in qualitative research methods, this book provides a comprehensive summary of the major qualitative traditions. Going beyond the philosophical assumptions, perspectives, and theories, in chapter 6, the focus turns to the introduction of a qualitative study and the key elements involved: stating the problem, formulating the purpose statement, and generating research questions. Consistent with the author's view throughout the book is the emphasis on how these three elements relate to the particular chosen tradition of inquiry and how this involves what he calls "encoding" specific terms and "foreshadowing" ideas to be developed later. The author illustrates how this might be accomplished by providing several examples from qualitative studies.

Creswell, J. W. (2003). *Research design: Qualitative, quantitative, and mixed methods approaches* (2nd ed.). Thousand Oaks, CA: Sage.

This book is accessible, readable, and useful in terms of providing clear guidelines for designing qualitative research. The chapters in Part II focus on the mechanics of composing and writing a scholarly introduction, explaining in great detail how to go about developing a researchable problem, setting the problem within an appropriate context, devising a purpose statement, and asking viable research questions. There also is discussion of limitations, delimitations, and the significance of a study. Each chapter concludes with writing exercises, allowing readers to practice the principles they learn.

Maxwell, J. (2005). *Qualitative research design: An interactive approach* (2nd ed.). Thousand Oaks, CA: Sage

Joseph Maxwell, one of the leading authors of qualitative research, reflects on the purpose for a qualitative dissertation. In so doing, he makes clear the various elements that constitute qualitative research design and provides a clear strategy for creating workable relationships among these design components. The design, logic, and coherence of a research study are crucial. Throughout the planning process, there are various issues to deal with. Maxwell clearly describes the considerations that inform your decisions about these issues. These design issues include clarifying the purpose of your study, creating a theoretical context for your research, and formulating strong research questions.

Morse, J. M., & Richards, L. (2002). *Read me first for a users guide to qualitative research*. Thousand Oaks, CA: Sage.

This book is useful for the beginning researcher to develop some understanding of the language of qualitative inquiry and, as the authors put it, "to start thinking qualitatively." This book provides a broad overview of qualitative traditions and the methods used within those traditions. The authors' intention is to emphasize that there are many ways of working qualitatively, and they offer suggestions for how best to go about identifying and selecting the most appropriate choice of inquiry tradition. These choices, as the authors explain, fit different research purposes and research questions, providing different research experiences and outcomes. Included are useful bibliographic references for each of the major qualitative research traditions.

Schram, T. H. (2003). *Conceptualizing qualitative inquiry: Mindwork for fieldwork in education and the social sciences*. Upper Saddle River, NJ: Merrill Prentice Hall.

This book aptly conveys the iterative and interconnected processes involved in the design of qualitative research. The focus is on the practical issues involved in conceiving of and connecting the ideas that prompt and guide a thoughtful and coherent research study. Most useful is the detailed description of the interplay among the various components involved in conceptualizing and designing the study: developing and situating a researchable problem, generating a research purpose, forming research questions, and clarifying researcher perspectives.

Developing and Presenting the Literature Review

OVERVIEW

This chapter provides a guide to what some see as one of the most daunting tasks involved in writing a dissertation—that of reviewing topic-specific literature. A dissertation demonstrates your ability to write a coherent volume of intellectually demanding work. A key part of the dissertation that illustrates your scholarship is the way in which you have analyzed, organized, and reported the relevant literature. With thoughtful preparation, careful planning of your work and time, and helpful guidelines, this *is* a manageable task.

In conducting a literature review, you are forced to think critically and consider the role of argument in research. Thus, reviewing the literature is research in and of itself. Because a dissertation is really about demonstrating your ability to conduct and carry out a research project, our intent throughout this book is to help you understand what it means to be a researcher. With regard to the literature review chapter, an underlying assumption is that if you can understand the ideas and master the techniques and methods inherent in the literature review, this will be helpful to you in your own research.

Often students put off doing their literature review because they do not fully understand its purpose and function or they are unsure of the procedures to follow in conducting a literature search. In this chapter, we attempt to address both of these issues. The chapter is divided into two sections. Section I, "Instruction," discusses the purpose and function of the literature review; the role the literature review plays in a dissertation, pointing out possible differences with respect to the different qualitative traditions; and the actual steps involved in conducting and presenting a thorough and systematic literature review. Section II, "Application," demonstrates how to organize and write an actual literature review chapter. Here we focus on the specific problem as outlined in chapter 1 and, using this as an example, explain and illustrate how to develop the associated literature review.

CHAPTER OBJECTIVES

Chapter 2 Objectives

Section I: Instruction

- Provide an understanding of the function and purpose of a literature review (the "*what?*").
- Describe the role of a research-based critical literature review in a dissertation (the "*why?*").
- Provide the skills related to the various steps involved in conducting and presenting a thorough and systematic review of the literature, including identifying and retrieving relevant material and sources; analyzing, evaluating, and synthesizing ideas found in the literature; and developing a conceptual framework (the "*how?*").

Section II: Application

- Presentation of a completed literature review chapter based on the process described previously.

SECTION I: INSTRUCTION

Function and Purpose of a Literature Review

The review of related literature involves the systematic identification, location, and analysis of material related to the research problem. This material can include books, book chapters, articles, abstracts, reviews, monographs, dissertations, research reports, and electronic media. A key objective of the literature review is to provide a clear and balanced picture of current leading concepts, theories, and data relevant to your topic or subject of study. The material, although consisting of what has been searched, located, obtained, and read, is not merely a simplistic summative description of the contents of articles and books, nor is it a series of isolated summaries of previous studies. Your readers are being asked to view this literature review as representing the sum of the current knowledge on the topic, as well as your ability to think critically about it.

Areas of inquiry within disciplines exist as ongoing conversations among authors and theorists. By way of your literature review, you join the conversation—first by listening to what is being said and then formulating a comment designed to advance the dialogue. The literature review thus involves locating and assimilating what is already known and then entering the conversation from a critical and creative standpoint. As Toracco (2005) defines it "The integrative literature review is a form of research that reviews, critiques, and synthesizes representative literature on a topic in an integrated way such that new frameworks and perspectives on the topic are generated" (p. 356). Ultimately, your review "tells a story" by critically analyzing the literature and arriving at specific conclusions about it.

A literature review requires a technical form of writing in which facts must be documented and opinions substantiated. Producing a good literature review requires time and intellectual effort. It is a test of your ability to manage the relevant texts and materials, analytically interpret ideas, and integrate and synthesize ideas and data with existing knowledge. One of the ways to improve your writing is to read as widely as possible. Look for examples of good and bad writing. Try to identify ways in which other authors have structured and built their arguments, as well as the methods and techniques they have used to express their ideas.

Role and Scope of the Literature Review in the Dissertation

The major purpose of reviewing the literature is to determine what has already been done that relates to your topic. This knowledge not only prevents you from unintentionally duplicating research that has already been conducted, but it also affords you the understanding and insight needed to situate your topic within an existing framework. As Boote and Beile (2005) explain:

> A substantive, thorough, sophisticated literature review is a precondition for doing substantive, thorough, sophisticated research. "Good" research is good because it advances our collective understanding. To advance our collective understanding, a researcher or scholar needs to understand what has been done before, the strengths and weaknesses of existing studies, and what they might mean. (p. 3)

A review of the literature enables you to acquire a full understanding of your topic; what has been already said about it; how ideas related to your topic have been researched, applied, and developed; the key issues surrounding your topic; and the main criticisms that have been made regarding work on your topic. Therefore, a thorough search and reading of related literature is, in a very real sense, part of your own academic development—part of becoming an "expert" in your chosen field of inquiry.

As Hart (2005) explains, "A literature review forms the foundation for the research proper" (p. 26). It is incumbent on you, as the researcher, to find out what already exists in the area in which you propose to do research before doing the research. You need to know about the contributions that others have made relative to your topic because this prior work, as well as current research and debate, will provide you with the framework for your own work. In reviewing the literature, areas of concentrated interest, as well as areas of relative neglect, will become apparent, and so you will begin to identify a "space" for your own work. You also will gain a deeper understanding of the interrelationships and intersections between the subject under consideration and other subject areas. Therefore, a review of the literature allows you to get a grip on what is known and to learn where the "holes" are in the current body of knowledge. A review of the literature also enables you to recognize previously reported concepts or patterns, refer to already established explanations or theories, and recognize any variations between what was previously discovered and what you are now finding as a result of your study.

Qualitative researchers use existing literature to guide their studies in various ways depending on the type of study being conducted. Depending on the research tradition you have adopted, there are subtle differences in the interplay between prior knowledge and discovery. As such, there are differences regarding the purpose and process for planning the research design and presenting the review of the literature with respect to each of the research traditions. There are some general guidelines regarding whether the literature is referred to *before* asking questions and data collection or *after* data collection and data analysis (Creswell, 1998). For example, in a phenomenological study, the literature is reviewed primarily following data collection so that the information in the literature does not preclude the researcher from being able to "bracket" or suspend preconceptions. If conducting a grounded theory study, some literature review is conducted initially to place the study in context and to inform the researcher of what has been done in the field. The main literature review is conducted *during* concept development, however, because the literature is used to define the concepts and further define and clarify the relationships in the theory developed from the empirical data. In grounded theory, the literature becomes a source for data (Strauss & Corbin, 1990). When categories have been found, the researcher trawls the literature for confirmation or refutation of these categories. The objective is to ascertain what other researchers have found and whether there are any links to existing theories. In conducting an ethnographic study, the literature is reviewed before data are collected, serving as a background for the research question and informing the researcher as to what will be studied and how it will be studied. With narrative inquiry and case study, both "before" and "after" approaches are employed: An initial review is conducted after the development of the research question to shape the direction of the study, and the literature also is reviewed on an ongoing basis throughout the study to compare and contrast with the data that have emerged and the study's conceptual framework.

No matter which qualitative tradition or genre you have adopted, the review of related literature is more than just a stage to be undertaken and a hurdle to be overcome. Whether the literature is referred to before asking questions and data collection data or after data collection and data analysis, the literature is, right from the beginning, an essential, integral, and ongoing part of the research process. Aside from the formal review of related and relevant literature of chapter 2 of the dissertation, which demonstrates that you show command of your subject area and an understanding of the research problem, you will more generally need to conduct reviews of the literature at various stages of the dissertation process.

At the initial stages, a preliminary search and analysis of the literature is usually necessary to focus on a researchable topic and evaluate its relevance. It is the progressive honing of the topic, by way of the literature review, that makes most research a practical consideration. Having done that and having developed a narrowly defined problem statement, you then set or situate your problem within a context. To do this, it is important to consult the literature to see whether the study's problem has been addressed and how and to what extent the issues surrounding the problem have been addressed.

Besides providing a foundation—a theoretical framework for the problem to be investigated—the literature review can demonstrate how the present study advances, refines, or revises what is already known. Knowledge of previous studies offers a point of reference for discussing the contribution that your study will make in advancing the knowledge base. As such, the literature review is a conscious attempt to keep in mind that the dissertation research emerges from and is contained within a larger context of educational inquiry. The literature that describes the context frames the problem; it provides a useful backdrop for the problem or issue that has led to the need for the study. The literature review also can assist you in refining your research questions. Furthermore, previous studies can provide the rationale for your research problem, and indications of what needs to be done can help you justify the significance of your study.

It is important to realize that the literature review does not formally end once you have written your introductory and literature review chapters, but carries over into subsequent chapters as well.

As a qualitative researcher, you must demonstrate the ability to assess the methodologies that you will be using in your research. This type of assessment is necessary to display a clear and critical understanding of how you will be conducting your study and why you have chosen to conduct it that way. The aim of the methodology chapter is to indicate the appropriateness of the various design features of your research, including your research approach and the specific methodology employed. In this regard, relevant references from the literature are necessary to illustrate the respective strengths and weaknesses of each of the data-collection methods you intend to employ.

Being familiar with previous research also facilitates interpretation of your study's findings because the latter will need to be discussed in terms of whether and how they relate to the findings of previous studies. If your findings contradict previous findings, you can describe the differences between your study and the others, providing a rationale for the discrepancies. However, if your findings are consistent with other findings, your report could include suggestions for future research to shed light on the relevant issues.

You might be asking: "What is the scope of a literature review?" Just how much literature you will need to cover is a difficult question to answer. As a rule of thumb, a literature review should represent the most current work undertaken in a subject area, and usually a 5-year span from the present is a tentative limit of coverage. For historical overviews, however, you might reach beyond the 5-year span. However, there is no formula that can be applied. Base your decision on your own judgment and the advice of your advisor. The following general guidelines can assist you:

- Avoid the temptation to include everything. Bigger does not necessarily mean better. A concise, well-organized literature review that contains relevant information is preferable to a review containing many studies that are only peripherally related to your research problem.
- When investigating a heavily researched and well-developed area, review only those works that are directly related to your specific research problem.
- When investigating a new or little-researched problem area, you need to gather enough information to develop and establish a logical framework for your study. Therefore, review all studies related in some meaningful way to your research problem.

As you continue reviewing the relevant and appropriate literature, you will know when you have reached a saturation point when you begin to encounter the same references over and again and can no longer find any new sources. Generally speaking, a literature chapter is usually between 30 to 50 pages. However, this number depends, to a large extent, on the complexity of your study and the preferences of your advisor. Therefore, take time to clarify this with her or him prior to writing the review.

Remember, because you are attempting to provide a comprehensive and up-to-date review of your selected areas, it is important to revisit the literature review toward the end of your study to make sure no new research has been overlooked. This step is especially important if much time has passed since you wrote the original literature review for your proposal. Thus, as your study comes to a close, it may be necessary to conduct a new literature search to make sure that all new studies conducted since you wrote the original literature review are included. Moreover, as we remind you in Part III of this book, the literature review is an important early task. Once you complete your study, you need to reread your literature review and ensure that everything therein is directly relevant to your study. Based on your findings and the analysis and interpretation of those findings, whatever is deemed irrelevant should be eliminated. Equally important, if a section of literature review is missing, it will need to be added.

Preparing for the Literature Review

Finding relevant material for a comprehensive literature review involves multiple strategies and a wide variety of sources. It is important to become familiar with your institution's library. You should check on what services your library provides, how to access these services, and the regulations and procedures regarding the use of library services and materials. In this regard, university libraries usually offer short informative seminars or courses.

Materials other than books, such as journals and conference papers, are generally obtainable through your library databases. This step is where your university library becomes an especially useful and efficient resource. Through their subscription to these databases, libraries have become gateways to information, and technological advancements have opened up a range of new possibilities to researchers. Some of the more commonly used online library databases for the social sciences are presented as Appendix A.

There are a few hundred databases that can link you to the relevant scholarly publications. Each database has its own unique features; familiarizing yourself with these features will enable you to access and conduct electronic searches. Once accessed, you can search according to your topic of interest and obtain either abstracts or full text articles. Search processes are not necessarily the same across all databases. The art of database searching involves learning how to input terms that will connect you with the material most related to your topic. Because database formats change frequently, you should check with librarians for recent information regarding new tools or strategies included in the latest versions of the databases. Appendix A offers an overview of some of the more commonly used databases.

Aside from online searches, you also should spend time in the library getting used to call numbers related to your topic in order to find the appropriate sections. To produce a comprehensive literature review, you have to be thorough. Many sources that are needed for review are not available online. Conducting a literature search using only online sources might mean that you miss some critical information.

Retrieval and review have their own set of requisite technical skills. A comprehensive literature search on a topic involves managing databases, references, and records. A common thread running through the discussion of the various stages involved in conducting a literature review is how to manage and organize information, materials, and ideas. Table 2.1 shows the various steps involved in constructing a well-developed literature review. Following is a more detailed explanation of each of the steps involved.

Step 1: Identify and Retrieve Literature

The literature review involves locating and assimilating what is already known. To do this, the writer must experience what Fanger (1985) describes as "immersion in the subject" by reading extensively in areas that either directly or indirectly relate to the topic under study. To begin, you need to select available documents, published and unpublished, on the topic. Through your search, you will begin to identify the relevant classic works and landmark studies, as well as the most current work available.

Primary source documents contain the original work of researchers and authors. Secondary sources are written by authors who interpret the work of others, including abstracts, indexes, reviews, encyclopedias, and textbooks. Secondary sources are useful because they combine knowledge from many primary sources and provide a quick way to obtain an overview of a field or topic. They also are a useful resource for obtaining other sources of information related to your research topic. At the same time, secondary sources cannot always be considered completely reliable. As such, as a serious graduate researcher, you should not rely solely on these, but should base your review on primary sources as much as possible. As you proceed in your search, note which authors are making significant contributions to increasing the knowledge base with regard to your chosen topic. In addition to seeking

Table 2.1   Roadmap for Conducting the Literature Review

1: Identify and Retrieve Literature

- Search library catalogues/library stacks.
- Familiarize yourself with online databases and identify those that are relevant for your field of study.
- Develop parameters that will yield focused results by selecting pertinent keywords or descriptors and specifying a limited range of publication dates (go back 5–10 years).
- Try out general descriptors and various combinations of subdescriptors. In this way, your search is refined and all possible yields are covered.
- Search the Internet for relevant information and resources.
- From all the sources that you use, try to obtain both theoretical and empirical (research-based) literature.
- Make sure to include primary as well as secondary sources.
- Identify and include the relevant classic works and landmark studies related to your topic.
- Also seek review articles that provide "state of the art" scholarship on a particular topic. In other words, review as much up-to-date work as possible.
- In collecting literature, be prepared to refine your topic more narrowly.
- Keep control: From the beginning, develop a system for recording and managing material.
- At the end of the study, revisit online databases to check for any new literature that may have emerged.

2: Review and Analyze the Literature

- Look for essential components in the literature.
- Extract and record information by asking systematic questions of the literature.
- Develop an analytic format and use it consistently.
- Write a short overview report on each piece of literature reviewed, including specific detailed information.
- For research articles, extract technical elements and establish tables or matrices.
- While analyzing the specifics, be on the lookout for broader themes and issues.

3: Synthesis: Write the Review

- Organize separate elements as one integrated, creative whole.
- Determine the patterns that have emerged, such as trends, similarities, and contradictions/contrasts.
- Identify themes and translate them into corresponding headings and subheadings.
- Write a first draft.
- Ensure that your argument flows logically and coherently, that it is written clearly, and that it is well supported by citations.
- Test the draft by inviting/soliciting feedback from colleagues and advisors.
- Edit, revise, and refine, incorporating feedback from others.

4: Develop the Conceptual Framework

- The conceptual framework becomes an integral part of your study. It is a repository for the findings as well as a tool for analysis. As such, careful development is essential.
- Establish categories that are directly tied to the research questions.
- Develop descriptors for each category that are based on the literature, pilot study findings, and personal "hunches."
- Be prepared to refine and revise your conceptual framework as the study progresses.

primary material, you might want to revisit the earlier studies of these writers to note the development of their theory or ideas.

With the tremendous amount of information available via electronic media, it is crucial that you learn to access this information. However, anyone anywhere can put information on the Web, so any information from the Internet should be cited with caution. The ease of access of Web-based articles makes these sources of materials attractive. If you cannot determine the author of information or the date it was produced, it has no place in academic research. Although many websites for government agencies, professional organizations, and educational institutions provide useful information, you should always evaluate information obtained from a website for currency, legitimacy, accuracy, and potential bias.

The retrieval effort consists of a series of stages:

Stage 1: Use keywords and combinations of keywords (descriptors) to identify potential sources: Using various combinations of keywords maximizes the possibility of locating articles relevant to your planned study. Seek and make records of citations that seem to be relevant to your topic.

Stage 2: Skim and screen the sources: Assess each piece of literature to ascertain whether the content is relevant to your study.

Stage 3: Acquisition: Print documents that are available electronically. In some cases, only an abstract is available. In those cases where the material seems relevant, you need to obtain the full text document. Check out books; copy articles from journals and chapters from books; and, if material is unavailable through your own library, order interlibrary loans.

A comprehensive literature search on a topic that covers all the necessary sources and resources is a demanding and rigorous process. It is seldom possible to find all the information required within the space of a few weeks. Often initial search strategies may not reveal what you are looking for; therefore, you will need to search more widely in the databases and also make use of more complex combinations of words and phrases. Proceed with persistence, flexibility, and tenacity. Persistence means being thorough in your search and keeping detailed records of how you have managed your search activities.

Following are some organizing strategies to assist you in the identification and retrieval process:

1. Because you will return to the library databases time and again to continue your review, it would be wise to develop a system of keeping track of key words (descriptors) and combinations of key words you have used. In the dissertation you will have to report on how the literature was selected and what procedures were used to select the material, so keeping a record of this information is important.

2. It is also important to keep track of each book or document that you consult. In this regard, you should keep diligent bibliographic citations. You will save much time by writing each reference in its proper form initially. There are various software programs available such as EndNote (www.end note.com), Citation (www.oberon-res.com), and Procite (www.procitecom/pchome.html) that enable you to create a list of bibliographic references. In our experience, however, maintaining an ongoing alphabetically arranged, accurate record by way of a Word document is the easiest and most efficient. We suggest that you prepare a typed list of each piece of literature reviewed, making sure that all details (authors, titles, dates, volume numbers, page numbers, etc.) are correct. This list then becomes a working draft of your references. To avoid the frustration of having to search for information at a later stage (and possibly not being able to track it

down), keep a close check on this list, making sure not to inadvertently omit any details as you go along. If the reference is a book, be sure to include the library call number because you may need to return to it later. This list will encompass all materials that you have retrieved, and thus will have some bearing on your study. In the final version of your dissertation, you will include only a reference list, not a bibliography (i.e., a list of texts that are cited in the body of the manuscript).

3. Collecting literature is an ongoing process. You need to develop some system for classifying sources into those that have a direct bearing on your topic and those that are more peripherally related to your topic. You need to be selective in choosing material most relevant to your study. Always keep in mind the problem that your study is addressing. As you gather and sort material, ask yourself how and in what ways the material relates to your research problem. You might categorize each piece of material as *very important*, *moderately important*, or *mildly important*. After locating pertinent material for review, you should store these files, especially those that are central to your topic and that you think you might cite. When possible, you should save material electronically to allow for efficient and easy retrieval.

Step 2: Review and Analyze the Literature

Once you have undertaken a comprehensive literature search, you will need to critically assess each piece of material to analyze its content. In other words, you read with the goal of producing a product—an analytical evaluation. Toward this end, you need to put yourself in the role of researcher and prepare a systematic and comprehensive method of critical analysis.

Analysis is the job of systematically breaking down something into its constituent parts to describe how they relate to one another. Analysis should not be viewed as a random dissection, but a methodological examination. Although there is a degree of exploration involved in analysis, you should aim to be systematic, rigorous, and consistent. In this way, the identification of the individual and similar elements in a range of materials can be compared and contrasted. Analysis lays the foundation for critique. Critique identifies the strengths and key contributions of the literature as well as any deficiencies, omissions, inaccuracies, or inconsistencies. By highlighting the strengths and identifying the deficiencies in the existing literature, critical analysis is a necessary step toward adding to the knowledge base. Analysis consists of two main stages:

Stage 1: Skim and Read

1. Skim the book or article first, noting its topic, structure, general reasoning, data, and bibliographical references.

2. Go back and skim the preface and introduction, trying to identify the main ideas contained in the work.

3. Identify key parts of the article or, if a book, identify key chapters. Read these parts or chapters, as well as the final chapter or conclusion.

Stage 2: Highlight and Extract Key Elements

What you are trying to do is understand the historical context and state of the art relevant to your topic. You are looking at what has been covered in the literature, but you are also looking for gaps and anomalies. Although there will be considerable variation among the different pieces of literature, it is imperative to develop a format and use it consistently. A consistent format will pay off when you begin to synthesize your material and actually write the review. Begin by asking specific questions of the literature. These questions will help you think through your topic and provide you with some idea of how to structure your synthesis discussion.

- What are the origins and definitions of the topic?
- What are the key theories, concepts, and ideas?
- What are the major debates, arguments, and issues surrounding the topic?
- What are the key questions and problems that have been addressed to date?
- Are there any important issues that have been insufficiently addressed or not addressed at all?

In analyzing research studies, you need to identify and extract some of the more technical elements common to all research studies, such as problem, purpose, research questions, sample, methodology, key findings, conclusions, and recommendations. The purpose of reading analytically is to identify and extract these pertinent components in the literature. However, as you read and analyze, you should be on the lookout for the broader themes, issues, and commonalities among the various authors. Also be aware of "outliers" (i.e., points of divergence and difference). Regarding research articles reviewed, make notes of major trends, patterns, or inconsistencies in the results reported. Also try to identify relationships between studies. These findings will all be important to mention in the final synthesis, which aims to integrate all the literature reviewed. As you continue to read and analyze the literature, also begin to think about what other information you might need so you can refine your search accordingly.

Following are some organizing strategies to assist you in analyzing your material:

1. Read your "very important" documents first. Highlight, make notations in the margins, or write memos on Post-it notes of inconsistencies, similarities, questions, concerns, and possible omissions as you go along.

2. Develop a computerized filing system of Word documents for your literature review. For every piece of material that you read, write a brief summary that covers the essential points: major issues, arguments, and theoretical models. Include conclusions that you can draw, and note any inferences that you can make regarding your own study.

3. As you read, be sure to jot down any pertinent comments or quotations that you think might be useful in the presentation of your review. In so doing, be careful to copy quotations accurately. Make sure to use quotation marks when extracting material directly, so as to avoid inadvertently plagiarizing others' ideas and/or words. Direct quotations also require page numbers, and it will save you considerable time and energy later in the process if you have noted these page numbers accurately.

4. Regarding primary research-based sources, you might consider preparing a summary sheet that compares important characteristics across all the studies that you have reviewed. A template for the analysis of research-based literature is provided in Table 2.2. A template for the analysis of theoretical literature is found in Table 2.3. These are both useful analytical tools for methodological analysis of the articles prior to beginning the review by conveying the results of your analysis, noting similarities and differences among research studies and/or theories. These tools also serve as a record of your literature search. Tables such as these can appear in the appendix of your dissertation. Alternatively, they can be included in the body of the literature review chapter to augment and clarify the narrative discussion.

5. When you have finished reviewing all the articles you have collected, be sure to revisit your entire (and rapidly growing) bibliography to make certain that it is complete and up to date.

You now have a complete record of what the literature states about key variables, ideas, and concepts related to your study. Reading through your summaries will serve to highlight important themes, issues, commonalities, and differences—in effect, these are the answers to your critical questions. The resulting insights will give you a sense of the forest as well as the trees. This sense will prepare you to integrate the material you are reading and proceed with writing a coherent and logical synthesis of the literature.

Table 2.2   Template for Analysis of Research-Based Literature

Study Details: Author, Date of Study, Publication.	Methodological Approach/Research Design:
	Theoretical/Conceptual Framework:
	Research Sample:
	Research Site:
	Research Problem:
	Research Purpose:
	Research Question:
	Subquestions:
	Key Findings:
	Conclusions:
	Recommendations:

Table 2.3   Template for Analysis of Theoretical Literature

Theorist	*Overview of Theory*	*Key Premises*
Theorist 1		• • •
Theorist 2		• • •
Theorist 3		• • •
Theorist 4		• • •

Step 3: Synthesis—Write the Review

After you select the literature and organize your thoughts in terms of critically analyzing the literature into discrete parts, you need to arrange and structure a clear and coherent argument. To do this, you need to create and present a synthesis—reorganizing and reassembling of all the separate pieces and details so that the discussion constitutes one integrated whole. This synthesis builds a knowledge base and extends new lines of thinking.

Whereas analysis involves systematically breaking down the relevant literature into its constituent parts, synthesis is the act of making connections between those parts identified in the analysis. Synthesis is not about simply reassembling the parts. Rather, it is about recasting the information into a new and different arrangement—one that is coherent, logical, and explicit. This process might mean bringing new insights to an existing body of knowledge. The intent is to make others think more deeply about and possibly reevaluate what may hitherto have been taken for granted.

A key element that makes for good synthesis is integration, which is about making connections between and among ideas and concepts. It is about applying what you are researching within a larger framework, thereby providing a new way of looking at a phenomenon. Your literature review is a demonstration of how your research problem is situated within the larger conversation and/or part of a broader theoretical scheme. To achieve a well-integrated literature review, you must be sure to emphasize relatedness and organize the material in a well-reasoned and meaningful way.

Synthesis is not a data dump; it is a creative activity. In discussing the literature review, Hart (2005) refers to what he calls "the research imagination." An imaginative approach to searching and reviewing the literature includes having a broad view of the topic; being open to new ideas, methods, and arguments; "playing" with different ideas to see whether you can make new linkages; and following ideas to see where they might lead. We see the literature review as somewhat of a sculpture—a work of art that, in its molding, requires dedication, creativity, and flexibility. It cannot be stressed enough that synthesis is an iterative and recursive process where drafts are refined, revised, and reworked until a final best version is crafted.

Presenting the Review

A literature review must be based on a well-thought-out design or plan that integrates the material discussed. The results of your analysis can provide you with ideas for the structure of your review. To present a coherent and logical review, it is important to create a detailed outline prior to writing. You cannot begin without this. An outline will save you time and effort in the long run and will increase your probability of having an organized review. Don't be surprised, however, if the outline changes as you write. In fact, this is quite often the case, as you will need to arrange and then rearrange to maintain a logical flow of thought.

To create the outline, you need to determine how various theorists define the topic and the themes and/or patterns that have emerged. Themes and patterns translate into headings and subheadings. Differentiating each major heading into logical subheadings gives structure to the review as a whole, helping to advance the argument and clarifying the relationships among sections. Headings and subheadings also enable the reader to see at a glance what is covered in the review. With a completed outline, you can begin to sort your references under their appropriate headings, and so begin to present your discussion. Following are some important guidelines for writing.

Be Selective

A comprehensive literature review need not include every piece of material that you have located and/or read. Include only material that is directly relevant to your research problem and the purpose of your study. Although all the material that you reviewed was necessary to help you to situate your own study, not every citation with respect to an issue need be included. The use of too many or nonselective references is an indication of poor scholarship and an inability to separate the central from the peripheral.

Provide Integration and Critique

It is your task as a writer to integrate, rather than just report on, the material you have read. Comment on the major issues that you have discovered. Never present a chain of isolated summaries of previous studies. We have stressed throughout this book that you will need to demonstrate an analytical and critically evaluative stance. Once you have pulled together all of the salient perspectives of other authors vis-à-vis your topics, you need to stand back and provide critique. However, providing a critique in an academic work does not mean you make a personal attack on the work of others. When it comes to writing a critical evaluation, you must treat that work with due respect.

Legitimacy

In using the literature on a topic, you are using the ideas, concepts, and theories of others. Therefore, it is your responsibility to cite sources correctly and comply with academic and legal conventions. This means being scrupulous in your record keeping and ensuring that all details of referenced works are accurately and fully cited. This includes work obtained via electronic media such as the Internet, although copyright protection for data on the Internet is currently in a state of flux.

Use of Quotations

As stated in the writing section of Section I, try to limit the use of direct quotations and quote only materials that are stated skillfully and are a clear reflection of a particular point of view. The practice of liberally sprinkling the literature review with quoted material—particularly lengthy quotations—is self-defeating; unessential quotations are a distraction from the line of thought being presented.

Academic Style

There are various conventions in academic writing, including such things as the use of certain words and phrases. Some words that might be common in everyday language and conversation are inappropriate for use in a dissertation. For example "it is obvious," "it is a fact," "everyone will agree," and "normally" are assumptions and presuppositions and, as such, are often imprecise. In addition, be sure to guard against using discriminatory language. Bear in mind at all times you are not writing an editorial column, but a piece of scholarly research to be read by the academic community. You can benefit from seeking feedback from others. It often takes a critical, objective eye to point out gaps, flaws, and inconsistencies in one's writing.

Revise, Revise, and Revise

A first draft should be just that—a preliminary, tentative outline of what you want to say based on a planned structure. Every writer goes through a series of drafts, gradually working toward something with which he or she can be satisfied. Often what is helpful is to distance yourself from your review and then go back and revisit. Time away for thinking and reflection tends to create "aha moments" and fresh insights. The final draft should be as accurate as possible both in terms of content and structure.

Step 4: Develop the Conceptual Framework

In our experience, graduate students seem to lack an understanding of the nature and role of the conceptual framework (CF); what it is, what its purpose is, where it is derived from, how it is developed, how it is used, and what effect it has on research. The reason for this knowledge gap is that the term is somewhat an abstract notion, conjuring up a model or diagram of some sort. Moreover, there does not appear to be a uniform and consistent definition, and discussions in the literature around CFs are not clear or precise. As we reviewed the qualitative research literature (Maxwell, 2005; Merriam, 1998; Miles & Huberman, 1994; Robson, 2002; Rossman & Rallis, 2003; Schram, 2003), it became clear to us that those writers who attempt to explain the notion of CFs do not do so conclusively, and therefore offer only vague or insufficient guidance to students in terms of understanding the actual role and place of the CF. In addition to students' confusion, even experienced researchers sometimes find themselves at a loss in the process of developing a CF (Anfara & Mertz, 2006).

Merriam (1998) argues that the CF affects every aspect of the study, from determining how to frame the problem and purpose to how the data are collected. Similarly, Miles and Huberman (1994) and Schram (2003) contend that, without some CF, there would be no way to make reasoned decisions in the research process. We tend to agree that the CF plays an extremely central role in the research process, as well as in the final analysis. Thus, in our view, because it is so central a component of your dissertation, and because its scope is far reaching throughout the subsequent chapters, development of the CF requires careful, logical, and thoughtful explication.

The review and critique of existing literature culminates in a CF that posits new relationships and perspectives vis-à-vis the literature reviewed. In this way, the CF becomes the scaffolding of the study. Most important, it becomes a working tool consisting of categories that emanate from the literature. These categories become the repository for reporting the findings and guiding data analysis and interpretation. The CF is described in narrative form and then displayed at the end of the literature review chapter. In the findings chapter, the categories and descriptors become the headings and subheadings for presentation of your findings. The CF is included in the dissertation's appendix. Here the title changes to "Coding Legend" or "Coding Scheme," as you assign symbols (codes) to each main category and each of the respective descriptors.

Following are the general guidelines for developing a CF. In Section II of this chapter, we explain development of the CF in greater detail and illustrate its application vis-à-vis a qualitative dissertation. A completed CF is included as Appendix B. The intent is that, based on this example, you will be able to craft a CF that is distinctively yours and unique to your own study. Following are the steps involved in constructing a conceptual framework. In the application section that follows, these steps are elaborated in greater detail.

Step 1: Developing Categories

You need to give careful thought to developing conceptual categories that are based on and directly tied to your study's research questions. To be comprehensive, you need to make sure there is one category that relates to each research question. These categories form the backbone of your study. As you will see, they become the repository for presenting your findings. They also translate into analytic categories later on in your study, and so become an essential analytic tool.

Step 2: Developing Descriptors for Each Category

Under each category, you need to lay out the categories' descriptors. These descriptors reflect what you have learned from the reviewed literature, data from your pilot studies, and your own best guesses or hunches about how people might respond to each of your research questions. Not all of your descriptors will be useful, and you will refine these as the study proceeds. The CF remains flexible. Based on the data you collect, some of the descriptors may remain intact, others may be deleted, or new ones may be added.

Having discussed the purpose and function of the literature review and the steps involved, we are now ready to introduce what a completed chapter 2 should look like. In the following section, we focus on the specific problem as outlined in chapter 1 and explain how to develop and present the associated literature review.

SECTION II: APPLICATION

Because of the nature of the literature review, it would be impractical to present here a full-blown literature review on our topic. Rather, what we have done is identify each of the actual steps that should be followed in completing your literature review and provide illustrative examples in an outline or skeleton form. The intent of presenting the application piece in this way is that you could use these steps as a template and present your own literature review in the same order. These steps include:

1. Provide a statement of purpose.

2. Identify the topics or bodies of literature.

3. Provide the rationale for topics selected.

4. Describe your literature review process, report all your literature sources, and identify the key words used to search the literature.

5. Present the review of each topic.

6. Present your conceptual framework.

7. Provide a brief chapter summary of the literature review and its implications for your study.

Steps 1 through 4 constitute all that is necessary to introduce the literature review to the reader. Steps 5 and 6 constitute the "meat" of the review. Step 7 is intended to highlight the main points, thereby providing some closure for the chapter. In the following pages, we put each of these steps into play and provide an illustration of what chapter 2, the literature review of a dissertation, should look like. Bear in mind that the application section that follows is a skeleton view of what a literature review chapter should look like. Were each section to be more completely and fully developed, as would be required in an actual dissertation, such a chapter would obviously be much longer and more detailed.

CHAPTER II
Review of the Literature
Overview

The purpose of this multicase study was to explore with 20 doctoral candidates their perceptions of why they have not managed to complete their dissertations. Specifically, the researcher sought to understand how the experiences of these individuals may have inhibited their progress in conducting and carrying out research. To carry out this study, it was necessary to complete a critical review of current literature. This review was ongoing throughout the data collection, data analysis, and synthesis phases of the study.

This critical review explores the interconnectedness of the experiences of participants and the resources that they perceived were available to them. In light of this, two major areas of literature were critically reviewed: (a) higher education/doctoral programs, and (b) adult learning theory. A review of the literature on higher education and doctoral programs provides an understanding of the context, history, structure, rules, and regulations under which candidates must work to obtain doctoral degrees. Adult learning theory is reviewed to provide a context for understanding what knowledge, skills, and attitudes were perceived as needed by the participants and how they attempted to learn what they perceived they needed.

In providing a rationale for your choice of topics, in some instances you might want to include an explicit assertion, a contention, or a proposition that relates to the research problem and that is substantiated by supporting literature. The assertion/contention should be broad and is based on the overall judgments you have formed thus far based on an analysis of the literature.

To conduct this selected literature review, the researcher used multiple information sources, including books, dissertations, Internet resources, professional journals, and periodicals. These sources were accessed through ERIC, ProQuest, Digital Dissertations, eduCAT, and CLIO. No specific delimiting time frame was used around which to conduct this search. Because of the nature of the three bodies of literature reviewed, the historical development, for example, of higher education/doctoral programs was considered significant and therefore an arbitrary criterion, such as a time frame might preclude the inclusion of substantial relevant material.

Throughout the review, the researcher attempted to point out important gaps and omissions in particular segments of the literature as and when they became apparent. In addition, relevant contested areas or issues are identified and discussed. Each section of the literature review closes with a synthesis that focuses on research implications. The interpretive summary that concludes the chapter illustrates how the literature has informed the researcher's understanding of the material and how the material contributes to the ongoing development of the study's conceptual framework.

The prior section included how the literature was selected, how information was accessed, what if any time delimitations you employed, what keywords and procedures were used to search the literature, what databases were used, and, if appropriate, what criteria were used for retaining or discarding the literature. You also may choose to explain the main ideas and themes from the literature that you identified and by which you carried out your analysis.

Topics Reviewed

Having introduced the reader to your review, go on to present each topic in the order in which you have introduced them in the prior section. For each topic, establish an outline for yourself. Typically, the outline is made up of three interrelated sections: (a) introduction, (b) discussion, and (c) summary/conclusions/implications that relate to the discussion.

For each topic, start off by putting the reader in the picture so that she or he understands where you are going with your review of a particular topic or subject and how you intend to tackle it. This becomes your introduction to the topic. Give the reader a rationale for the topic and a brief overview of how you have organized the discussion. You also should preview the main points that you will make in the body of the discussion.

The introduction is followed by a systematic review of the material and is subdivided by headings and subheadings based on your analysis and synthesis of the literature.

Think carefully about how you would like to organize the discussion. Usually you would start with general material to provide the reader with a comprehensive perspective. You would then proceed to discuss the material that is closely related to your own particular study. Thus, in planning how you will write, arrange your headings and subheadings accordingly because these will allow the reader to follow your train of thought. When appropriate, and especially with research-based literature, you also might employ the summary tables that you constructed when analyzing the literature because these tables reflect the variables or themes inherent in your discussion. At the end of the discussion of each topic, you should offer a concise and cohesive summary that highlights and clarifies the salient points discussed.

Summary

To provide some form of clarity and closure for the reader, you also need a final concluding summary at the end of the discussion that identifies all the key points mentioned in the review. This final summary should make reference to the line of argumentation that was specified in the introduction and pull the entire discussion together. The point of all the summaries—both those at the end of each topic as well as the final chapter—is to tell the reader what your review yielded in terms of informing your study.

Conceptual Framework

The review and critique of the literature, combined with the researcher's own experience and insights, has contributed to developing a conceptual framework for the design and conduct of this study. The conceptual framework developed for this study helps to focus and shape the research process, informing the methodological design and influencing the data-collection instruments to

be used. The CF also becomes the repository for the data that were collected, providing the basis for and informing various iterations of a coding scheme. As such, this framework provides an organizing structure both for reporting this study's findings as well as the analysis, interpretation, and synthesis of these findings. In this way, the CF is essentially a "working tool."

Each of the categories of the CF is directly derived from the study's research questions as outlined in chapter 1. The first research question seeks to determine the extent to which participants perceived they were prepared to conduct research and write the dissertation following the completion of their coursework. Therefore, the logical conceptual category to capture responses to this question would be "Preparedness for Dissertation Process." The second research question seeks to identify what candidates perceive they need to learn to carry out the dissertation process. The category entitled "KSA" is all-encompassing and thus appropriate. The third research question is intended to uncover how candidates go about acquiring the KSA they perceive they need. Hence, the appropriate categorization is "How They Learn." Research questions four and five attempted to get at the factors that either help or hinder people's progress in the dissertation process; thus, "Facilitators" and "Barriers" are appropriate categories. To further explain each of the categories, the researcher drew on the literature, pilot test data, as well as her own educated guesses about potential responses to the research questions, which resulted in the various bulleted descriptors under each of the respective categories. During the course of data collection and analysis, some of the descriptors within each of the major categories were added, some were deleted, and others were collapsed. The CF was thus continually revised and refined.

As you may note, the prior narrative introduces your CF and describes what you mean by a conceptual framework, how you have developed it, and how it will be used in your study; that is, its nature, role, and function vis-à-vis your own particular study. You should be aware, like so many aspects of the dissertation, that the CF takes time to develop. As with the literature review, you will go through various iterations until you finally arrive at a workable, tight conceptual framework for your study. A completed CF, based on the example used in this book, is included as Appendix B.

SUMMARY DISCUSSION FOR CHAPTER 2

Broadly speaking, a literature review is a narrative that integrates, synthesizes, and critiques the research and thinking around a particular topic. It sets the broad context of the study, clearly demarcates what is and is not within the scope of the investigation, and justifies those decisions. A literature review should not only report the claims made in the existing literature, but should also examine it critically. Such an examination of the literature enables the reader to distinguish what has been and still needs to be learned and accomplished in the area of study. Moreover, in a good review, the researcher not only summarizes the existing literature, but also synthesizes it in a way that permits a new perspective. Thus, good literature review is the basis of both theoretical and methodological sophistication, thereby improving the quality and usefulness of subsequent research. As the foundation of the research project, a comprehensive review of the literature in a dissertation should accomplish several distinct objectives:

- Frames the research problem by setting it within a larger context;
- Focuses the purpose of your study more precisely;

- Leads to the refinement of research questions;
- Forms the basis for determining the rationale and significance of your study;
- Enables you to convey your understanding of your research approach, as well as the specific data-collection methods employed;
- Links your findings to previous studies;
- Places research within a historical context to show familiarity with state-of-the-art developments;
- Enables you to justify, support, and substantiate your study's findings;
- Contributes to analysis and interpretation of your study's findings; and
- Enables you to develop a conceptual framework that can be used to guide your research.

It should be apparent to you that the literature review is a sophisticated form of research in its own right that requires a great deal of research skill and insight. You are expected to identify appropriate topics or issues, justify why these are the appropriate choice for addressing the research problem, search and retrieve the appropriate literature, analyze and critique the literature, create new understandings of the topic through synthesis, and develop a CF that will provide the underlying structure for your study.

Thinking about the entire literature review process may initially be overwhelming and intimidating. Instead of viewing it as one big whole, think of it as a series of steps—and steps within those steps. Tackle each topic one by one and set yourself small achievable goals within each topic area. Be sure to subdivide your work into manageable sections, taking on and refining each section one at a time. The important point, and one that we stress throughout, is that you should proceed in stages. Like the skier traversing the terrain, the best way to be successful is to divide and conquer.

Chapter Checklist

Preparing for the Literature Review

✓ Are you clear about the role and scope of the literature review vis-à-vis the qualitative research tradition that you have adopted?

✓ Are you familiar with all possible resources, including library indexing systems and electronic databases?

✓ Have you set up your own systems of identifying, retrieving, organizing, and storing your information?

✓ Have you made sure that all information is securely saved by way of backup systems?

Writing the Literature Review

✓ Do you have a clear introduction to this chapter that includes your purpose statement (if required), as well as an explanation of how the chapter will be organized?

✓ Does your overall review show a clear understanding and critique of each topic?

✓ Is the review comprehensive? Does it cover the major points of each topic?

✓ Have you included historical as well as current coverage?

✓ Is the review well organized?

✓ Does the path of your argument flow logically?

✓ Is the review analytical and critical, and not merely summative and descriptive?

✓ Is there an introductory paragraph outlining the organization of the bodies of literature?

✓ Are the methods for conducting the literature review sufficiently described?

✓ Does the order of headings and subheadings seem logical?

✓ Are there summary paragraphs at the end of each major section, as well as an overall summary at the end of the chapter?

✓ Are there too many direct quotations that detract from the readability of the chapter?

✓ Are all citations included in the reference list?

✓ Have all citations that you have not included been eliminated from the reference list?

✓ Have you checked your recommended style manual for format, punctuation, grammar, and correct use of citations?

✓ Have you edited and reedited your work?

Developing the Conceptual Framework

✓ Are the categories directly tied to the research questions?

✓ Do you have at least one category per research question?

✓ Have you included descriptors that are based on the literature, pilot studies, and your own hunches?

✓ Do the descriptors make sense?

✓ Are there any other descriptors you may have forgotten to include?

ANNOTATED BIBLIOGRAPHY

Boote, D. N., & Beile, P. (2005). Scholars before researchers: On the centrality of the dissertation literature review in research preparation. *Educational Researcher, 34*(6), 3–15.

These authors posit that acquiring the skills and knowledge to analyze and synthesize the research in a field of specialization should be the focal, integrative activity of pre-dissertation doctoral education. Moreover, they argue that a thorough, sophisticated literature review is the foundation for substantial research. Indeed, the academic community should be able to assume that a dissertation literature review indicates a doctoral candidate's ability to locate and evaluate scholarly information and synthesize research in his or her field. Yet as these authors indicate, despite the assumption that dissertation literature reviews are comprehensive and up to date, in many instances, literature reviews are poorly conceptualized and written. This article discusses in detail the various functions of the dissertation literature review and suggests criteria for evaluating the quality of dissertation literature reviews.

Booth, W. G., Colomb, G. G., & Williams, J. M. (2003). *The craft of research* (2nd ed., pp. 75–164). Chicago: University of Chicago Press.

This book includes useful guidelines regarding how to locate printed and recorded sources, as well as sources found on the Internet; how to gather data directly from people; how to assess the reliability of sources; how to read and take notes accurately; and how to make arguments and claims and how to support them.

Galvan, J. L. (2004). *Writing literature reviews: A guide for students in the social and behavioral sciences* (2nd ed.). Glendale, CA: Pyrczak.

This book offers instruction on how to plan and implement the various stages involved in completing a major writing assignment such as the literature review chapter of a dissertation. Useful information is provided on how to search databases for reports of original research and related theoretical literature, critically analyze these types of literature, and synthesize them into a cohesive narrative. Included are detailed, step-by-step instructions, and these are illustrated with examples from a wide range of academic journals.

Hart, C. (2005). *Doing a literature review*. Thousand Oaks, CA: Sage.

This book is a practical and detailed guide to researching, preparing, and writing a literature review at the doctoral level. This accessible text offers advice on good practices with regard to searching for existing knowledge on a topic; understanding arguments; analyzing and synthesizing ideas; managing information; and writing up and producing a well-crafted, critical, and creative review.

Merriam, S. B. (1998). *Qualitative research and case study application in education*. San Francisco: Jossey-Bass.

As Merriam rightfully suggests, the literature review is not a linear process, but rather an iterative and interactive one. This book includes an extensive discussion about the use of literature in qualitative studies. The author identifies the steps in reviewing the literature and provides useful criteria for selecting references. These include checking to see whether the author is an authority on the topic, how current the material is, whether the material is relevant to your topic, and the quality of the resource.

Presenting Methodology and Research Approach

OVERVIEW

Chapter 3 of the dissertation presents the research design and the specific procedures used in conducting your study. A research design includes various interrelated elements that reflect its sequential nature. This chapter is intended to show the reader that you have an understanding of the methodological implications of the choices you made and, in particular, that you have thought carefully about the links between your study's purpose and research questions and the research approach and research methods that you have selected.

Note that in the proposal's chapter 3, you project *what you will do* based on what you know about the particular methods used in qualitative research, in general, and in your tradition or genre, in particular; hence, it is written in future tense. In the dissertation's chapter 3, you report on *what you have already done*. You write after the fact; hence, you write in past tense. As such, many of the sections of chapter 3 can be written only after you have actually conducted your study (i.e., collected, analyzed, and synthesized your data).

To write this chapter, you need to conduct literature reviews on the methodological issues involved in qualitative research design.

You need to show the reader that you (a) have knowledge of the current issues and discourse, and (b) can relate your study to those issues and discourse. In this regard, you need to explain how you have gone about designing and conducting your study while making sure that you *draw supporting evidence from the literature* for the decisions and choices that you have made.

This chapter, which is usually one of the dissertation's lengthiest, is essentially a *discussion*, in which you explain the course and logic of your decision making throughout the research process. In practice, this means describing the following:

- The rationale for your research approach
- The research sample and the population from which it was drawn
- The type of information you needed
- How you designed the study and the methods that you used to gather your data
- The theoretical basis of the data-collection methods you used and why you chose these
- How you have analyzed and synthesized your data
- Ethical considerations involved in your study
- Issues of trustworthiness and how you dealt with these
- Limitations of the study and your attempt to address these

Following are the two sections that make up this chapter. Section I offers instruction on how to develop each section of chapter 3. Section II illustrates application by way of the example used throughout this book and gives you some idea of what a complete chapter 3 should look like. Note that Section I includes various "how-to" matrices, charts, and figures. Although not all of these may make their way into the main body of your final dissertation, they can and often do appear as "working tools" in the dissertation's appendix.

CHAPTER OBJECTIVES

Chapter 3 Objectives

Section I: Instruction

- Identify the key components of the methodology chapter:
(a) Introduction and overview,
(b) research sample, (c) overview of information needed, (d) research design, (e) methods of data collection, (f) methods for data analysis and synthesis, (g) ethical considerations, (h) issues of trustworthiness, (i) limitations of the study, and (j) chapter summary.
- Provide explanation of how each component of the research methodology must be developed and presented.
- Show that you understand how all of the components combined form a logical, interconnected sequence and contribute to the overall methodological integrity of the study.

Section II: Application

- Presentation of a completed methodology chapter based on the content and process as described previously.

SECTION I: INSTRUCTION

The dissertation's third chapter—the methodology chapter—covers a lot of ground. In this chapter, you document each step that you have taken in designing and conducting the study. The format that we present for this chapter covers all the necessary components of a comprehensive methodology chapter. Universities generally have their own fixed structural requirements, and so we recommend that, before proceeding to write, you discuss with your advisor how to structure the chapter as well as the preferred order of the sections and how long each section should be. Most important, make sure (a) your sections are in a logical sequence, and (b) what you write is comprehensive, clear, precise, and sufficiently detailed so that others will be able to adequately judge the soundness of your study. Table 3.1 is a roadmap intended to illustrate the necessary elements that constitute a sound methodology chapter and a suggested sequence for including these elements.

As pointed out previously, although qualitative research as an overall approach is based on certain central assumptions, it is characterized by an ongoing discourse regarding the appropriate and acceptable use of terminology. Current thinking over the years has caused some qualitative researchers to develop their own terminology to more effectively reflect the nature and distinction of qualitative research, whereas others still borrow terminology from quantitative research. Throughout this chapter, we point out instances in which you should be aware of these differences so that you can make an informed choice.

Introduction and Overview

The chapter begins with an opening paragraph in which you restate the study's purpose and research questions and then go on

Table 3.1 Roadmap for Developing Methodology Chapter: Necessary Elements

---

1: Introduction and Overview

Begin by stating purpose and research questions. Go on to explain how the chapter is organized. Then provide a rationale for using a qualitative research approach, as well as a rationale for the particular qualitative tradition/genre you have chosen. Provide a brief overview of your study.

2: Research Sample

Describe the research sample and the population from which that sample was drawn. Discuss the sampling strategy used. (Depending on the qualitative research tradition, a sample can include people, texts, artifacts, or cultural phenomena.) In this section, describe the research site if appropriate (program/institution/organization).

3: Overview of Information Needed

Describe the kinds of information you will need to answer your research questions. Be specific about exactly what kind of information you will be collecting. Four general areas of information are needed for most qualitative studies: contextual, perceptual, demographic, and theoretical information.

4: Research Design Overview

This section outlines your overall research design/methodology. It includes the list of steps in carrying out your research from data collection through data analysis. The two sections that follow elaborate in greater detail on the methods of data collection and the process of data analysis. The narrative in this section is often augmented by a flowchart or diagram that provides an illustration of the various steps involved.

5: Data-Collection Methods

Explain that a selected literature review preceded data collection; although this informs the study, indicate that the literature is not data to be collected. Identify and present all the data-collection methods you used, and clearly explain the steps taken to carry out each method. Include in the discussion any field tests or pilot studies you may have undertaken. To show that you have done a critical reading of the literature, you may be required to discuss the strengths and weaknesses of each method of data collection used. In this regard, you may either include in this section what the literature says about each of the methods you will be using, or the literature on methods may be a separate section.

6: Data Analysis and Synthesis

Report on how you managed, organized, and analyzed your data in preparation to report your findings (chap. 4) and then how you went on to analyze and interpret your findings (chap. 5). It is important to note that this section of chapter 3 can thus be written only *after* you have written up the findings and analysis chapters of your dissertation.

7: Ethical Considerations

This section should inform the reader that you have considered the ethical issues that might arise vis-à-vis your study and that you have taken the necessary steps to address these issues.

8: Issues of Trustworthiness

This section discusses the criteria for evaluating the trustworthiness of qualitative research—credibility, dependability, and transferability. Moreover, you must indicate to the reader that you have a clear understanding of the implications thereof vis-à-vis your own study and the strategies you employed to enhance trustworthiness.

(Continued)

Table 3.1 (Continued)

9: Limitations of the Study
Cite all potential limitations and your means to address these limitations. The discussion should include problems inherent in qualitative research generally, as well as limitations that are specific to your particular study. Regardless of how carefully you plan a study, there will always be some limitations, and you need to explicitly acknowledge these.

10: Chapter Summary
A final culminating summary ties together all the elements that you have presented in this chapter. Make sure that you highlight all the important points. Keep your concluding discussion concise and precise.

---

to explain the chapter's organization. You then proceed to discuss how your research lends itself to a qualitative approach and why this approach is most appropriate to your inquiry. Critical to a well-planned study is the consideration of whether a qualitative approach is suited to the purpose and nature of your study. To convey this notion to the reader, it is necessary to provide a rationale for the qualitative research approach, as well as your reasons for choosing a particular qualitative tradition—namely, case study or multiple case study, ethnography, phenomenology, biography, or grounded theory.

In your discussion, you begin by defining *qualitative inquiry* as distinct from quantitative research. Then you go on to discuss the values and benefits derived from using a qualitative approach; in other words, its strengths. You would not talk about its weaknesses here; you will do that in the last section of the methodology chapter called "Limitations." Make sure that this first section flows logically and that you structure your discussion well by using appropriate headings and subheadings. Once the overall approach and supporting rationale have been presented, you can move on to explain who the research participants are, the sampling strategies you used to select the participants, what kind of data were needed to inform your study, and the specific data-collection and data-analysis strategies employed.

The Research Sample

In this section, you need to identify and describe in detail the methods used to select the research sample. This provides the reader with some sense of the scope of your study. In addition, your study's credibility relies on the quality of procedures you have used to select the research participants. Note that some qualitative researchers object to the use of the word *sample* in qualitative research, preferring terms such as *research participants* or *selected participants*. This is another example of the discourse among qualitative researchers that was mentioned previously.

Some research is site-specific, and the study is defined by and intimately linked to one or more locations. If you are working with a particular site, be it a particular place, region, organization, or program, the reader needs some detail regarding the setting. Although it is typically mentioned briefly in the beginning pages of chapter 1, in this section of chapter 3 you need to talk more specifically about how and why the site was selected.

After discussing the site, if applicable, you proceed to tell the reader about the research sample—the participants of your study. You also need to explain in some detail how the sample was selected and the pool from which it was drawn. This discussion should include the criteria used for inclusion in the sample, how participants were identified, how they were contacted, the number of individuals contacted, and the percentage of those who agreed to participate (i.e., the response rate). You also need to discuss why the specific method of sample selection used was considered most appropriate.

In qualitative research, selection of the research sample is purposeful (Patton 1990, 2002). This type of sampling is sometimes referred to as *purposive sampling* (Merriam, 1998) or *judgment sampling* (Gay, Mills, & Airasian, 2006). The logic of purposeful sampling lies in selecting information-rich cases, with the objective of yielding insight and understanding of the phenomenon under investigation. This method is in contrast to the random sampling procedures that characterize quantitative research, which is based on statistical probability theory. Random sampling controls for selection bias and enables generalization from the sample to a larger population—a key feature of quantitative research. Remember, one of the basic tenets of qualitative research is that each research setting is unique in its own mix of people and contextual factors. The researcher's intent is to describe a particular context in depth, not to generalize to another context or population. Representativeness in qualitative research is secondary to the participants' ability to provide information about themselves and their setting.

As its name suggests, a qualitative researcher has reasons (purposes) for selecting specific participants, events, and processes. The purposeful selection of research participants thus represents a key decision in qualitative research. Thus, in this section, you need to identify and provide a brief rationale for your sampling strategy. The strategy that you choose depends on the purpose of your study, and you need to make that clear in your discussion. For example, in a phenomenological study, you might employ "criterion-based sampling." Criterion sampling works well when all the individuals studied represent people who have experienced the same phenomenon. In a grounded theory study, you would choose the strategy known as *theoretical sampling* (or *theory-based sampling*), which means that you examine individuals who can contribute to the evolving theory. In a case study, you might use the strategy of *maximum variation* to represent diverse cases to fully display multiple perspectives about the cases. Appendix C presents an overview of the variety of purposeful sampling strategies used in qualitative research.

Once you have offered a rationale for your sampling strategy, you need to go on to discuss the nature and makeup of your particular sample. Describe who these individuals are, disclose how many individuals constitute the sample, and provide relevant descriptive characteristics (e.g., age, gender, occupation, level of education, etc.). It is helpful to include charts to augment and complement the narrative discussion. Providing information regarding selection procedures and research participants will aid others in understanding the findings. Having provided a description of the research sample and the setting, you are now ready to proceed to explain exactly what types of information you will need from the participants.

Overview of Information Needed

This section briefly describes the kinds of information you need to answer your research questions and thus shed light on the problem you are investigating. Four areas of information are typically needed for most qualitative studies: contextual, perceptual, demographic, and theoretical. The following sections define the content and the specific relevancy of each of these areas.

Contextual Information

Contextual information refers to the context within which the participants reside or work. It is information that describes the culture and environment of the setting, be it an organization or an institution. It is essential information to collect when doing a case study set in a particular site or multiple similar sites because elements within the environment or culture may, as Lewin (1935) reminds us, influence behavior. Lewin's fundamental proposition is that human behavior is a function of the interaction of the person and the environment. This theory is particularly relevant when one is trying to understand the learning behaviors of a discrete segment of a population in a particular organizational or institutional setting.

Given the nature of contextual information, such a review would provide knowledge about an organization's history, vision, objectives, products or services, operating principles, and business strategy. In addition, information on an organization or institution's leaders and its structure, organizational chart, systems, staff, roles, rules, and procedures would be included in this area of information. The primary method of collecting contextual information is through an extensive review of organization/institutional internal documents, as well as a review of relevant external documents that refer in some way to the organization or institution. Documentation can be of a descriptive and/or evaluative nature.

Demographic Information

Demographic information is participant profile information that describes who the participants in your study are—where they come from, some of their history and/or background, education, and personal information such as age, gender, and ethnicity. Such demographic information is needed to help explain what may be underlying an individual's perceptions, as well as the similarities and differences in perceptions among participants. In other words, a particular

data point (e.g., age) may explain a certain finding that emerged in the study.

Demographic information is typically collected by asking participants to complete a personal data sheet either before or after the interview or other data-collection methods take place. The information is then arrayed on a matrix that shows participants by pseudonym on the vertical axis and the demographic data points (age, gender, education, etc.) on the horizontal axis, as illustrated in Table 3.2. This demographic matrix, which is usually presented in the prior section, in which you discuss your research sample, can also later be used in conjunction with frequency charts. The latter, to be explained further later on, table the findings to help you with cross-case analysis, which is required later in the dissertation process. A sample completed participant demographics matrix appears as Appendix D.

Perceptual Information

Perceptual information refers to participants' perceptions related to the particular subject of your inquiry. Particularly in qualitative research when interviews are often the primary method of data collection, perceptual information is the most critical of the kinds of information needed. Perceptual information relies, to a great extent, on interviews to uncover participants' descriptions of their experiences related to such things as: how experiences influenced the decisions they made, whether participants had a change of mind or a shift in attitude, whether they described more of a constancy of purpose, what elements relative to their objectives participants perceived as important, and to what extent those objectives were met.

It should be remembered that perceptions are just that—they are not facts—they are what people perceive as facts. They are rooted in long-held assumptions and one's

Table 3.2   Participant Demographics

Participant (by pseudonym)	Age	Male %	Female %	Ethnicity	Education	Years Enrolled In . . .
Participant 1						
Participant 2						
Participant 3						
Participant 20						
N = 20						

own view of the world or frame of reference. As such, they are neither right nor wrong; they tell the story of what participants believe to be true.

Theoretical Information

Theoretical information includes information searched and collected from the various literature sources to assess what is already known regarding your topic of inquiry. Theoretical information serves to:

- Support and give evidence for your methodological approach;
- Provide theories related to your research questions that form the development and ongoing refinement of your conceptual framework;
- Provide support for your interpretation, analysis, and synthesis; and
- Provide support for conclusions you draw and recommendations you suggest.

It is recommended that you create a matrix that aligns your research questions with the information you assess is needed and the methods that you will use to collect that information. Creating this type of alignment ensures that the information you intend to collect is directly related to the research questions, therefore providing answers to the respective research questions. For planning purposes, the alignment indicates the particular methods you will use to collect the information. It is useful to array a table similar to Table 3.3, which illustrates how you might go about setting up such a matrix. A sample matrix showing a completed overview of information needed is presented as Appendix E.

Research Design

Once you are clear about the information you need and the methods you will use to obtain that data, you are ready to develop and present your research design. Whatever combination of methods you choose to use, there is a need for a systematic approach to your data. The main objectives of this section are to identify and present the data-collection methods and explain clearly the process you undertook to carry out each method. Be sure to include in your discussion any field tests or pilot studies you may have undertaken to determine the usefulness of any instruments you have developed. Because the research design in qualitative research is flexible, also mention any modifications and changes you

Table 3.3 Overview of Information Needed

Type of Information	What the Researcher Requires	Method*
(a) Contextual To provide context and background	Organizational background, history, and structure; mission; vision; values; products; services; organizational culture; leadership; staff and site description	Document Review, Observation
(b) Demographic	Descriptive information regarding participants, such as age, gender, ethnicity, discipline, etc.	Survey
(c) Perceptual	Participants' descriptions and explanations of their experiences as this relates to the phenomenon under study.	
Research Question 1. Write out question	Write out what you specifically want to know regarding this question. - -	Interview Critical Incidents Focus Group

Do the same for all your subsequent research questions

*List of documents and instruments for all data collection methods should appear as appendices.

might have made to your design along the way. That is, describe all the steps that you took as you moved through the study to collect your data. Indicate the order in which these steps occurred, as well as how each step informed the next. The narrative can be accompanied by a flowchart or diagram that illustrates the steps involved. A sample research design flowchart appears in Appendix F.

Appropriate methods are derived from having done your analysis of the kinds of information you need to answer your research questions. The discussion of methods and process is preceded by a brief statement concerning your literature review. The purpose of this brief pre-data-collection literature review statement is to underscore: (a) the theoretical grounding for the study, (b) that the review of the literature was ongoing and related research was continually updated, and (c) that the conceptual framework

developed from the literature review was used to guide the data analysis, interpretation, and synthesis phases of the research. This literature review statement comes before the identification and description of methods because, although the literature review is ongoing, generating new information and supporting evidence, it is not a data-collection method per se. You are now ready to discuss the methods you will use in your study.

Methods of Data Collection

Qualitative researchers are concerned about the validity of their communication. To reduce the likelihood of misinterpretation, we employ various procedures, including redundancy of data gathering and procedural challenges to explanation. These procedures, called *triangulation*, are considered a process of using multiple perceptions to clarify meaning. Keep in mind that the use of multiple methods of data collection to achieve triangulation is important to obtain an in-depth understanding of the phenomenon under study. There are several methods used in qualitative research to choose from: interviews (often the primary method), summative focus groups, document review, observation, and critical incident reports. A variety of combinations of methods can be employed. Surveys and questionnaires, which are traditionally quantitative instruments, also can be used in conjunction with qualitative methods to provide corroboration and/or supportive evidence. Appendix G provides a summary overview of the qualitative data-collection methods from which to choose.

A common pitfall in writing this section is the tendency to describe the data-collection methods chosen as if they exist in a vacuum without explaining the logical connections among the methods you have chosen, your research questions, and your research approach. Following are the sequential steps that must be covered in this section. Be specific and precise in your discussion as you:

1. Describe each data-collection method you used.

2. Provide a rationale for each of the methods selected.

3. Provide complete information about how you used each method.

4. Describe how you developed each of your instruments.

5. Describe how you field tested your instruments.

6. Describe how you recorded and safeguarded your data.

7. Describe the steps you took to preserve confidentiality and anonymity of data.

A note of clarification: *Methodology* refers to how research proceeds and encompasses a range of logistical, relational, ethical, and credibility issues. The term *methods* commonly denotes specific techniques, procedures, or tools used by the researcher to generate and analyze data. Unlike the overview of methodology discussed earlier, which reflects an overall research strategy, this section describes what the literature says about each of the methods you used in your study. In other words, you discuss how the instruments you have chosen are appropriate to your study, making use of the literature to support each of your choices.

To show that you have done a critical reading of the literature and to acknowledge that data-collection methods, although certainly useful, are not without some disadvantages, the discussion should include some detail regarding the strengths and weaknesses of each method. In your discussion, present the methods of data collection in the order in which you use them, and be sure to structure the discussion well by having a separate heading for each method.

Based on the research questions, specific data-collection methods are chosen to gather the required information in the most appropriate and meaningful way. Remember too that triangulation strengthens your study by combining methods. Having presented the methods that you have used to gather data, you are ready to go on and explain how the data have been recorded and managed, as well as your strategies for data analysis.

Because interviews are, in most cases, the primary method of data collection, it is useful at this point to explain how interview questions are developed. To carry out the purpose of your study, all the research questions must be satisfied. Therefore, designing the right interview questions is critical. To ensure that the interview questions are directly tied to the research questions, type out in bold font each of your research questions and then underneath each brainstorm three or four questions that will get at that research question. When you have done this for each of your research questions, you should have a list of 12 to 15 interview questions. To do a preliminary test of your interview questions, think about all probable responses you might get from each interview question, and reframe the questions until you are satisfied they will engender the kind of responses that refer directly to the research questions. A sample of a completed interview schedule or interview protocol based on research questions is presented as Appendix H.

Constructing a matrix that lists the research questions along the horizontal axis and the interview questions down the vertical axis can further indicate the extent to which your interview questions have achieved the necessary coverage of your research questions. Table 3.4 is an illustration of this approach. This type of matrix, which allows a visual overview of the required coverage of the research questions via the interview schedule, in conjunction with pilot interviews, can help you further refine your interview questions.

Data Analysis and Synthesis

In this section, you report on how you managed, organized, and analyzed your data in preparation to write up and present your findings (chap. 4) and then how you went on to analyze and interpret your findings (chap. 5). Thus, it is important to note that this section of chapter 3 can be written only *after* you have written up the findings and analysis chapters of your dissertation.

The process of data analysis begins with putting in place a plan to manage the large volume of data you collected and reducing it in a meaningful way. You complete this process to identify significant patterns and construct a framework for communicating the essence of what the data revealed given the purpose of your study. Here your conceptual framework becomes the centerpiece in managing the data. The categories that comprise your conceptual framework become the repositories of your data. Thus, as you look at your raw data, categorize them within the construct of your conceptual framework and assign initial codes to relevant quotes. This iterative process of open coding leads to the ongoing refinement of what will become your final coding schema. Generally, include your coding schema or coding legend as an appendix. Appendix I is a completed coding scheme sample. In addition, it is useful to show the reader how your coding

Table 3.4 Research Questions/Interview Questions Matrix

| Interview Questions | Research Questions | | | |
	1:	2:	3:	4:
1				
2				
3				
4				
5				

Do the same for all your subsequent research questions.

scheme developed. Appendix J offers such an illustration.

Therefore, the process of analysis is both deductive and inductive. The initial categories of your conceptual framework were deductively obtained from the literature. From your own experience and the data as they emerged from pilot tests, you begin to see patterns and themes. In this way, coding occurs inductively. As the coding schema continues to emerge, you must obtain inter-rater reliability by requesting colleagues, usually three, to read one of your interview transcripts to test your codes. Any discrepancies that result from the independent review by your colleagues must be discussed and reconciled with each of them. Such discrepancies may result in additional exploration of the data. Exploration of such discrepancies in which further clarification is needed will help you as the researcher to refine how you state your findings, as well as subsequent analysis and recommendations (Creswell, 1998). You also can have these same colleagues act as "devil's advocates" or peer reviewers throughout data collection, analysis, and interpretation.

Computer software programs can be useful in both managing and analyzing your data. Various programs (e.g., *ATLAS ti, NUD.IST, NVivo*) enable the researcher to store, categorize, retrieve, and compare data. At the same time, there are other researchers who prefer to manage and analyze their data manually—to see visual displays of the data as they move through the analysis process. These researchers also are concerned with what they perceive as a limitation related to mechanical handling of data (Berg, 2004; Merriam, 1998), and so they may feel more comfortable using flip charts, tables, charts, and matrices. We are not suggesting one approach over the other because the method you select to manage and analyze your data is a matter of personal preference and depends on what you are most comfortable with and/or institutional requirements.

Whether you use a computer-based system or a manual one, the development of visuals—tables and/or figures—can be useful in helping you organize your thinking in preparation for writing. Aside from helping you develop your own thinking, visuals also are useful for displaying your data so your readers can better understand them. Various types of charts can be constructed, and you can indeed be quite creative in devising these charts. For presenting and analyzing findings, we have found three charts to be particularly effective: data summary tables, the analysis outline tool, and consistency charts.

Data summary tables, discussed in more detail in chapter 4, can help you in preparing to present the findings from the data. These tables are used for recording the number and types of participant responses, tracking the frequency of participant responses against the categories on your conceptual framework, and formulating overall finding statements with respect to each of your research questions. Sample data summary tables are presented as Appendices R through V.

To further help in the analysis and interpretation of findings, we suggest using what we call an interpretation outline tool. This tool, discussed in more detail in chapter 5, prompts you to probe beneath the surface of your findings to uncover the deeper meanings that lie beneath them. A sample interpretation outline tool appears as Appendix Y. Consistency charts, discussed further in chapter 4, help align your thinking with respect to how each finding can generate suitable conclusions and recommendations. A sample completed consistency chart is presented in Appendix Z.

Because qualitative research is, by its nature, flexible and because there are no strict guidelines and standards for qualitative analysis, every qualitative researcher will approach the analytic process somewhat differently. Therefore, it is necessary to

(a) provide a detailed description of how you went about analyzing your data, (b) refer to the matrices that you used to display your data, and (c) identify the coding processes used to convert the raw data into themes for analysis. Your description should include specific details about how you managed the large amount of data. Include information about the computer software, Post-it notes, index cards, flip charts, or other processes that you used. This list helps the reader clearly understand how and in what ways you reduced or transformed your data.

As a last point in this section, it is important that researchers understand what is meant by *synthesis of the data*. Whereas analysis splits data apart, synthesis is the process of pulling everything together: (a) how the research questions are answered by the findings, (b) how the findings from interviews are supported from all other data-collection methods, (c) how findings relate to the literature, and (d) how findings relate to the researcher's going-in assumptions about the study. This process is not linear; rather, you describe your findings, interpret and attach meaning to them, and synthesize throughout your discussion.

Ethical Considerations

As researchers, we are morally bound to conduct our research in a manner that minimizes potential harm to those involved in the study. We should be as concerned with producing an ethical research design as we are an intellectually coherent and compelling one.

Colleges, universities, and other institutions that conduct research have institutional review boards (IRBs) whose members review research proposals to assess ethical issues. Although all studies must be approved by your institution's IRB committee, there are some unique ethical considerations surrounding qualitative research because of its emergent and flexible design. Ethical issues can indeed arise in all phases of the research

process: data collection, data analysis and interpretation, and dissemination of the research findings. For the most part, issues of ethics focus on establishing safeguards that will protect the rights of participants and include informed consent, protecting participants from harm, and ensuring confidentiality. As a qualitative researcher, you need to remain attentive throughout your study to the researcher–participant relationship, which is determined by roles, status, and cultural norms.

In this section of chapter 3, you need to show the reader that you have considered the ethical issues that might arise vis-à-vis your own study, you are sensitive to these issues, and you have taken the necessary steps to address these issues. In most instances, you will be talking in generalities; the potential issues that could arise apply to any qualitative research study and are usually not specific to your own. Because protection of human subjects is such an important issue in social science research, the main point is that you acknowledge and convey to the reader that you have considered and taken heed of the issues involved. Remember, informed consent is central to research ethics. It is the principle that seeks to ensure that all human subjects retain autonomy and the ability to judge for themselves what risks are worth taking for the purpose of furthering scientific knowledge. In this regard, it is important that you include in your appendix a copy of the consent form that you used in your study. A sample consent form appears in Appendix K.

Issues of Trustworthiness

In quantitative research, the standards that are most frequently used for good and convincing research are validity and reliability. If research is valid, it clearly reflects the world being described. If work is reliable, then two researchers studying the same phenomenon will come up with compatible observations. Criteria for evaluating qualitative research differ from those used in quantitative research, in that the focus is on how well the researcher has provided evidence that her or his descriptions and analysis represent the reality of the situations and persons studied. In this section of chapter 3, you need to clarify to the reader how you have accounted for trustworthiness regarding your own study.

As mentioned previously, qualitative research is characterized by an ongoing discourse regarding the appropriate and acceptable use of terminology. Current thinking has led some qualitative researchers to develop alternative terminology to better reflect the nature and distinction of qualitative research, whereas others still feel comfortable borrowing terminology from quantitative research. While some qualitative researchers argue for a return to terminology for ensuring rigor that is used by mainstream science (Morse, Barrett, Mayan, Olson, & Spiers, 2002), others object to the use of traditional terms such as *validity* and *reliability*, preferring instead *credibility* and *dependability*. This contrast is a matter of institutional and/or personal preference, and we recommend that you check with your advisor in this regard. Lincoln and Guba (1985) and Guba and Lincoln (1998), among others, belong to the latter camp, proposing various criteria for evaluating the trustworthiness of qualitative research:

1. Credibility: This criterion refers to whether the participants' perceptions match up with the researcher's portrayal of them. In other words, has the researcher accurately represented what the participants think, feel, and do? Credibility parallels the criterion of validity (including both validity of measures and internal validity) in quantitative research. Evidence in support of credibility can take several forms:
   a. Clarify up front the bias that you, as the researcher, bring to the study. This self-reflection creates an open and honest attitude that will resonate well with readers. You should continually monitor their own subjective perspectives and biases by recording reflective field notes or keeping a journal throughout the research process.
   b. Discuss how you engaged in repeated and substantial involvement in the field. Prolonged involvement in the field facilitates a more in-depth understanding of the phenomenon under study, conveying detail about the site and the participants that lends credibility to your account.
   c. An aspect of credibility involves checking on whether your interpretation of the processes and interactions in the setting is valid. Typically, qualitative researchers collect multiple sources of data. The information provided by these different sources should be compared through triangulation to corroborate the researcher's conclusions.
   d. Triangulation of data-collection methods also lends credibility. Using multiple methods corroborates the evidence that you have obtained via different means.
   e. Present negative instances or discrepant findings. Searching for variation in the understanding of the phenomenon entails seeking instances that might disconfirm or challenge the researcher's expectations or emergent findings. Because real life is composed of different perspectives that do not always coalesce, discussing contrary information adds to the credibility of your account.
   f. To ensure that the researcher's own biases do not influence how participants' perspectives are portrayed, and to determine the accuracy of the findings, you can make use of "member checks," which entails sending the transcribed interviews or summaries of the researcher's conclusions to participants for review.
   g. Use "peer debriefing" to enhance the accuracy of your account. This process involves asking a colleague to examine

your field notes and then ask you questions that will help you examine your assumptions and/or consider alternative ways of looking at the data.

2. Dependability: This criterion parallels reliability, although it is not assessed through statistical procedures. Dependability refers to whether one can track the processes and procedures used to collect and interpret the data:

    a. Provide detailed and thorough explanations of how the data were collected and analyzed, providing what is known as an "audit trail." Although it is not possible to include all of your data in the findings chapter, many qualitative researchers make it known that their data are available for review by other researchers.

    b. Ask colleagues to code several interviews, thereby establishing inter-rater reliability. This process of checking on the consistency between raters reduces the potential bias of a single researcher collecting and analyzing the data.

3. Transferability: Although qualitative researchers do not expect their findings to be generalizable to all other settings, it is likely that the lessons learned in one setting might be useful to others. Transferability is not whether the study includes a representative sample. Rather, it is about how well the study has made it possible for the reader to decide whether similar processes will be at work in their own settings and communities by understanding in depth how they occur at the research site. Thus, transferability refers to the fit or match between the research context and other contexts as judged by the reader. As a criterion of trustworthiness, transferability is assessed by the following factors:

    a. The richness of the descriptions included in the study give the discussion an element of shared or vicarious experience. Qualitative research is indeed characterized generally by "thick description" (Denzin, 1989/2001). Thick description is a vehicle for communicating to the reader a holistic and realistic picture.

    b. The amount of detailed information that is provided by the researcher regarding the context and/or background also offers an element of shared experience.

This section of the dissertation's chapter 3 addresses this central question: How do we know that the qualitative study is believable, accurate, and plausible? To answer this question, one must have some knowledge of the criteria of trustworthiness in qualitative research and the approaches to addressing these criteria. You need to discuss the criteria for evaluating the trustworthiness of qualitative research and to indicate to the reader that you have a clear understanding of the implications thereof vis-à-vis your own study. As the researcher, you are expected to display sensibility and sensitivity to *be* the research instrument. Begin this section by discussing what validity and reliability in qualitative research involves, using references from the literature to support your statements. Then go on to talk about the strategies that you have employed to enhance the trustworthiness of your own study vis-à-vis validity (credibility), reliability (dependability), and generalizability (transferability).

Limitations of the Study

Confusion sometimes exists around the terms *delimitations* and *limitations*, and this issue deserves some clarification. *Delimitations* clarify the boundaries of your study. They are a way to indicate to the reader how you narrowed the scope of your study. As the researcher, you control the delimitations, and you should make this clear. Typical delimitations are selected aspects of the problem, time and location of the study, sample selected, and so on. *Limitations* of the study expose the conditions that may weaken the study (Locke, Spirduso, & Silverman, 2000; Rossman & Rallis, 2003).

In this section of chapter 3, you cite potential limitations and your means of addressing/guarding against these limitations. Regardless of how carefully you plan a study, there are always some limitations, and you need to explicitly acknowledge these. This section describes the problems inherent in qualitative research and how you can control for these limitations to the extent possible. In most instances, you can control for limitations by acknowledging them. Limitations arise from, among other things, restricted sample size, sample selection, reliance on certain techniques for gathering data, and issues of researcher bias and participant reactivity. Discussing limitations is intended to show the reader that you understand that no research project is without limitations, and that you have anticipated and given some thought to the shortcomings of your research. Stating the limitations also reminds the reader that your study is situated with a specific context, and the reader can make decisions about its usefulness for other settings.

Chapter Summary

The purpose of a final culminating summary is to tie together everything that you have presented in this chapter. Provide a short summary overview, making sure to cover all the sections of this chapter, recapping and highlighting all the important points. Keep the discussion concise and precise.

The application section that follows is a skeleton view of what a methodology chapter should look like. The methodology chapter, as evidenced from the prior instructions, is lengthy, and much detail is required in each section. In an actual dissertation, each section of this chapter would be more

thoroughly elaborated, and hence would require a much more extensive discussion.

SECTION II: APPLICATION

CHAPTER III
Methodology
Introduction

The purpose of this multicase study was to explore with a sample of doctoral candidates their perceptions of why they have not managed to complete their dissertations. The researcher believed that a better understanding of this phenomenon would allow educators to proceed from a more informed perspective in terms of design and facilitation of doctoral programs. In seeking to understand this phenomenon, the study addressed five research questions: (a) On completion of their coursework, to what extent did participants perceive they were prepared to conduct research and write the dissertation? (b) What did participants perceive they needed to learn to complete their dissertation? (c) How did participants attempt to develop the knowledge, skills, and attitudes they perceived are necessary to complete the dissertation? (d) What factors did participants perceive might help them to complete the dissertation? (e) What factors did participants perceive have impeded and/or continue to impede their progress in working toward completing their dissertation?

This chapter describes the study's research methodology and includes discussions around the following areas: (a) rationale for research approach, (b) description of the research sample, (c) summary of information needed, (d) overview of research design, (e) methods of data collection, (f) analysis and synthesis of data, (g) ethical considerations, (h) issues of trustworthiness, and (i) limitations of the study. The chapter culminates with a brief concluding summary.

Rationale for Qualitative Research Design

Qualitative research is grounded in an essentially constructivist philosophical position, in the sense that it is concerned with how the complexities of the sociocultural world are experienced, interpreted, and understood in a particular context and at a particular point in time. The intent of qualitative research is to examine a social situation or interaction by allowing the researcher to enter the world of others and attempt to achieve a holistic rather than a reductionist understanding (Bogdan & Biklen, 1998; Locke et al., 2000; Mason, 1996; Maxwell, 2005; Merriam, 1998; Merriam & Associates, 2002; Patton, 1990; Schram, 2003; Schwandt, 2000). Qualitative methodology implies an emphasis on discovery and description, and the objectives are generally focused on extracting and interpreting the meaning of experience (Bogdan & Biklen, 1998; Denzin & Lincoln, 2003; Merriam, 1998). These objectives are contrasted with those of quantitative research, where the testing of hypotheses to establish facts and to designate and distinguish relationships between variables is usually the intent.

It was the researcher's contention that purely quantitative methods were unlikely to elicit the rich data necessary to address the proposed research purposes. In the researcher's view, the fundamental assumptions and key features that distinguish what it means to proceed from a qualitative stance fit well with this study. These features include (a) understanding the processes by which events and actions take place, (b) developing contextual understanding, (c) facilitating interactivity between researcher and participants, (d) adopting an interpretive stance, and (e) maintaining design flexibility.

Rationale for Case Study Methodology

Within the framework of a qualitative approach, the study was most suited for a case study design. As a form of research methodology, case study is an intensive description and analysis of a phenomenon, social unit, or system bounded by time or place (Berg, 2004; Creswell, 1998; Merriam, 1998; Merriam & Associates, 2002; Miles & Huberman, 1994; Stake, 1994, 1995, 2000, 2001). As Merriam (1998) indicates, qualitative case study is an ideal design for understanding and interpreting educational phenomena. As she describes it,

> A case study design is employed to gain an in depth understanding of the situation and meaning for those involved. The interest is in process rather than outcomes, in context rather than a specific variable, in discovery rather than confirmation. Insights gleaned from case studies can directly influence policy, practice, and future research. (Merriam, 1998, p. 19)

The present research fit well with Merriam's criteria because it sought to better understand why certain people who complete the coursework do not go on to complete the dissertation and hence do not graduate with a doctoral degree.

The Research Sample

A purposeful sampling procedure was used to select this study's sample. To yield the most information about the phenomenon under study, purposeful sampling is a method that is typical of case study methodology (Patton, 1990; Silverman, 2000). The researcher sought to locate individuals at a variety of universities. Thus, a snowball sampling strategy, sometimes referred to as network or chain sampling (Miles & Huberman, 1994; Patton, 2002), was employed, whereby participants were asked to refer other individuals whom they knew to be ABD. The criteria for selection of participants were:

- All participants were enrolled in a doctoral program for at least 3 years, and
- All participants completed the coursework and passed the certification examination.

A delimiting time frame of 3 years was decided on by the researcher to ensure adequate experience in a doctoral program. Purposeful sampling allowed for sampling across various locations in the United States. The research sample included 20 individuals. Included in the sample were individuals from doctoral programs at nine universities, including Columbia University, Wayne State University, University of Massachusetts, University of Georgia, University of Southern California, University of Michigan, Rutgers University, Fordham University, and Northwestern University. Purposeful selection also was based on variation across certain distinguishing characteristics. Although participants were all ABD doctoral candidates, there were differences among them along the following parameters: length of time spent in doctoral program, university and discipline, gender, age, and occupation.

Information Needed to Conduct the Study

This multicase study focused on 20 doctoral candidates from nine universities located in different regions of the United States. In seeking to understand why these doctoral candidates have not obtained doctoral degrees, five research questions were explored to gather the information needed. The information needed to answer these research questions was determined by the conceptual framework and fell into three categories: (a) perceptual, (b) demographic, and (c) theoretical. This information included:

- Doctoral candidates' perceptions of what they needed to know and how they went about obtaining what they needed to conduct their research and complete their dissertations.
- Demographic information pertaining to participants, including years in program, doctoral program concentration/discipline, age, gender, and ethnicity.
- An ongoing review of the literature providing the theoretical grounding for the study.

Overview of Research Design

The following list summarizes the steps used to carry out this research. Following this list is a more in-depth discussion of each of these steps.

1. Preceding the actual collection of data, a selected review of the literature was conducted to study the contributions of other researchers and writers in the broad areas of higher educational programs and adult learning theory.

2. Following the proposal defense, the researcher acquired approval from the IRB to proceed with the research. The IRB approval process involved outlining all procedures and processes needed to ensure adherence to standards put forth for the study of human subjects, including participants' confidentiality and informed consent.

3. Potential research participants were contacted by telephone, and those who agreed to participate were sent a questionnaire by mail. The survey was designed to collect demographic as well as perceptual data.

4. Semistructured, in-depth interviews were conducted with 20 ABD doctoral candidates in nine universities located across the United States.

5. Interview data responses were analyzed within and between groups of interviewees.

6. Critical incident instruments were given to participants at the end of each interview to check data collected through other means. Of the 20 participants, 12 responded.

7. A focus group was conducted with six ABDs who were drawn from the pool of participants identified for this study to cross-check data from that group with the data collected through interviews.

Literature Review

An ongoing and selective review of literature was conducted to inform this study. Two topics of literature were identified: higher education doctoral programs and adult learning theory. The focus of the review was to gain a better understanding of what prompted participants to enroll in doctoral programs, the requirements and challenges inherent in these programs, and the effect on participants and the means they took to meet the requirements and overcome the challenges they faced.

IRB Approval

Following the literature review, the researchers developed and successfully defended a proposal for this study that included: the background/context, problem statement, purpose statement, and research questions outlined in chapter 1; the literature review included in chapter 2; and the proposed methodological approach as outlined in chapter 3.

Data-Collection Methods

The use of multiple methods and triangulation is critical in attempting to obtain an in-depth understanding of the phenomenon under study. This strategy adds rigor, breadth, and depth to the study and provides corroborative evidence of the data obtained (Creswell, 1998; Denzin & Lincoln, 2000). Therefore, this study employed a number of different data-collection methods, including survey, interviews, critical incident reports, and a focus group.

Phase I: Survey

Potential participants were contacted. Of those who were contacted to participate, three individuals declined. The 20 individuals who agreed to participate were sent a questionnaire by mail and were asked to return the completed forms by way of a self-addressed envelope. The questionnaire was designed to collect profile data and also asked participants their purposes for enrolling in a doctoral program. The survey appears as Appendix L.

An advantage of survey methodology is that it is relatively unobtrusive and relatively easily administered (Fowler, 1993). It must be acknowledged, however, that surveys can be of limited value for examining complex social relationships or intricate patterns of interaction. In keeping with the qualitative research tradition, the surveys used in the present study included some open-ended questions that sought to tap into personal experiences and shed light on participants' perceptions. For the purposes of the present study, surveys had a distinct place in the study's methodological design and served as a useful complement or adjunct to other data-collection methods.

Phase II: Interviews

The interview was selected as the primary method for data collection in this research. The interview method was felt to be of the most use in the study because it has the potential to elicit rich, thick descriptions. Further, it gives the researcher an opportunity to clarify statements and probe for additional information. Creswell (1994), Marshall and Rossman (2006), and Denzin and Lincoln (2003) state that a major benefit of collecting data through individual, in-depth interviews is that they offer the potential to capture a person's perspective of an event or experience.

The interview is a fundamental tool in qualitative research (Kvale, 1996; Merriam, 1998; Seidman, 1998). Kvale (1996) describes the qualitative research interview as an "attempt to understand the world from the subject's point of view, to unfold the meaning of peoples' experiences, to uncover their lived world ..." (p. 1). As Patton (1990) similarly claims, "qualitative interviewing begins with the assumption that the perspective of others is meaningful, knowable, and able to be made explicit" (p. 278). The researcher's logic for using this data-collection method is that a legitimate way to generate data is to interact with people (i.e., talk to and listen to them), thereby capturing the meaning of their experience in their own words.

Although interviews have certain strengths, there are various limitations associated with interviewing. First, not all people are equally cooperative, articulate, and perceptive. Second, interviews require researcher skill. Third, interviews are not neutral tools of data gathering; they are the result of the interaction between the interviewer and the interviewee and the context in which they take place (Fontana & Frey, 2003; Rubin & Rubin, 2005; Schwandt, 1997).

Interview Schedule of Questions and Pilot Interviews. With guidance from her advisor, the researcher used the study's five research questions as the framework to develop the interview questions. Matrices were constructed to illustrate the relationship between this study's research questions and the interview questions as they were being developed. Three doctoral colleagues were then asked to review and provide feedback to the researcher. Their comments were incorporated, and the researcher resubmitted the schedule of questions to her advisor. With the advisor's approval, two pilot interviews were conducted by phone. The preliminary themes that emerged from the pilot interviews revolved around reasons that individuals enroll in doctoral programs and their learning during the process. From the pilot interviews, a series of open-ended questions was developed, which enabled the researcher the flexibility to allow new directions to emerge during the interview. The final interview schedule is included as Appendix H.

Interview Process. The researcher sent individual e-mails to prospective participants describing the purpose of the study, inviting their participation, and requesting a convenient date and time for a telephone interview. The researcher sent confirming e-mails to the 20 individuals who agreed to be interviewed. The interviews took place between August and October 2006. Before the interview commenced, the interviewee was asked to review and sign a university consent form required for participation in this study (see Appendix I). All interviews were conducted telephonically and were tape recorded in their entirety. At the end of each interview, the interviewee was asked to complete and return by e-mail the critical incident instrument, which had been prepared by the researcher. On completion of the interview, the audio tape was transcribed verbatim.

Phase III: Critical Incidents

The researcher selected critical incident instruments with the intention of corroborating interview data and, further, to allow the uncovering of perceptions that might not have been revealed through the interviews. Critical incident reports,

a data-collection method first formulated by Flanagan (1954), are useful because qualitative research methodology emphasizes process and is based on a descriptive and inductive approach to data collection (Bogdan & Biklen, 1998). Of particular importance is that written critical incident reports probe assumptions, allowing time for reflection (Argyris & Schon, 1996; Brookfield, 1991; Marshall & Rossman, 2006).

Although there is support in the literature for the use of the critical incident as an effective technique for enhancing data collection, with several authors noting its advantages (Bogdan & Biklen, 1998; Brookfield, 1986, 1987, 1991; Flanagan, 1954), the researcher was mindful of Brookfield's repeated caution that critical incidents cannot be the sole technique for collecting data. Critical incidents are too abbreviated to provide the rich descriptions that can be obtained in interviews and observations. A further concern regarding the use of critical incident reports has to do with the accuracy of data because this technique relies solely on the respondents' recall. A related concern is that, although reporting information that respondents perceive is important, the researcher may fail to report salient incremental data and the information, as such, may be incomplete.

The critical incident instrument was developed by the researcher and further refined by her advisor. The instrument was field tested in conjunction with the pilot interviews. The results of the field test called for minor revisions, and these were incorporated into a final critical incident form/instrument. This instrument is included as Appendix M.

The critical incident instrument was subsequently given to the 20 participants in this study at the end of each interview by the researcher. The instrument asked respondents to think about a specific time when they felt ill-prepared to conduct some part of the dissertation process. Specifically, participants were asked to briefly describe the incident, indicating who was involved, what they learned, and how they thought their learning would influence how they would handle similar situations in the future. Participants were given a self-addressed envelope and were requested at the end of the interview to return completed critical incidents to the researcher as soon as possible. The researcher received 12 completed critical incidents from among the 20 participants. Although the researcher had hoped for a greater response, when analyzed, the returned critical incidents served as a "validity check" on some aspects of the data uncovered in the interviews.

Phase IV: Focus Group

Focus groups, or group interviews, possess elements of both participant observation and individual interviews, while also maintaining their own uniqueness as a distinctive research method (Morgan, 1997). A focus group is essentially a group discussion focused on a single theme (Kreuger, 1988). The goal is to create a candid conversation that addresses, in depth, the selected topic. The underlying assumption of focus groups is that, within a permissive atmosphere that fosters a range of opinions, a more complete and revealing understanding of the issues will be obtained. Focus groups are planned and structured, but are also flexible tools (Vaughn, Schumm, & Sinagub, 1996). Kreuger and Casey (2000) list various uses of focus groups, many of which fit well with this study's purpose. These are to: (a) elicit a range of feelings, opinions, and ideas; (b) understand differences in perspectives; (c) uncover and provide insight into specific factors that influence opinions; and (d) seek ideas that emerge from the group.

It must be acknowledged that focus groups, while serving a useful function, are not without disadvantages. Among these disadvantages is "groupthink" as a possible outcome (Fontana & Frey, 2003). Furthermore, logistical difficulties might arise from the need to manage conversation while attempting to extract data, thus requiring strong facilitation skills.

One 1½-hour formative focus group was convened with six participants who were not part of the study sample. These participants were purposefully selected based on the established criteria. The purpose of this focus group interview was twofold:

(a) to augment the information obtained, and (b) to provide additional data to ensure trustworthiness and credibility. In the open-ended format that was used, the researcher asked the group to explore two issues. First, what did they feel helped them the most in the research process? Second, what challenges and obstacles did they encounter that impeded their progress?

The researcher contacted the 20 study participants seeking their interest in joining a focus group discussion. The study participants were advised of the purpose and were told that the discussion would be held over an Internet Conference Call System and would be audiotaped. Eleven of the 20 participants responded that they would be willing to join the discussion, and the first 6 respondents were selected. A general e-mail was sent by the researcher thanking the participants who had expressed interest. Following that, the researcher contacted each of the focus group members to schedule a convenient time to hold the discussion.

Methods for Data Analysis and Synthesis

The challenge throughout data collection and analysis was to make sense of large amounts of data, reduce the volume of information, identify significant patterns, and construct a framework In this regard, Merriam (1998) cautions researchers to make data analysis and data collection a simultaneous activity to avoid the risk of repetitious, unfocused, and overwhelming data.

The formal process of data analysis began by assigning alphanumeric codes according to the categories and descriptors of the study's conceptual framework. The researcher prepared large flip chart sheets. These sheets were color coded and taped on the wall. Each sheet identified the descriptors under the respective categories of the conceptual framework. As the process of coding the transcripts proceeded, new flip chart sheets were prepared to capture other themes as they emerged.

Before cutting and pasting coded participant quotations, the researcher shared samples of coded interviews with two colleagues. Discussion with both colleagues confirmed the researcher's designations. The researcher also prepared written narratives on each of the sheets after all the data had been assigned. These narratives were helpful in cross-checking the data and served as a secondary analysis.

As a final step, to see whether there were any variables that would account for similarities or differences among participants, the researcher tested the coded data on the sheets against the frequency charts prepared for each finding and the numerically coded profile data on the participants. This step aided the researcher in her cross-case analysis of the data, which is described more fully later.

The coding process fragments the interview into separate categories, forcing one to look at each detail, whereas synthesis involves piecing these fragments together to reconstruct a holistic and integrated explanation. Overall, the researcher's approach was to come up with a number of clusters, patterns, or themes that were linked together, either similarly or divergently and that collectively described or analyzed the research arena. Toward this end, the researcher essentially followed a three-layered process in thinking about the data. First, she examined and compared threads and patterns within categories. Second, she compared connecting threads and patterns across categories. Third, the current work was situated with respect to prior research and was compared and contrasted with issues that had been raised by the broader literature. These three layers were not separate, but were interlocked and iterative throughout the synthesizing process.

Based on analysis and synthesis, the researcher was able to move forward and think about the broader implications of this research. Toward this end, she formulated several conclusions and developed various practical and research-related recommendations.

Ethical Considerations

In any research study, ethical issues relating to protection of the participants are of vital concern (Berg, 2004; Marshall & Rossman, 2006; Merriam, 1998; Pring, 2000; Punch, 1994; Schram, 2003). A social science researcher is responsible for both informing and protecting respondents. The research process involves enlisting voluntary cooperation, and it is a basic premise that participants are informed about the study's purpose. The central issue with respect to protecting participants is the ways in which the information is treated. Although it was anticipated that no serious ethical threats were posed to any of the participants or their well-being, this study employed various safeguards to ensure the protection and rights of participants.

First, informed consent remained a priority throughout the study. Written consent to voluntarily proceed with the study was received from each participant. Second, participants' rights and interests were considered of primary importance when choices were made regarding the reporting and dissemination of data. The researcher was committed to keeping the names and/or other significant identity characteristics of the sample organizations confidential. Cautionary measures were taken to secure the storage of research-related records and data, and nobody other than the researcher had access to this material.

Issues of Trustworthiness

In qualitative research, trustworthiness features consist of any efforts by the researcher to address the more traditional quantitative issues of validity (the degree to which something measures what it purports to measure) and reliability (the consistency with which it measures it over time). In seeking to establish the trustworthiness of a qualitative study, Guba and Lincoln (1998) use the terms *credibility*, *dependability*, *confirmability*, and *transferability*, arguing that the trustworthiness of qualitative research should be assessed differently from quantitative research. Regardless of the terminology used, qualitative researchers must continue to seek to control for potential biases that might be present throughout the design, implementation, and analysis of the study.

Credibility

The criterion of credibility (or validity) suggests whether the findings are accurate and credible from the standpoint of the researcher, the participants, and the reader. This criterion becomes a key component of the research design (Creswell, 2003; Creswell & Miller, 2000; Marshall & Rossman, 2006; Mason, 1996; Maxwell, 2005; Merriam, 1998; Merriam & Associates; 2002; Miles & Huberman, 1994). Seeking not to *verify* conclusions, but rather to *test the validity* of conclusions reached, entails a concern with both methodological and interpretive validity (Mason, 1996).

Methodological validity involves asking how well matched the logic of the method is to the kinds of research questions that are being posed and the kind of explanation that the researcher is attempting to develop. Dealing with this type of validity involves consideration of the interrelationship between the research design components—the study's purpose, conceptual framework, research questions, and methods. Interpretative validity involves asking how valid the data analysis is and the interpretation on which it is based. Although this step is somewhat dependent on methodological validity, it goes further in that it directs attention to the quality and rigor with which the researcher interprets and analyzes data in relation to the research design (Mason, 1996).

To enhance the methodological validity of the study, the researcher triangulated data sources as well as data-collection methods. Gathering data from multiple sources and by multiple methods yields a fuller and richer picture of the phenomenon under review. To enhance the interpretive validity of this study, the researcher employed various strategies. First, she clarified her assumptions up front, and the steps through which interpretations were made also were charted through journal writing. Second, the researcher used various participatory and collaborative modes of research, including the search for discrepant

evidence and peer review, which has been discussed at length by Lincoln and Guba (1985). This entails looking for variation in the understanding of the phenomenon and seeking instances that might challenge the researcher's expectations or emergent findings. Reviewing and discussing findings with professional colleagues was a further way of ensuring that the reality of the participants was adequately reflected in the findings.

Dependability

Reliability in the traditional sense refers to the extent that research findings can be replicated by other similar studies. Qualitative research usually does not cover enough of an expanse of subjects and experiences to provide a reasonable degree of reliability. As argued by Lincoln and Guba (1985), the more important question becomes one of whether the findings are consistent and dependable with the data collected. As the researcher understood it, in qualitative research the goal is not to eliminate inconsistencies but to ensure that the researcher understands when they occur. Thus, it becomes incumbent on the researcher to document her procedures and demonstrate that coding schemes and categories have been used consistently.

Toward this end, inter-rater reliability (Miles & Huberman, 1994) was established by asking colleagues to code several interviews. Although coding was generally found to be consistent, there were certain instances where the raters made some inferences that could not be fully supported by the data. In these cases, the researcher reviewed the data and reconciled differences in interpretations. In addition, the researcher maintained an audit trail (Lincoln & Guba, 1985) that chronicled the evolution of her thinking and documented the rationale for all choices and decisions made during the research process. This trail, which Merriam & Associates (2002) describe as offering "transparency of method," depended on the researcher keeping a journal as well as a record of memos that included detailed accounts of how all the data were analyzed and interpreted.

Confirmability

The concept of *confirmability* corresponds to the notion of objectivity in quantitative research. The implication is that the findings are the result of the research, rather than an outcome of the biases and subjectivity of the researcher. To achieve this end, a researcher needs to identify and uncover the decision trail for public judgment. Although qualitative researchers realize the futility of attempting to achieve objectivity, they must nevertheless be reflexive and illustrate how their data can be traced back to its origins. As such, the audit trail (Lincoln & Guba, 1985) used to demonstrate dependability, including ongoing reflection by way of journaling and memo, as well as a record of field notes and transcripts, served to offer the reader an opportunity to assess the findings of this study.

Transferability

Although generalizeability is not the intended goal of this study, what was addressed was the issue of *transferability* (Lincoln & Guba, 1985)—that is, the ways in which the reader determines whether and to what extent this particular phenomenon in this particular context can transfer to another particular context. With regard to transferability, Patton (1990) promotes thinking of "context-bound extrapolations" (p. 491), which he defines as "speculations on the likely applicability of findings to other situations under similar, but not identical, conditions" (p. 489). Toward this end, the researcher attempted to address the issue of transferability by way of thick, rich description of the participants and the context. Depth, richness, and detailed description provide the basis for a qualitative account's claim to relevance in some broader context (Schram, 2003).

Limitations of the Study

This study contains certain limiting conditions, some of which are related to the common critiques of qualitative research methodology in general and some of which are inherent in this study's research design. Careful thought has been given to ways of accounting for these limitations and to ways of minimizing their impact. Unique features of qualitative research methodology present potential limitations in its usage.

Because analysis ultimately rests with the thinking and choices of the researcher, qualitative studies in general are limited by researcher subjectivity. Therefore, an overriding concern is that of researcher bias, framing as it does assumptions, interests, perceptions, and needs. One of the key limitations of this study is the issue of subjectivity and potential bias regarding the researcher's own participation in a doctoral program first as a student and currently as a faculty member.

A related limitation was that interviewees may have had difficulty adjusting to the researcher taking on the role of interviewer, a phenomenon referred to by Maxwell (1996) as *participant reactivity*. Because a few of the participants knew the researcher, their responses may have been influenced or affected. They may have tried overly hard to cooperate with the researcher by offering her the responses they perceived she was seeking or which they perceived might be helpful to her. Alternatively, because of familiarity with the researcher, these few participants might have been guarded and therefore less candid in their responses.

Recognizing these limitations, the researcher took the following measures. First, she acknowledged her research agenda and stated her assumptions up front. Coding schemes were scrutinized by advisors and through peer review, as were coded documents and transcripts. To reduce the limitation of potential bias during data analysis, the researcher removed all participant names and coded all interview transcripts blindly so as not to associate any material or data with any particular individual. To address the problem of participant reactivity, the researcher continued to reflect on how and in what ways she might be influencing participants. Furthermore, she made a conscious attempt to create an environment that was conducive to honest and open dialogue. Experience as an interviewer, as well as prior research experience, was helpful in this regard.

Aside from issues pertaining to bias and reactivity, a further major limitation of this study was that the research sample was restricted. Therefore, a critique of this research might be the limited possibility of generalizing this study to other groups and other programs. Although generalizability was not the intended goal of this study, what the researchers addressed is the issue of transferability (Lincoln & Guba, 1985). By way of thick, rich description, as well as detailed information regarding the context and background of the study, it was anticipated that knowledge could be assessed for its applicability and applied appropriately in other contexts.

Chapter Summary

In summary, this chapter provided a detailed description of this study's research methodology. Qualitative case study methodology was employed to illustrate the phenomenon of why some people who complete all the doctoral coursework do not go on to complete the dissertation, never obtain the doctoral degree, and hence remain ABD. The participant sample was made up of 20 purposefully selected individuals. Three data-collection methods were employed, including individual interviews, critical incidents, and a focus group. The data were reviewed against literature as well as emergent themes. Credibility and dependability were accounted for through various strategies, including source and method triangulation.

A review of the literature was conducted to devise a conceptual framework for the design and analysis of the study. A process analysis enabled the key themes from the findings to be identified. Through a comparison with the literature, interpretations and conclusions were drawn, and recommendations were offered for both educational practice and further research. The intent was that this study would make a contribution to the understanding of doctoral students, current and future, with regard to their completing a dissertation. Additionally, it is hoped that this study will be of value to those educators who are responsible for doctoral programs.

SUMMARY DISCUSSION FOR CHAPTER 3

Writing the methodology chapter requires time, mind work, and a great deal of reflection about the nature of your inquiry. You most certainly want to present well-reasoned research that will illustrate the integrity of your study. Be sure to give careful thought to how you present the discussion, and, as always, remember to work from an outline. Your headings and subheadings in this chapter are contingent on your particular university's requirements. How well you present this chapter illustrates to the reader that you have carefully designed and produced a sound study based on the principles of qualitative research.

As emphasized throughout this book, writing a dissertation is not a linear process. Rather, it is an iterative and recursive one that requires much back and forth, reminder notes to yourself, and memos to change, revise, and update what you have already written. Chapter 3 is one of those chapters that must remain flexible and open to change right up to the very end. Frustration is inevitable, but don't despair! This is all part and parcel of managing and organizing the research and writing process.

Chapter Checklist

✓ Do you have a clear introduction to this chapter that includes your purpose statement (if required), as well as an explanation of how the chapter will be organized?

✓ Does the discussion have a logical flow?

✓ Does the discussion illustrate that you have a good understanding of the assumptions and principles of qualitative research?

✓ Do you offer a convincing argument for choosing a qualitative approach?

✓ Do you provide a convincing argument for the particular qualitative tradition or genre (or combination of traditions) that you have chosen?

✓ Have you made it clear how the research sample was selected from the population, as well as the specific criteria used in selection?

✓ Have you provided a sufficiently detailed description of the site and research sample?

✓ Have you discussed issues of access and consent?

✓ Is the information that is needed to conduct the study clearly and specifically outlined?

✓ Are you clear how and from whom the necessary information will be obtained?

✓ Is there a logical connection between the type of information needed and the methods you have selected to obtain that information?

✓ Are the data-collection methods sufficiently described? The description of each instrument should relate to the function of the instrument in the study and what the instrument is intended to measure.

✓ Have you provided a comprehensive literature review of the data-collection methods used and included details regarding the strengths and limitations of each method?

✓ Are the data-collection methods congruent with the problem being investigated and the specific qualitative tradition employed?

✓ Do you explain the procedures you use for recording, managing, and storing information?

✓ Has triangulation of the data-collection methods been achieved?

✓ Is the study's methodology/research design documented in sufficient detail? Have you described in chronological order each step taken in conducting the study?

✓ Is there a sequential progression inherent in the methodological design? That is, is the reader able to see how each stage of the study's design builds on and flows logically from the stage preceding it?

✓ Have you discussed all decisions made during the course of the study, and, if applicable, have you mentioned any changes or modifications in focus, direction, and design?

✓ If applicable, have you described all field tests or pilot tests that you have used?

✓ Are your methods of data analysis, synthesis, and interpretation sufficiently described and detailed?

✓ Are your methods of data analysis congruent with the principles of qualitative research?

✓ Are the ethical considerations that you have identified clear and acceptable, and have you discussed the procedures followed to address them?

✓ Does your discussion of the key issues pertaining to trustworthiness in qualitative research show that you have a clear understanding of these issues?

✓ Does your discussion around trustworthiness show how you have considered and accounted for credibility, dependability, and transferability vis-à-vis your own study?

✓ Do you acknowledge potential limitations of your study?

✓ Do you indicate how you have attempted to address these limitations?

✓ Are headings and subheadings used effectively to structure and present the discussion?

✓ Does the discussion in each section flow logically?

✓ Are the transitions from one section of the chapter to another clear and logical? Have you made use of effective segues?

✓ Are tables, figures, and appendices used effectively and appropriately?

✓ Do tables and figures follow the format specified by your required style manual?

✓ Are the columns and rows of each table labeled correctly?

✓ Does the title of each table and/or figure indicate exactly (clearly and concisely) what the table or figure is intended to represent?

✓ Have you checked for institutional and/or program-related differences regarding the content and structure of chapter 3?

✓ Have you checked for institutional and/or program-related differences regarding the appropriate use of qualitative language and terminology?

ANNOTATED BIBLIOGRAPHY

Berg, B. L. (2004). *Qualitative research methods* (5th ed.). Boston: Allyn & Bacon.

The author covers the entire research design process from sampling strategies to collecting, organizing, and making sense of qualitative data. This book provides a solid grounding in the mainstream qualitative methods, with chapter 2 providing a discussion of purposeful sampling and its many different types of strategies, and chapter 3 providing a thorough overview of ethical issues. Chapters 4 and 5 offer detailed information pertaining to interviews and focus groups. Chapter 11 provides an in-depth overview and description of content analysis—the basis of the qualitative analytical approach. There are extensive lists of references presented at the end of each chapter, which offer the reader a variety of primary sources. Overall, the book focuses on current issues in the world of social research, which include a serious concern about ethical behavior and a more reflexive and sensitive role for the researcher.

Creswell, J. W. (1998). *Qualitative inquiry and research design: Choosing among five traditions.* Thousand Oaks, CA: Sage.

Creswell uses the metaphor of a "circle of interrelated activities" to describe a process of engaging in activities that include but go beyond collecting data. In chapter 7, he introduces each activity: locating a site, sampling purposefully to obtain a research sample, collecting data (interviews, observation, document review, and audiovisual material), recording information, exploring field issues, and storing data.

Furthermore, he explores how each of these activities varies by tradition of inquiry. In chapter 8, Creswell discusses generally, as well as more specifically for each of the five traditions, the different procedures for data analysis and the representation of data in both narrative and visual forms. Chapter 10 focuses on the intricacies involved in the issue of trustworthiness: establishing standards of quality and verification.

Denzin, N. K., & Lincoln, Y. S. (Eds.). (2003). *Collecting and interpreting qualitative materials* (2nd ed.). Thousand Oaks, CA: Sage.

This comprehensive collection of chapters written by experts in the field covers a variety of qualitative methodological issues related to gathering, analyzing, and interpreting data. Unlike most of the other books recommended in this section's annotated bibliography, this book is not a "how-to" handbook. Rather, it uncovers and examines the philosophical and political implications of qualitative research methodology, addressing issues of equity and social justice. Part I includes discussion of data-collection methods, including interviews, observation, documents and material culture, and focus groups. Also included is a chapter on software and qualitative research. Part II includes discussion of issues pertaining to the practices of interpretation, evaluation, and representation.

Kvale, S. (1996). *Interviews: An introduction to qualitative research interviewing.* Thousand Oaks, CA: Sage.

Interviewing is an essential tool in the repertoire of any qualitative researcher, yet the hows and the whys of the interview process are not always easily understood. This book does a good job of explaining the theoretical underpinnings and practical aspects of the interview process. After examining the role of the interviewer in the research process, the author considers some of the key philosophical issues related to interviewing. He then takes the reader through what he calls "the seven stages of the interview investigation"—from designing a study to writing it up. Particularly useful are the chapters on analysis (chap. 11) and validity (chap. 13).

Marshall C., & Rossman, G. B. (2006). *Designing qualitative research* (4th ed.). Thousand Oaks, CA: Sage

These authors offer comprehensive instruction as well as outline the challenges involved in the design and conduct of a sound qualitative study. Chapter 4 offers useful guidelines about the various qualitative data-collection methods, with a particular focus on interviews, observation, and document review as primary methods. The authors also provide good discussion of secondary methods, including survey, life history, and narrative inquiry. The focus is on how to design a data-collection strategy by way of thoughtfully combining methods so that they build on and complement one another. Chapter 5 deals with recording, managing, and analyzing data. This chapter defends the value and logic of qualitative research and offers some useful insights and background reading around issues of trustworthiness in qualitative inquiry. Particularly useful are the exhaustive and well-organized bibliographies found at the end of each of these chapters.

Mason, J. (1996). *Qualitative researching.* Thousand Oaks, CA: Sage.

The intent of this book is to provide qualitative researchers with a set of tools and a mode of critical thinking to help them plan and develop a sound research design. It is based on the notion that qualitative researchers need to think and act strategically in ways that combine intellectual, philosophical, technical, and practical concerns. Chapter 2 deals with questions about planning and designing a qualitative study. Chapters 3 and 4 cover the various methods for generating qualitative data: interviews, observation, and document analysis. The author uses the medium of posing questions around pertinent issues related to the choice and use of methods. These questions are not designed to probe qualitative research in the abstract, but represent the active thinking-and-doing skills required to make informed and thoughtful choices.

Merriam, S. B. (1998). *Qualitative research and case study applications in education*. San Francisco: Jossey-Bass.

The primary focus of this book is on qualitative research in general, with applications to case study as a secondary emphasis. Part I includes discussion of the different types of qualitative research and how to design a qualitative case study, including sample selection. Part II consists of four chapters that detail data-collection techniques: These chapters include how to record and evaluate interview data, how to conduct observations and record observation data in the form of field notes, and how to use documents, including their strengths and limitations. Chapter 6 illustrates the application of all three methods of data collection with regard to case study methodology. Chapter 10 in Part III deals with issues of trustworthiness and research ethics.

Morgan, D. L. (1997). *Focus groups as qualitative research* (2nd ed.). Thousand Oaks, CA: Sage.

This book is an excellent guide to focus groups. It covers how focus groups compare with other qualitative methods of data collection, pointing out the strengths and weaknesses of this method and outlining the many uses of focus groups vis-à-vis qualitative research. The author offers clear instructions regarding how to plan a research design that includes focus groups, as well as how to actually go about conducting the group interview and analyze the data that are generated.

Patton, M. Q. (2002). *Qualitative research and evaluation methods* (3rd ed.). Thousand Oaks, CA: Sage.

Patton's classic book brings together theory and practice, offering many useful strategies for designing and conducting qualitative studies. Examples serve to clarify and deepen understanding of the qualitative research process in its many facets. Especially useful are the sections on the defining characteristics of qualitative research, the variety of qualitative research traditions, sampling procedures, methods and techniques of data collection (there are detailed and thorough chapters dealing with observation and interview), data analysis and interpretation (including computer-assisted analysis), ethical issues, and criteria for enhancing credibility. Patton is one of the forebearers of qualitative research. This often-quoted book set the standards for the field in the 1980s and 1990s. Recently revised, it brings readers up to date with the variety of current perspectives about (as well as the variety within) qualitative inquiry.

Robson, C. (2002). *Real world research: A resource for social scientists and practitioner-researchers* (2nd ed.). Malden, MA: Blackwell.

This book deals with qualitative design issues and data-collection methods. The book is wide ranging and offers the reader an appreciation of the complexities and issues involved in designing, carrying out, analyzing, and reporting on different kinds of studies. Particularly useful for dissertation writers are discussions in Part III around the use of surveys/questionnaires, interviews, observation, and document analysis, and instruction in Part IV around preparing for data analysis and synthesis. This text, which emphasizes the importance of a flexible research design for qualitative inquiry, is a useful reference to use along the way as you conduct your research and begin to write the dissertation.

Seidman, I. (1998). *Interviewing as qualitative research: A guide for researchers in education and the social sciences.* New York: Teachers College Press.

Most qualitative research employs interviewing as a primary method of data collection. This book is a concise yet one of the most informative overviews on the art of interviewing, with the author offering concrete examples of interviewing techniques, as well as discussion of the complexities involved, including technical, logistical, and ethical issues. What are especially useful are the guidelines to analyzing and interpreting interview data, which are presented in the final chapter. Here the author gives clear instruction on how to manage the data (interviews usually generate an enormous amount of text), as well as studying, reducing, analyzing, and interpreting the text. Particularly helpful are the suggestions regarding transcription, as well as the different ways in which interview data can be displayed. In this regard, the author discusses two basic ways in which to do this: creating profiles and developing themes.

Vaughn, S., Schumm, J. S., & Sinagub, J. (1996). *Focus group interviews in education and psychology.* Thousand Oaks, CA: Sage.

This book illustrates the specific steps to take in conducting focus groups in educational and psychological settings. By way of numerous examples, the authors explain how to prepare for focus groups: create a moderator's guide, select a setting, and understand, analyze, and interpret the focus group findings. This book is extremely reader-friendly; it is clearly written, and instructions and guidelines are easy to follow. Each chapter contains numerous procedural tables, as well as ideas for applications of trial runs of the techniques discussed.

Analyzing Data and Reporting Findings

OVERVIEW

Once you have collected your data by way of the various data-collection methods that you have chosen to use, your next step is to manage, organize, and make sense of all the separate pieces of accumulated information. Qualitative data include excerpts from documentation, interview transcripts, survey comments, focus group transcripts, critical incident forms, field notes from observations, and so on. Additionally, you may have collected some quantitative data by way of survey methodology, yielding numbers, frequencies, and percentages. All of these data are called *raw data* because they are as yet untouched by you. Your task is to transform them into something meaningful by analyzing them and making inferences from these discrete pieces of information.

Many students become overwhelmed at this point of the dissertation process, having completed or still being immersed in data collection and faced with mounds and mounds of "stuff" and unsure about what needs to be done first. Frequently, the comment is that they are overloaded with data and drowning. Many students have some notion of *what* they must do, but are uncertain about *how* to really go about doing it. A common problem facing qualitative

researchers is the lack of agreed-on approaches for analyzing qualitative material. Although there is some information regarding how and why to use qualitative research methodologies, there is considerably less information on the actual "nuts and bolts" of what to do with the data after the research has been conducted.

Although most research courses and textbooks describe the basic structure of research, few move the student into the areas of data organization and analysis. Much is made of the process of *coding*—assigning an alphanumeric system to segments of transcripts. Less attention is paid, however, to application; that is, how to use coded material. Typically, the results are that students come up with excellent ideas for research, conduct solid literature reviews, produce what sound like viable research designs, and even collect massive amounts of data. The problem arises, however, at this point: What do you do with the collected data? In this chapter, we provide the "what" as well as the "how" regarding transforming raw data into meaningful findings. Section I, "Instruction," describes what needs to be done and explains in a series of steps how to go about this. Section II, "Application," provides an example of what a findings chapter should look like. Using the research problem carried throughout this book, we present the actual findings of the research that we conducted.

When you reach this point in the research process, it is essential to keep an open mind, remembering that qualitative research is all about discovery. You need to look carefully at all of your data, seeking to uncover important insights regarding the phenomenon that you are researching. These are your "findings." The procedures you use to accomplish this need to be well thought out, explicitly documented, and directly connected to your research questions. Subsequently, in the following chapter, "Analyzing and Interpreting Findings," you will synthesize all your data sources and insights, creating an interpretation that is holistic and integrated.

There is often confusion around the idea of data analysis in qualitative research and what it actually entails. Qualitative data analysis is the process of bringing order, structure, and meaning to the masses of data collected. Broadly speaking, qualitative data analysis is an attempt by the researcher to summarize all the collected data in a dependable and accurate manner. This process is based on induction: The researcher starts with a large set of data and seeks to progressively narrow them into smaller important groups of key data. There are no predefined variables to focus analysis as there are in quantitative research. Qualitative data analysis requires the researcher to be patient and reflective in a process that strives to make sense of multiple data sources. The analytic procedure falls essentially into the following sequential phases: organizing the data, generating categories, identifying patterns and themes, and coding the data.

We want to draw your attention to the fact that, although chapter 5 deals with analysis and interpretation, it should become evident to you that the process of analysis begins occurring in this chapter by way of organizing and transforming raw data into what are called the "research findings."

Essentially, this chapter involves the analysis of data to produce findings. The following chapter involves the analysis, interpretation, and synthesis of those findings. Both chapters involve analytic decisions. These two chapters together should convince you that you are sufficiently knowledgeable about the interlocking analytic processes that constitute qualitative research.

CHAPTER OBJECTIVES

Chapter 4 Objectives

Section I: Instruction

- Provide a conceptualization of qualitative data analysis.
- Identify the specific strategies involved in analyzing qualitative data.
- Explain how to organize, reduce, and prepare raw data through coding and categorization.
- Explain how to formulate clear and precise findings statements based on analysis of the data.
- Describe how to report and present findings in a clear, comprehensive, and systematic manner.

Section II: Application

- Presentation of a completed findings chapter based on the content and process as described earlier.

SECTION I: INSTRUCTION

Organizing and Preparing Your Data for Analysis

Data Management Strategies

The data generated by qualitative methods are voluminous, and the sheer quantity of raw data can indeed be quite daunting. If data are to be thoroughly analyzed, they must be well organized. Understanding the ways in which the data can be organized and managed is hence important. As mentioned in Part I, attention to detail in managing data is important at every stage of the research process. This notion becomes all too clear when it is time to write up the research. Once you are sure that your data are well organized, the analysis can begin in earnest.

Transcribe your interviews as soon as possible, and assign identification codes to each transcript. Bear in mind that you must know your data intimately. Although extremely tedious, transcribing your interviews yourself is one way of immersing yourself in your data and becoming more familiar with it. Remember that doing your own transcriptions, or at least checking them by listening to the tapes as you read them, can be quite different from just working off transcriptions done by somebody else.

Although extremely time consuming, it is imperative that interviews be transcribed verbatim. The exact words of participants must be recorded, along with any aspects of nonverbal communication, such as pauses, laughter, or interruptions. These nonverbal nuances are usually noted within parentheses as they occur. If you are having your transcriptions done by a professional transcriber, you need to make these instructions clear. Also, if computerized data analysis tools are going to be used, the data might have to be converted into a format that is compatible with the software program to be used.

Make sure all your information is complete and legible. Write dates on all transcriptions and field notes. Label all notes according to type (observers' notes, memos, transcriptions, etc.). Be sure to make copies of all your material; from an early stage, find a way to securely store the data in well-labeled computer files so that you know where to locate the different pieces of information. It is prudent—and indeed highly advisable—to make back-up copies of all your data, putting one master copy away someplace for safekeeping. As mentioned in Part I, it is essential to sort and order your data for easy retrieval. Safely storing the data also ensures that you are honoring the confidentiality of participants—an essential ethical consideration.

If you have collected any quantitative material, you need to summarize the data to illustrate patterns. In a qualitative study, quantitative findings are secondary and are used to supplement and/or augment the primary qualitative findings. We recommend that you "chunk" your data and prepare the quantitative component at the outset prior to embarking on qualitative data analysis. While you analyze quantitative and qualitative data separately and in different ways, as you see later in this chapter, in qualitative research, reporting the findings means that data from all sources are seamlessly woven to provide an overall integrated and holistic presentation.

In a qualitative study, usually simple descriptive statistics will suffice vis-à-vis quantitative data. Measures of central tendency include such things as mean, mode, and/or median. Measures of variability include such things as range and standard deviation. Raw scores must first be converted to percentages, and graphical or mathematical procedures such as tables, graphs, or bar charts (histograms) are then used to depict patterns in the data. Various references in this chapter's annotated bibliography (namely, Huck's *Reading Statistics and Research* and Rea & Parker's *Designing and Conducting Survey Research*) might be useful in the analysis and presentation of survey results. If you intend to use more sophisticated quantitative measurement procedures, we suggest that you seek professional advice and consult with the appropriate quantitative references.

Deciding on an Analytic Approach

It must be pointed out at the outset that different qualitative research traditions or genres promote specific strategies for data analysis. Data analysis in the different traditions is similar, but there are some fundamental differences. For example, grounded theory is systematic in its approach: Categories of information are generated (open coding), one of the categories is selected and positioned within a theoretical model (axial coding), and a story is explicated from the interconnection of the categories (selective coding). Coding and categorizing involve the "constant comparison" method that continues throughout the study. Through the emergence of major categories, theory can evolve. Case study and ethnographic research involve a detailed description of the setting or individuals, followed by analysis of the data for themes, patterns, or issues (Stake, 1995; Wolcott, 1994). Phenomenological research makes use of significant statements, the generation of meaning units, and the development of an "essence" description (Moustakas, 1994). Researchers who use this approach are reluctant to describe specific analytic techniques, fearing that these might be seen as rules and become inflexible (Hycner, 1985). As such, the focus is on attitude and the response to the phenomenon under study. The aim is to achieve an analytic description of the phenomena not affected by prior assumptions.

Whatever tradition or genre one adopts, perhaps the most fundamental underlying operation in the analysis of qualitative data is that of discovering significant classes or sets of things, persons, and events and the properties that characterize them. In qualitative research, we are interested in the language of the participants or texts. We work with the data (words) to identify units of information that contribute to themes or patterns—the study's findings. Therefore, analysis has to do with data reduction and data display.

In qualitative research, interviewing is often the major source of data needed for understanding the phenomenon under study. This process generates an enormous amount of text. To make the data more readily accessible and understandable, the vast array of words, sentences, and paragraphs has to be reduced to what is of most importance and interest and then transformed to draw out themes and patterns. Most important in qualitative research is that the analytic process is an interweaving of inductive and deductive thinking.

Although committed to empathy and multiple realities, the researcher decides what story will be reported. As Stake (2000) puts it, "This is not to dismiss the aim of finding the story that best represents the case, but to remind that the criteria of representation ultimately are decided by the researcher" (p. 441). All researchers enter the field with a certain perspective and certain assumptions, yet the material should not be addressed with a set of hypotheses that you set out to prove or disprove. Rather, you need to approach your transcripts with an open mind, seeking what emerges as significant from the text. As Seidman (1998) writes, "The interviewer must come to the transcript prepared to let the interview breathe and speak for itself" (p. 100). Your assumptions are usually articulated in your conceptual framework. Theories and prior research inform this framework, offering potential categories. At the same time, the conceptual framework remains flexible and open to the unexpected, allowing the analytic direction of the study to emerge.

The following classification of Crabtree and Miller (1992) illustrates one view of how analytic approaches might differ:

1. Quasi-statistical approaches: Use word or phrase frequencies to determine the relative importance of terms and concepts. This approach is typified by content analysis—the process of converting qualitative data into a quantitative format.

2. Template approaches: Key codes are determined either on an a priori basis (i.e., derived from theory or research questions or from an initial read of the data). These codes serve as a template or "bins," remaining flexible as the data analysis process proceeds. This approach makes use of matrices, networks, flow charts, and diagrams that supplement descriptive summaries of the text.

3. Editing approaches: These are more interpretive and flexible than the above. There are no (or few) a priori codes. Codes are emergent. This is typified by the grounded theory approach.

4. Immersion approaches: This approach is the least structured and most interpretive, emphasizing researcher insight, intuition, and creativity. Methods remain fluid and are not systematized.

Although there are some specific analytic differences according to the qualitative tradition or genre that is adopted, qualitative analysis, as we see it, is somewhat of a stepwise procedure that involves a blend of approaches. Our view is that tightly organized and highly structured schemes can filter out the unusual and serendipitous. The approach we adopt in explaining this chapter, as is seen, is essentially a combination of the template and editing approaches. We see this balance as the most readily applicable to the flexibility that characterizes all types of qualitative research.

Remember that whatever approach you choose to use should be based on what you feel most comfortable with and which is most suited to the research tradition that you have adopted. In addition, the preference of your advisor and your department will of course need to be taken into consideration. Remember, too, that you are expected to be able to describe in detail your analytic approach and to show that you are able demonstrate how you got from your data to your conclusions. This step is necessary to enhance both the credibility (validity) and dependability (reliability) of your study.

A Systematic Procedure for Data Analysis

Although we offer a stepwise procedure to prepare and analyze the data, please bear in mind that we are *not* implying in any way that the interrelationship among these steps is necessarily linear. Each phase in this multistage process leads logically to the next, yet the process is essentially an iterative and somewhat messy one. You will most likely cycle through the phases more than once, looping back and revisiting earlier phases in an ongoing effort to narrow and make sense of what is in the data. The steps that you take will overlap each other as you continue to read and collect data. As you increasingly internalize and reflect on your data, the initial ordered sequence will most likely lose its structure and become more flexible.

Just how long the analytic process lasts is difficult to predict. It depends largely on the nature of the study, the amount of data collected, as well as the analytic and synthesizing abilities of the researcher. The process can be repetitious, tedious, and time-consuming. However, there is no substitute for fully immersing yourself in your data. Take the time to read and reread. Really live with your data. Getting to know intimately what you have collected, and struggling with the nuances, subtleties, caveats, and contradictions, is an integral part of the process. Keep an open mind, and be prepared for the unexpected. Remain patient. Accept that the process in its entirety will take time, and be aware of not making premature judgments. Figure 4.1 includes the iterative steps of the analytic process. Following the figure is a more detailed discussion of the key activities involved in the process.

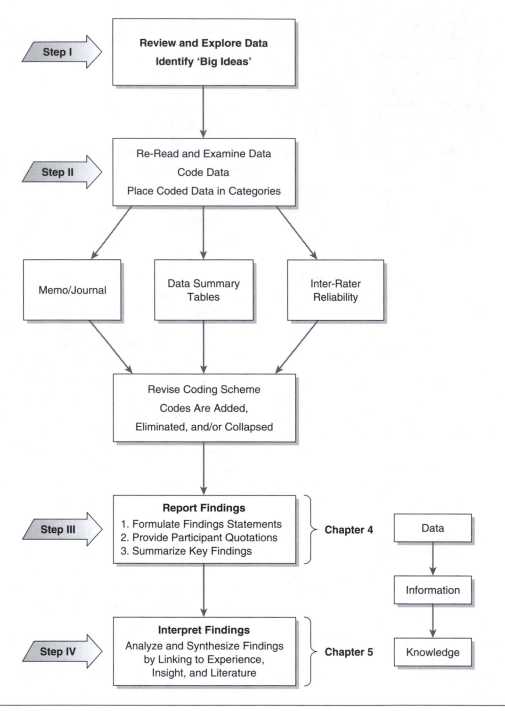

Figure 4.1 Roadmap for the Process of Qualitative Data Analysis: An Outline

Review and Explore the Data

You need to examine each piece of information and, building on insights and hunches gained during data collection, attempt to make sense of the data as a whole. To achieve this goal, begin by carefully reading over all the data provided by the various data-collection sources. Read the transcriptions of your interviews, critical incidents, and/or focus groups. If you have used document review, read over your documentation too. What you are really doing is reading to get some feel for the "storyline," including the major and minor stories that are being told within the data. This initial reading of all the data is done to gain an overall sense of the whole before you break it into its constituent parts.

It is important that you get a good feel for your data—an experience that usually generates emergent insights. In reading over the data, try to make sense of what people are saying. Also try to integrate what different people are saying. The more familiar you are with the details of your data, the better you will be able to present it, and the better your analysis of it will be. In this first go-around, read through each transcript and try to identify the "big ideas." Although the big ideas are likely to become altered or refined, they provide an initial framework for the development of the study's findings.

As Merriam (1998) points out, qualitative analysis usually results in the identification of recurring patterns and themes that "cut through the data" (p. 11). Data analysis demands a heightened awareness of the data and an open mind to recurring and common threads, some of which may be subtle. The real purpose of this initial read is to immerse yourself in your data and gain a sense of their possibilities. As you read, make notes of or highlight relevant words and phrases that you think capture important aspects of the data. Remember that these should bear some relationship to the research questions and should not simply be some random words that seem to occur with regular frequency. Ask yourself: What is this about? What seems to be emerging? Check these ideas against the categories and descriptors of your conceptual framework.

In addition to highlighting parts of the text and underlining sections and issues that seem important and relevant, also jot down in the margins any ideas, thoughts, reflections, and comments that come to mind. This process will provide you with a record of your initial sense of the data. Later, when you are deeper into the analytic process, you may find that some of these early impressions are useful and hold up throughout.

If your study includes document review, a useful tool to help collate and organize all the information that you are able to glean from documents is a document summary form. With regard to interviews, critical incidents, and focus groups, after reading each transcript carefully, make summary notes for each participant. Summarizing data in this way is important because it creates a profile of each document and/or each individual research participant. Moreover, much of what occurs in later analytical steps requires reducing the data to units. Reduction of data requires a researcher to think about smaller bits of data, and this step runs the risk of missing the forest for the trees. Templates for the document summary form and the participant summary form are included as Appendices N and O, respectively.

Reread and Code the Data

The first step in the analytic process was to consider the "big ideas" or themes. The second step is to dissect and classify the data and place sections of material into categories. Although it is important initially to become familiar with your data, you do not want to drown in it. Thus, an important step is to reduce all that you have collected to a manageable database, grouping it in useful ways. This step is essentially what Seidman (1998) and Creswell (1998) refer to as a "winnowing process." From your large stacks of papers that contain your raw data, you have to find ways to distill the information into smaller sets of notes that characterize your total data. To do this, you need to develop some manageable system of classification (i.e., a coding scheme).

The reduction process includes questioning the data, identifying and noting common patterns in the data, creating codes that describe your data patterns, and assigning these coded pieces of information to the categories of your conceptual framework. Your conceptual framework is the centerpiece in managing and reducing the data. A sample conceptual framework is included as Appendix B. The categories that comprise your conceptual framework become the repositories of your data. In effect, you turn your conceptual framework into a coding scheme/legend by assigning codes to each category and each subcategory (or descriptor). That coding scheme is included in your dissertation's appendix. At the same time, the uncoded conceptual framework should remain intact and is usually presented at the end of your literature review chapter. A sample coding scheme is included as Appendix I.

Much is made about coding. However, there is really nothing that mysterious about it. Coding is essentially a system of classification—the process of noting what is of interest or significance, identifying different segments of the data, and labeling them to organize the information contained in the data. Codes are, in effect, a type of shorthand; the names or identifiers that you attach to chunks or segments of data that you consider relevant to your study. As such, you can use any system that works for you, be it alphanumeric or some form of symbol. Some people find it useful to use highlighting pens

to color code their data. Whatever system you choose to use, as you read your material, the codes that you assign signals what you think is going on in a piece of data.

As you read your material, reference segments or units of text by highlighting or bracketing them. These segments can be single words, phrases, sentences, or even whole paragraphs. Codes can be written in the margins or alongside the appropriate segments of text. A sample coded transcript segment is presented as Appendix P. As with all aspects of the research process, precision is key. It is of the utmost importance to know who said what. Therefore, do not forget to include participant identification with each unit of information. In addition, label each passage with a notation system that will designate its position in the original transcript. Later, when considering an excerpt taken from its original context, you may want to check the accuracy of the text, perhaps going back to the audiotape. Specific labeling of each excerpt allows for such retracing.

At this point in the reading/marking/labeling process, it is important to keep labels tentative. As you read and mark units or sections from the material, one way is to begin to label them using terms based on the actual language of the participants—known in the language of grounded theory as an *in vivo* term. This process is called *open coding*, a grounded theory concept where the descriptors emerge from the data, and is essentially the same as what Patton (1990, 2002) refers to as *inductive analysis*. While using in vivo labels, note whether there is something in the data that might fit one of the descriptors of your conceptual framework. The procedure of using predetermined coding categories and seeking to fit the data into such categories is against the spirit of pure grounded theory. Although we make use of some concepts from grounded theory, please note that the approach we adopt in this book is not a pure grounded theory approach.

If you use predetermined categories, you run the risk of analyzing data by coding text units according to what you expect to find. Your conceptual framework must remain flexible and open to change throughout the entire analytic process. Remember, the reason you have spent so much time and energy talking to participants is to find out what *their* experience is and to endeavor to understand it from *their* perspective. In the process of working with excerpts and seeking connections among them, be aware that not all your data will fit your predetermined categories. Rather than trying to force data into categories, you will most likely have to create some new, emergent descriptors and/or collapse and/or eliminate some of them. As you go along, you will see too that some coded excerpts might fit under more than one category. For now, place them wherever seems most appropriate. Instead, you might choose to place the same excerpt of text under more than one category. When making tentative placements, make notes. Later on you will proceed to sort coded text more specifically.

At this stage of the process, you, as the researcher, are exercising judgment as to what you think is significant in each interview transcript. Some passages stand out because they are striking to you in some way. Others stand out because they are contradictory and seem inconsistent with your conceptual framework. Although it may be tempting to put those aside, you should exercise caution and not submit to researcher bias. In this regard, you must be vigilant in not seeking only material that supports your own opinions and remaining open to the unexpected.

As you will come to realize, too, any given segment of data might be viewed differently by two different researchers or even coded using more than one label by one researcher. There is no single "correct" way to organize and analyze the data. Therefore, it is necessary that you read, reread, and reexamine all

of your data to make sure that you have not missed something or coded something in a way that is inappropriate given the experience of participants. At this point, inter-rater reliability is also required. Have a colleague review your work to see whether your codes are appropriate and relevant to your research questions. Alternatively, have a colleague code some of the same transcripts that you have been working on to check for consistency. Compare and discuss similarities and differences. There are many reasons that different researchers would view and interpret the data in different ways, including researcher bias, personal interests, style, and interpretive focus. Indeed, important insights can emerge from the different ways in which people look at the same set of data.

As you read, sort, and code, two other processes should be occurring simultaneously: (a) preparing data summary charts, and (b) writing memos and/or journaling.

The first thing you need to do is fill out data summary tables—one for each research question. These tables are tools that help you compile what participants have said about each of the categories in the conceptual framework and record how many participants' comments fall under the same categories. These tables are a way to summarize participant data. They provide a way to highlight the evidence to support what the researcher says she or he has found. In the absence of such a summary, identification of pervasive themes and findings is either up to the discretion of the researcher or the interpretation of the reader.

To accurately report and analyze the findings of your research, you have to be rigorous about recording participant responses. Get in the habit of filling out data summary tables as you code. Perform the two activities in tandem so that no information is lost. It is useful to array data summary tables as outlined in Table 4.1. These tables are essentially matrices in which the participants (under pseudonyms) are listed down the vertical axis, with the descriptors (the different aspects of each category) being listed along the horizontal axis. These descriptors should be listed exactly as they appear under each category of your conceptual framework. How each participant responds to each of the descriptors on the horizontal axis is then checked off, and tallies (raw frequencies as well as percentages) are noted at the bottom of each column. A data summary table should be developed in this same format for each category of the conceptual framework. In this way, you have a consistent record of findings regarding all your participants' responses across all of your categories. The categories are directly tied to your research questions. Samples of completed data summary tables are presented as Appendices R through V.

Although qualitative research is not essentially about quantifying data, and although the intent is not to reduce the data to numeric representations, tallies and frequencies in qualitative research are essentially a supplement to the narrative. Data summary tables are working tools that create a record of who said what and how many times a particular response occurs. As such, these tables are an essential precursor to interpretation, where you will need to look closely at both individual participants and the overall group of participants—that is, cross-case analysis.

As you read through your data, different ideas come into your mind. These ideas might be the basis for interpretations or even conclusions and recommendations later on. Therefore, you need to record all these thoughts so that you do not lose them. You might consider keeping a journal and/or some system of memo as to what is going on with the data. *Memoing*, a concept originally referred to by Strauss (1987), involves recording and writing notes about certain

Table 4.1 Template for Data Summary Table

	Descriptor 1	*Descriptor 2*	*Descriptor 3*	*Descriptor 4*	*Descriptor 5*	*Descriptor 6*	*Descriptor 7*
Pseudonym 1							
Pseudonym 2							
Pseudonym 3							
Pseudonym 4							
Pseudonym 5							
Pseudonym 6							
N = X	# = x %	# = x %	# = x %	# = x %	# = x %	# = x %	# = x %

occurrences or sentences that seem of vital interest. Memos can trigger thinking processes and, as Strauss explains, is the written version of an internal dialogue going on during the research. By recording what you think is going on, you can capture new descriptors as they emerge through your reading and coding, which descriptors seem to overlap, and which descriptors are not appearing, thus needing to be eliminated. In this way, your notes serve to inform your coding scheme and become the basis for a coding scheme development chart (see Appendix J). The notes that you jot down, either in the form of memos or as part of a research journal, also can form the basis for an interpretation outline tool (see Appendix Y), as well as for a consistency chart of findings, interpretations, and conclusions (see Appendix Z). These charts are working tools that help guide and clarify your thinking and, as such, can be included in your appendix of your dissertation. These charts also form part of your audit trail—a necessary element for establishing your study's validity.

Sort and Categorize Quotations

Once you have coded your material, you are ready to copy and paste or cut out and place the quotes in their appropriate analytic categories (i.e., categorize your units of information). In categorizing material, some people prefer pasting quotes to index cards and stacking these in piles. Others prefer cutting out quotes and placing these in manila envelopes marked with the category name. We like the idea of flip charts—either actual or electronic—because they are visual. Whatever system you choose, make sure that, before you begin cutting, you have made photocopies of your original data and that these are safely stored.

If you decide to use our method of flip charts, you need to create a separate flip chart for each category. On each flip chart,

list the category name and underneath that the category's descriptors. Bear in mind that the categories of your conceptual framework are the superordinate headings that provide the organization for the units of data. The descriptors within each category become the subordinate headings. Actual flip charts can be pasted to your walls, and the quotes can be pasted to these. "Electronic flip charts" are essentially a computerized version, whereby the flip charts are Word documents on your computer, and quotes from your transcripts are copied and pasted electronically. Whichever mode you choose to use—be it actual or electronic—is a matter of personal preference. In either case, what is useful about the flip chart approach is that it enables you to visualize your data, live with it, and think about it. Appendix W contains a photograph of what a set of manual flip charts pasted to one's walls actually looks like when one of us (Marie Volpe) was writing her own dissertation.

As you paste quotations in the appropriate categories, look for any units of information that do not fit any of your existing descriptors. Keep these in a pile marked "Miscellaneous." Once you have finished going through all your transcripts, revisit these and see where they should fit or, alternatively, create a new place for them under emergent descriptors. When you identify passages that are important, but you are unsure of which category in which they should fall, write a memo about those passages. In writing about them, their properties might become clearer, leading you to discover what it is you find important in them both individually and relatively. This step becomes important for interpretation.

Once all the units of information have been placed under categories, review the descriptors for any overlap. Sometimes descriptors have similar characteristics or properties; that is, they really mean one and the same thing. Splitting two descriptors is sometimes arbitrary, and they can be better collapsed into one. At other times, a descriptor may be too broad or too nuanced and would make more sense if it were subdivided into more than one.

Reread your miscellaneous units of information and reconsider them in the light of the newly revised categories. First, if any can be appropriately placed under any of the new descriptors, do so. Second, it is possible that some units of information are still simply not relevant, and in these cases discard them. Third, some units provide relevant information that contributes to understanding of the research problem but still does not fit with any of the existing categories. These information units do not warrant being discarded. Rather, they might become categories of their own. In other words, to accommodate your findings, it is imperative that your coding scheme and conceptual framework remain flexible throughout.

Using Computer Software for Data Analysis

As you can see, the approach used in this book for data analysis is a manual one. We have explained the process of data analysis as it is done traditionally to highlight the thinking and the mechanics involved. You also need to be aware that, although there are various computer-aided qualitative data analysis software (CAQDAS) programs available, the principles of the analytic process are the same whether one is doing it manually or with the assistance of a computerized program.

Computer-aided software can indeed be of great assistance in classifying, sorting, and filing data. The software programs currently available are useful in mechanically organizing data and performing a number of analytic operations. With the use of these programs, for instance, you can create shorthand versions of themes or categories. After you sort your data, how many times a theme has been placed in a given category can be done automatically, and some programs can make connections among the categories to develop higher order conceptual structures.

Software analytical packages are a tool that can make the numerous tasks of the analytic process efficient and are certainly useful in assembling and locating information. However, there are various limitations involved with this method that you should be aware of. Software cannot interpret the emotional tone that is often critical to understanding the findings, and therefore neglects to take into account the contextual basis of information. In our experience, we have found that in searching out and producing every coded item each time these appear, the software tends to produce data—mostly in the form of discrete words and phrases—in the absence of their surrounding context. In so doing, although precise and concise, some of the richness of the data can become lost in the process. Moreover, with so many instances of discrete items, this method can produce a data glut, which can be overwhelming to the researcher. A further caveat regarding the use of computer-aided analysis is that, although books for learning the programs are widely available (e.g., Weitzman & Miles, 1995), qualitative software programs require time and skill to learn and employ effectively. As Weitzman and Miles (1995) point out, when contemplating the use of software, you should consider how computer literate you are, how at ease you are with the prospect of exploring and learning new software, as well as what kind of analysis you intend to do.

The method you select to manage and analyze your data is ultimately a matter of personal preference and depends on what you are most comfortable with and/or institutional requirements. Therefore, we do not advocate one way over another. If you are choosing software, it is important that you differentiate between programs that manage data and programs that actually perform data analysis. The former allows the researcher to store, index, sort, and retrieve data, whereas the latter actually does content analysis. Information on the different types of available software and the features of each is offered by various authors (Creswell, 1998; Merriam, 1998; Robson, 2002; Silverman, 2000).

Presenting the Findings of Your Research

Overview

You, the researcher, are the storyteller. Your goal is to tell a story that should be vivid and interesting while also accurate and credible. In your report, the events, the people, and their words and actions are made explicit so that readers can experience the situation as real in a similar way to the researcher and experience the world of the participants. It must be remembered that the reader cannot always see the hard work that has gone into the development of the story or the complexity of strategies and procedure that produced it.

Qualitative analysis is a creative and ongoing process that requires thoughtful judgments about what is significant and meaningful in the data. Your study is only as good as the data you have to analyze and the care that you take in analyzing the data. What you have done up until now is transform your raw data into some format that will facilitate your analysis. Through coding, you have reduced your data and created groupings and subgroupings of information. Reducing is the first step toward presenting your data. Having reduced your data, you now have to shape it into a form in which it can be shared or displayed (Miles & Huberman, 1994). What you share and display are essentially the multiple perspectives

supported by the different quotations that are yielded by your research. The goal is to provide rich descriptions, often referred to as "thick description" (Denzin, 1989/2001)—an essential aspect of qualitative research. Exemplary studies indeed make readers feel as if they are *living* the experiences described. This is the real power of qualitative research.

As a general rule, findings should be presented as objectively as possible and without speculation; that is, free from researcher bias. Presentation of findings also is extremely important. Your presentation will hopefully lead your readers to understand your findings as clearly as you do. Therefore, the way you set up and structure this chapter must be neat and precise. Moreover, if your findings chapter is well organized, the analysis chapter that follows will be much more easily accomplished.

In qualitative research, interviewing is usually the major source of the data needed for understanding the phenomenon under study. The findings of qualitative research are typically reported in a narrative manner. Reports of qualitative studies usually include extensive samples of quotations from participants. These quotations provide the detail and substantiate the story that you are telling. By using the participants' own words, the researcher aims to build the reader's confidence that the reality of the participants and the situation studied is accurately represented. In a qualitative study, quantitative findings, if there are any, are secondary and are used to supplement and/or augment the qualitative findings. The quantitative material should therefore be seamlessly woven into the discussion, either in narrative form (where you would state explicitly how the quantitative results either support or refute the qualitative findings) or in graphic form (tables and charts can be used to augment the discussion by way of clear visual depictions).

Be aware that findings are often written up in different ways depending on the research tradition or genre adopted. If you have used a pure approach, we suggest that you consult with your advisor and the relevant literature regarding appropriate and distinctive forms of presentation.

The narrative can be presented by way of several different formats, and various authors have offered suggestions as to how qualitative research findings might be presented (Creswell, 2005; Glesne, 2005; Rubin & Rubin, 2005; Seidman, 1998). One way to present your findings is to develop and craft profiles or vignettes of individual participants and to group these into categories. Miles and Huberman (1994) describe a vignette as "a concrete focused story" (p. 83). Van Maanen (1988) recommends presenting ethnographic research through different styles of "tales" as a way of presenting truthful cultural portraits. Yet another approach to presentation—one that is often used in case study research—is to mark individual passages or excerpts from the transcripts and group these in thematically connected categories. The latter is the more conventional and commonly used way of presenting qualitative findings. Because it is a flexible format that fits a wide range of topics, we recommend this approach and adopt it in this chapter.

A Stepwise Procedure for the Presentation of Findings

Begin with an introductory paragraph or two in which you restate the purpose of your study (if required) and tell the reader how the chapter will be organized. Provide the reader with an outline that illustrates the way in which you will go about discussing your findings. This outline enables the reader to create a mental map of your presentation and then find that information as he or she peruses your text. If you have used computer software to aid you in your data analysis, you need to identify the program that you used and the steps you undertook in its use. You will tell the reader what your intention was in choosing the software and what it accomplished.

If you have a bounded case study, that is, if your research takes place at a particular site or location or if it is tied to a particular institution, organization, or program, you need to offer the reader a detailed description of the physical setting. In some cases, where appropriate, an entire chapter is devoted to describing the setting. In others, a section of several pages in the findings chapter is set aside for this; usually this precedes a presentation of the themed participant responses classified by way of coded categories. In some instances, the identity of the research setting is required to remain anonymous. In the interest of confidentiality, you need to account for anonymity by assigning the research setting a pseudonym.

Description of the setting is drawn primarily from the review of available documents. Documents can be of a public or private nature and can include descriptive and/or evaluative information pertaining to the research context. A review of the available documents provides descriptions and factual evidence regarding the context and its culture, and it also uncovers environmental factors and issues that may impact participants' perceptions about this context. Following a review of each document, you should summarize the relevant findings and record these systematically. A template of a document summary form is included as Appendix N. An examination of all the summaries of all your documents will provide the information you need to write this section of your findings chapter.

Description of the setting should incorporate all the important aspects of the context/environment in which the study takes place, including such things as descriptions of the organizational structure, background/history, mission, vision, policies and procedures, culture/environment, and the population from which the research sample was drawn. In describing the setting, be sure to clarify what is unique about it, as well as what characteristics of the setting are compelling and/or unusual. Thus, discussion of the setting serves to situate your study within a context. In addition, in your analysis, data revealed from the document review can be used to confirm or disconfirm data collected by other methods.

The most common means of organizing a findings chapter, and the approach that we use in this book, is through a discussion of the research questions one by one and the evidence you have from the data about how they might be answered. As you prepare to present your findings, remember that you should have at least one finding per research question. Because you are seeking to shed light on your problem, no research question should be left unanswered. All research questions must be answered. Formulating strong comprehensive finding statements requires that you study your data summary tables. Look at what each participant says in terms of each of the aspects of each finding, and ask yourself: What do I see here? What do I now understand is the answer to each research question?

To plan and lay out the discussion that should follow each of your findings statements, we suggest doing an outline or what we call a "findings roadmap." A sample findings roadmap is presented as Appendix X. This tool is constructed from the conceptual framework in conjunction with your data summary tables. The overall intent is not to quantify qualitative data; tallies and frequencies are essentially a supplement to the narrative. What *is* important to report is the concentration of individual responses and the concentration of responses across individuals.

The headings and subheadings on the findings roadmap provide the organizational structure for the discussion. In constructing

your roadmap, keep in mind that nobody wants to read pages and pages of findings. The tension is this: When reporting findings, the idea is to be concise. Yet the idea is also not to split hairs too finely. Therefore, look for any headings that overlap and can be collapsed.

In qualitative research, you as the researcher are telling the story of what you learned from participants. As such, participants' quotes are used to illustrate the points that you are making. In other words, you are telling the story of your research as you see it; as you make your points, you are giving "clues" to the reader about what people said. It is important to mention this because those clues or lead-in sentences are the very points that you are making. You cannot leave it to the reader to decide what the point is; you have to tell the reader the gist of what the research participant is saying that supports the points in your story. If you took the quotes out of your findings chapter, however, one would still have to be able to see the story. Remember that, although the quotes are your support and your evidence, if you had to remove all your quotes, your clues should be able to stand alone and "tell the story." Therefore, make sure that all your lead-in sentences are, in each case, specific. Your careful choice of words will reflect your clear understanding of your findings. If you mislead the reader or cause readers to "do the work" themselves, you jeopardize your study, introducing the possibility of it being misinterpreted or, worse still, rejected.

With short quotes (those that are no longer than a sentence or two), lead in with the participant's name (pseudonym) and be sure that the quoted material is placed within quotation marks. With longer quotes (those that are 40 words or more), use block indentation rather than quotation marks, and place the participant's name at the end of the quote. For example, some participants claimed that. . . . Then if you have two strong quotes, indent each with respective names at the end of the quotes. Two strong quotes can and should be presented one after the other with no sentence in between. Your lead-in sentence makes your point, and it represents what some of the participants said. In effect, therefore the two (or three) quotes that you use are representative of what has been said by some others as well. In reporting the findings, what we are not doing is reporting what every individual said, but rather how various individuals, even though they are expressing it in a slightly different way, are making the same point.

Following are some further useful pointers in planning your discussion:

- Under each findings statement, report your findings from the highest to the lowest frequency. That is, talk first about those aspects of the finding that are most prominent and continue to report on findings in descending order.

- Make sure that percentages and words that you use match (e.g., 100% would translate to "all," 95% would be an "overwhelming majority," 75% would be "a majority," 30% would be "some," 10% would be "a few," etc.).

- Be selective in your choice of quotes. Remember, the function of quotes is not to illustrate the perceptions or experiences of just one single individual, but rather to be representative of a group of people who share the same sentiment. That is, quotes are intended essentially to demonstrate and give examples of patterns that have emerged in the research. In selecting quotes, therefore, aim for richness and precision. Use only the strongest quotes that clearly show evidence of the points you are trying to make.

- Make sure that all the quotes you use are focused on the point you are trying to make. Be concise. Get to "the meat of the quote"—the essence that refers to and supports the point you are making—by eliminating redundancy, wordiness, and repetition. Use ellipses (. . .) to connect

supportive phrases that you want to use. Only tell the reader that which she or he needs to know; only that which is directly related to the points you are making. Although there is usually a lot of interesting information, and although much of it might be tempting to include, be sure to include only that which is relevant in terms of providing answers to your research questions.

- Quotations never stand on their own, but are linked to the context in which they occur and the claim that the researcher wishes to make. This way, they provide evidence for their assertions. As such, great care should be taken not to take quotes out of context or to mislead the reader about their meaning.

- Exercise skill in dissecting quotes in the right places. Be careful not to change or distort the quote in any way, but rather to pick out those phrases that highlight or stress the main point/idea you are making.

- Participants' words should always be used verbatim, including errors of speech and repetition. Irrelevant sentences and comments can be removed, and this is indicated by ellipses within the quotation. Indicate laughter, coughing, pauses, facial expressions, or any other gestures or emotions by way of including these instances within parentheses when these occur within the quote. Use italics where a word or phrase is emphasized.

- Do not repeat the same quotes.

- Try not to over- or under-quote any one individual. That is, make sure there is fair representation among participants.

When you reach the end of the presentation of your findings, which is usually extremely detailed, you owe it to the readers to tie the whole chapter together, reminding them of what they have learned in the preceding pages. Write a concluding paragraph, in which you briefly explain what you have found. Explain in summary form what the chapter has identified, and also prepare the reader for the chapters to follow by offering some foreshadowing as to the intent and content of the final two chapters.

The application section that follows is a skeleton view of what a findings chapter should look like. Essentially, our intention is to provide you with only a "snapshot" of a findings chapter. Were it to be more completely and fully developed, as would be required in an actual dissertation, such a chapter would usually be 40 to 60 pages. As emphasized throughout this book, requirements vary among institutions and programs, and so, as with other components of the dissertation, this is something you will need to check on with your advisor and/or department.

SECTION II: APPLICATION

CHAPTER IV
Findings
Introduction

The purpose of this multicase study was to explore with a sample of doctoral candidates their perceptions of why they have not managed to complete their dissertations. The researchers believed that a better understanding of this phenomenon would allow educators to proceed from a more informed perspective in terms of design and facilitation of doctoral programs. This chapter presents the key findings obtained from 20 in-depth interviews and seven critical incidents, as well as from a focus group conducted with six additional participants who were not part of the study sample. Five major findings emerged from this study:

1. The overwhelming majority of the participants indicated that the coursework did not prepare them to conduct research and write their dissertations.

2. All 20 participants expressed the need to know the content and understand the process involved in conducting research and writing their dissertations.

3. The majority of participants attempted to learn what they needed to know by reaching out in dialogue with colleagues and others, rather than through more formal means.

4. The majority of participants indicated that they relied on their own personal characteristics to facilitate their progress. More than half of these same participants also said colleagues were instrumental in helping.

5. The majority of participants cited lack of good, timely, and consistent advisement as a major barrier standing in the way of their progress.

Following is a discussion of the findings with details that support and explain each finding. By way of "thick description" (Denzin, 1989/2001), the researcher set out to document a broad range of experiences, and thereby provide an opportunity for the reader to enter into this study and better understand the reality of the research participants. The emphasis throughout is on letting participants speak for themselves. Illustrative quotations taken from interview transcripts attempt to portray multiple participant perspectives and capture some of the richness and complexity of the subject matter. Where appropriate, critical incident data are woven in with interview data to augment and solidify the discussion. Following is a further discussion that includes the focus group data.

Finding 1: The overwhelming majority (19 of 20 [95%]) of the participants indicated that the coursework did not prepare them to conduct research or write their dissertations.

The primary and overriding finding of this study is that the coursework did not prepare participants to conduct research or write their dissertations. This finding is highly significant in terms of the overwhelming number of participants (19 of 20 [95%]) who found the coursework ineffective in preparing them for the dissertation process. Based on participant descriptions, there appeared to be a lack of connection between the first part of the doctoral program—the coursework—and the second part—actually conducting research and writing and presenting it in a completed dissertation. Participants expressed this disconnect in the following ways:

> The dissertation and the coursework are two totally different ballgames. And so success in one does not make for success in another. The coursework gives you knowledge of the field, it gives you the theory but it doesn't prepare you to write the dissertation. And it doesn't really prepare you to analyze the research you conduct. And I think anyone going in to it needs to understand what a dissertation looks like. How big (emphasis) it is! And consider the other parts of it—not just writing it, but defending it, revising it, editing it—the whole process—you don't really know—no one tells you. (Debbie)

> The coursework was confined. The dissertation process didn't have a structure built into it—it wasn't explained and you find out it is much bigger, and more unwieldy. The process of actually doing it is much more time consuming—and that's if you know what you're doing—which in my case was less than half the time. It is a shame that the coursework is not more directed. Ultimately, everything is indirectly associated with the dissertation and so I think there could have been a better job done explaining what to expect, what you would have to know and be able to do by the end of the coursework, and you don't get that so it is like you've fallen off a cliff. (Fay)

> During the coursework, I got only an inkling of what a dissertation represents. But the sheer magnitude of it—it's mind-boggling really, in terms of research. And nothing prepared you for that. Knowing what I know now, I probably would not have gone into it at all in the first place! (Laughs) (Angela)

All 19 participants described their perception of the ineffectiveness of the coursework. Among the comments cited were those by Hank, who said:

"The coursework did not prepare me for what I had to do in this dissertation; it didn't prepare me for the process that lay ahead," and those by Morris, who commented, "I didn't get the practical information during the coursework and when it was given, it was so poorly explained and so unnecessarily complex as to what we were to do, I just go lost, I never got it."

Most of the participants also spoke unfavorably about the research courses. Anthony recalled: "The coursework was not in any way related to the dissertation. I took some research courses but they were not helpful; they were not related to my dissertation." Another participant said specifically of the research courses: "They never gave us the formula in those classes; you couldn't see it or understand it as a step-by-step process—something I found out the hard way" (Anne). Another participant commented: "...even in those (research) classes intended to explain the process, it was conveyed in a way by complex language, you know, and that kept it shrouded in some kind of mystery" (Frank). Only 1 participant of the 20, while acknowledging that it did not fully prepare her, described the research courses as being somewhat helpful. She said:

> I took the research courses and I learned a lot. It was difficult. And while I got something out of those courses, I didn't really know how I was going to go about actually doing the research, and I was very apprehensive. You know, the steps in the process were still unclear to me. So when I started out it was scary, almost debilitating. (Lin)

Although most participants appreciated the theoretical foundation the coursework provided, they also expressed the need for more focus on the practical aspects of conducting research. Two participants conveyed this view when they said:

> The academic work was certainly expected and I had to grapple with some difficult theoretical concepts and it was hard but it was also stimulating but what was missing is seeing the whole picture—I didn't understand how I was going to be able to apply those concepts to my research— they didn't really focus on that; they didn't make that clear. (Mollie)

You can't do this work if you don't have a solid basis, a theoretical foundation but you also need to know how to use theory to frame your research, and they don't really focus on that. They didn't really teach the "how to." They said like you have to have a conceptual framework; well, what is that? How will I know it when I see it? You know, what do I have to do to make one? So while there is certainly a lot to be said for knowing the theories, I think more of the "how tos" would have been helpful. (Julia)

Finding 2: All 20 participants (100%) expressed a need to know the content and understand the process involved in conducting research and writing their dissertations.

The order of magnitude in terms of the number of participants who raised the issue of the coursework not having prepared them is not only surprising, but may account for subsequent participant perceptions regarding what they needed to successfully carry out their work. This notion can be seen specifically in the finding that all 20 of the participants (100%) described that they needed knowledge and understanding of the content and/or the process required to conduct research and write the dissertation.

A few participants (3 of 20 [15%]) described the difficulty they had, and are having, in selecting a good, researchable problem. On this point, Anthony commented: "What I'm finding most difficult is to pinpoint exactly what I want to research—the research problem." As another student put it:

I have never given up when it comes to education and I really do not understand why I am having such a tough time finding the right topic and thinking clearly about it. You see they don't help you develop the topic but when you bring one forward, they're ready to tell you all the reasons why it won't work. I know if I could develop a narrowly defined topic, I could collect the data, analyze it and write it up but I just can't seem to get off the ground and this has been very distressing and depressing for me. (Shana)

Other participants (4 of 20 [20%]) spoke more poignantly about needing help in developing their proposal:

The problem really was and still is how to develop a problem and purpose and research questions that are concrete and that I can stick with and I still seem to be having this problem. I'm also not sure what will get me over this impasse and what is at the source of it, I know I need help. (Mollie)

I just cannot seem to get my proposal done. Every time I hand in a section, there seem to be so many revisions especially with the methodology. I never realized the proposal was such a hurdle.... This has been going on too long, and part of it is my own fault because I just don't seem to be able to stay with it. If I could just get past the proposal, I could probably move on. (B.J.)

There were some students (2 of 20 [10%]) who had completed their proposals and found themselves stuck in the beginning stages of the research process:

Looking back to the long process of the dissertation research, one critical stage for me started after my proposal defense when I had the pilot data and wanted more guidance for how to code it so as to pave the way for may later data analysis. I tried myself and coded every line of the pilot interviews based on my initial conceptual framework which was not very effective. I felt totally lost until another colleague was able to explain in language I understood what a conceptual framework really was and how to use it. If it weren't for him, I would still be stuck. (Sal)

I was doing life history interviews and they had no structure—None! And so when I went to analyze the data I was having a very, very difficult time identifying emerging categories because I had over twelve hundred pages of script that had to be analyzed and I didn't know where to begin, how to get started. And I was so stuck that I thought about giving up but somehow I just kept at it. But I can tell you it was nerve-wracking. (Doris).

Other participants (3 of 20 [15%]) said they knew what they were supposed to do with regard the research, but were not sure about how to carry it out. Following are some of the ways these participants expressed their frustrations in not knowing the process they needed to follow:

> I feel like I'm in limbo. The process and what is required is not clear. Basically, once you pass the certification exam, you get a letter of congratulations and then—boom—that's it! You are alone. I was alone. I feel very alone. (Lin)

> The method of doing a dissertation really stood in my way—the method—how to do it. I mean you know something from the theory and you've got all those books but you still don't know *how*. You know a lot of *what* but you still don't know how. And who is going to show you how? (Jane)

> I wish I knew what I needed to do sooner. Then I would have been much further along than I am. But I guess everybody has to have the experience of the process of searching, of exploring *how*. And while you are trying very hard, it is important to have somebody direct you. Especially because you will have a lot—and I mean a lot of data. I was lucky to have found someone who helped me. (Carin)

In addition to needing to understand the process, two students also spoke about the need to be assertive. In this regard, Lin said: "I learned there is help out there. Nobody tells you where the help is, you have to go and look for it." In this same vein, Angela said, "I have learned not to wait for professors but to seek them out, make appointments with them, and ask questions, and go after what you need to know."

A few of the participants (3 of 20 [15%]) talked about learning to carry out the research process on their own or, as several said, "the hard way." This idea is best illustrated by the comment of one participant who said:

> When I started out, I went to the doctoral office and I picked up some brochures, and the manual

helped me understand the process as far as what was required. Then I started reading other dissertations and sort of took them apart to figure out what others had done, and I pieced it together, piece-by-piece. Nobody told me, I had to find that all out by myself. I learned about the research process in a really hard way. (Brad)

A few of the inactive students (3 of 20 [15%]) reflected on their past experience in trying to understand the process and offered some insights into the complexities involved:

> The truth is that I feel that people get engaged in dissertation work without being really absolutely clear as to what it would take in terms of research, in terms of the support we were going to get, in terms of the type of writing we were going to have to do, the time frame as to how long it was going to take. There were so many unknowns. (Angela)

> A master's degree is very structured. You know exactly what you are supposed to do and how you are supposed to do it. But when you are in a doctoral program, all of a sudden you are expected to be very independent. And while people may like to be independent there still needs to be some kind of structure. Doctoral students need clear instructions in terms of both the presentation of their subject matter but also in terms of how to do the actual data collection, analysis, and the rest. Advisors should plan with students more and guide the students more. They should start exploring topics and the literature review early on—it would make it all so much better, so much less confusing, so much less agonizing. (Julia)

Finding 3: The majority of participants (15 of 20 [75%]) attempted to learn what they needed to know by reaching out in dialogue with colleagues, rather than through more formal means.

The overriding finding that the coursework did not prepare participants to carry out the practical aspects of conducting research and writing their dissertations was further reflected by the informal, rather than formal, ways by which the majority of students went about trying to get the help and guidance they needed. Half of all participants (50%) spoke of their experiences reaching out to other students. Connie described the value of interacting with colleagues: "The colleagues I met along the way were so helpful; we were supportive of one another. I was so lucky to be part of a cohesive and collaborative group, and we continue to help each other figure things out." Other participants were even more explicit in describing their positive interaction with colleagues:

> After the coursework, I looked to some of my classmates for help, especially those who were further along than I was, and that helped me a lot. It wasn't that they were experts but they knew more about the process than I did. They already had approved proposals and they were collecting data and I wasn't nearly there yet and they filled in some gaps for me. And I continue to keep in touch with them and sometimes I am able to help them, and you know, they understand, because it's like, we're all in this together. (Anne)

> Everybody is very busy. In every program they enroll too many students, and the professors don't have the time to give the students enough attention. So, in our department the doctoral students get together and we help each other. We shouldn't really have to do that! But we're all frustrated. (Lin)

In addition to reaching out to others, a number of participants (6 of 20 [33%]) also described how they went about learning informally in self-directed ways. Brad described his strategy in this way: "I spent a lot of my time doing research; I was either in the library or on the Internet and I just kept digging until I found what I needed." Similarly, another participant said:

> I did an awful lot of reading on my own. I read so many dissertations, I can't even tell you how many, particularly those related to my topic and that was helpful to me to understand what others had done, how they went about their research. So by reading I had some mental models I could follow. (Anthony)

A fewer number of participants (5 of 20 [25%]) said they found the post-coursework dissertation seminars offered at their universities of help in understanding the practical aspects of doing research. One of these participants described the benefits of these seminars in this way:

> I found the dissertation seminar very helpful. I went regularly and I learned a lot and it gave me a very clear outline of how to proceed. Finally, I understood how everything fits together, how the research questions are related to the purpose and how they must fit with your conceptual framework. I finally understood it because we had a faculty person who had a very pragmatic approach—she was so clear in her explanations. I think just about everyone in the seminar felt that way. (Sal)

Only 4 of the 20 participants (25%) mentioned that they got the direction they needed from their advisors. At the same time, these participants also said it was not always easy to get an appointment with their advisors. One of these participants described it in this way:

> It seemed I was always tracking my advisor down when she was on campus. Almost every other week, I tried to contact her. And when I did reach her, and when she had time, she would sit down with me and talk and every time after talking with her, I clarified a lot of stuff. I would tell someone to start as early as possible to build up a collegiate relationship with their advisor—it's so important. (Jane)

Only 1 of the 20 participants (5%) indicated that the coursework was somewhat helpful to her. She said: "The coursework helped me to some extent but not enough—it points you in the right direction but it doesn't fill in the missing pieces" (Lin).

To deal with her frustration, one participant (5%) reached out to other experts in her field. In this regard, she described how she reached out to a faculty person outside her university:

> I was fortunate, I met a professor in (another city) at a conference and I took it upon myself to e-mail her and she was kind enough to write

back—as a matter of fact we had countless e-mails going back and forth and she helped me form some initial ideas about how to develop the problem and how to carry out the research. And she didn't have to do that—she didn't know me all that well. I'm just grateful because I don't know what I would have done if I hadn't found her. (Jane)

Finding 4: The majority of participants (15 of 20 [75%]) indicated that they relied on themselves to facilitate their progress. More than half of these same participants (8 of 15 [53%]) also said that colleagues were instrumental in helping them.

It was not surprising that, in the absence of formal guidance during coursework and because of inconsistent advisement, a majority of participants relied on themselves and their colleagues to help facilitate their progress. Participants framed the need to be self-reliant as follows:

You need to have perseverance, patience, and basically a very independent spirit, someone who really pretty much knows how to go about finding out what they need to know and doesn't feel disheartened by lack of support and caring. (Angela)

What helped me was my single-mindedness. I was and am determined—you know, relentless. I think that's how one has to be. You can't sit back and wait for someone to come along to help you, it doesn't work that way, you have to rely on yourself mostly. (Connie)

The need to reach out to colleagues was expressed by many students. On this point, B.J. commented: "When I'm really stuck I call on some of my classmates. . . . And even if they don't have the answers, they provide moral support." Similarly, another participant said:

You have to have faith in yourself, you have to believe in yourself, you have to have confidence and it's about having a positive attitude—you know, one that says I can do this. Sometimes, when I hit a roadblock and my confidence dips, that's when I call on my colleagues and they give

me support and encouragement and I hope I do that for them when they need it. (Brad)

A few participants (3 of 20 [15%]) said they received help from faculty other than their advisors. This notion was illustrated by one participant who went outside her department for help:

I went to Professor X when I had questions. And she was great because she's very structured and she had examples of the way to do things. And you could sit with her. She would go over things. She took the time. I believe that to really make this work you have to have advisors who like to advise, who have the skills to advise and they have to have patience with people. And they need to be trained. It's almost as if they need to be counselors. I didn't have that in my department, with my advisor, so I had to go outside. (Debbie)

Only two participants (10%) described the guidance and direction they received from their advisors in positive ways. In his description of his relationship with his advisor, Dexter said: "I have a very good rapport with my advisor, he's always willing to go over things with me and he tries to find the time for me and I know that is not the case with all advisors so I really appreciate him." Jane corroborated these sentiments when she said: "I developed a very positive relationship and rapport with my advisor, and this was a big plus for me."

Finding 5: The majority of participants (14 of 20 [70%]) cited lack of good, timely, and consistent advisement as a major barrier standing in the way of their progress.

Given that only two participants described the guidance and direction they received from their advisors in positive terms, it is not surprising that the quality, access, and availability of advisors would be described by the majority of participants as a major impediment to their progress. (It should be noted that four participants did not share their perceptions of the advisement that they received.) The negative view of advisement is illustrated by the following participant comments:

Most of them (advisors) don't put much into it because they're not really interested in what their students are doing. If they can't share in getting the credit for it to bolster their tenure . . . I have a kind of jaded view of advisors at this point! I think it's the university structure and the bureaucracy. You know they have to publish or perish. And also I don't know if advisors come into it with the skills, the people skills. I think you really have to be able to work with the student, to understand their frustrations, their issues, the things that block them, and to help them to be able to overcome those things. In a lot of ways it's a mentoring relationship. And so you have to be authentic. (Debbie)

He (my advisor) really didn't help me at all. Every time I went in to see him, he would say to me "I'm here to help you." I was yelling silently, "help me, help me, tell me what to do!" In the end I was so frustrated. I wanted him to give me some specific work. I didn't know what I was supposed to do, instead of just reading the literature. That went on for a long, long time, about three to four years. (Lin)

I couldn't get anywhere with my first advisor. And I did three proposals with an advisor who kept saying, "Well, that's not it yet . . . I'll know it when I see it." So it was that kind of response. . . . I think when he said he'd know it when he saw it, he really didn't have a clue himself. He did well with advisees who could find a different way of dealing with that. I really needed some help and more structure, a framework in which to get it done and that wasn't forthcoming. (Anne)

Related to the disappointment that participants expressed concerning advisement, other faculty and administration and the rigidity of the process also were cited by eight of the participants (40%). Some of the ways participants summed up their experiences were as follows:

Nobody was really clear, not the faculty, not the administration. The really annoying thing from my perspective is that nobody is really there to give you guidelines. This is a very difficult process, a very lengthy one and while it is so rigid, so many things that are so vague. Most of the time,

the feeling is one of loneliness. Hanging out in the wind; it was so overwhelming. (Angela)

It was the constantly changing expectation among the Committee Members about what I was expected to do and how I was expected to do it. I was writing various chapters and I had constant and conflicting messages about what I was supposed to write and how I was supposed to write it. . . . It seemed like a useless exercise in control. (Hank)

I understand now, which I did not at the beginning, that writing a dissertation is an exercise whose value does not lie in its creative expression nor revelation of new knowledge, but merely in its approved execution in accordance with a particular set of rules. (Morris)

In addition to describing structural impediments, such as ineffective advisement, lack of faculty and administration support, and the rigidity of the process, participants also described personal factors that impeded their progress. Among these were professional work demands, personal and family issues, financial constraints, and lack of confidence in ability.

Ten of the 20 participants (50%) talked about the stress and challenges involved in managing their jobs and the time required to work on their dissertations. Following are illustrations of participants' comments regarding professional and work demands:

I found that having a demanding full-time position and a commute on top of it, I just couldn't fit it in. So I don't know if I lost the drive along the way, or if it was just that some other things became more of a priority. I mean, I had to work—that was the priority. So, I would say that people need to really think it through and dedicate the time to do it. (Doris)

Losing my job, that was a huge distracter. And the job that I took was a job that didn't pay me enough. I took it out of necessity, so there was a lot of financial strain imposed. Another thing about losing my job was that I lost the context of where I was thinking of doing my research. So I lost focus on what I actually was going to be doing, and I felt overwhelmed with trying to find something else. (Frank)

Six of the 20 participants (30%) focused on family issues and described these as impeding their progress. As Julia said: "Just when I felt I was beginning to make progress my mother died, and that really set me back." Various other comments illustrate the difficulties involved in managing family commitments:

My wife and I both work and we have three kids. There's always something going on, you know. Juggling all our schedules, managing everybody's plans and all the family issues is difficult. There's a lot of pressure. (Carin)

My job changed and I adopted children. And the combination of these two things meant that I just couldn't do it (the dissertation) and there wasn't anything anybody could do to help me with it at that point in time. (Debbie)

A few other participants (5 of 20 [25%]) expressed concern around funding their doctoral work:

I'm always running around and worrying about how I'm going to pay next semester's tuition. There's little scholarship money available, and I'm digging myself deeper in a hole every year. This has gone on for nine years. If I didn't have this worry maybe I would have finished. (Doris)

Some participants (5 of 20 [25%]) indicated that they struggled with the lack of confidence they had in their ability to do the work. Shana expressed her self-doubt by saying: "I would tell someone not to be afraid of it (the dissertation) like I was; I spent too much time being afraid." Another participant was even more explicit in explaining her doubts about being able to do the work:

I think it's [the dissertation] a terrifying process, I really do. And I worried so much about whether I could actually do this kind of work; I had a hard

time shaking off those self-doubting negative thoughts when they took hold of me. And I don't know that faculty really wants to disarm anybody of what it's all about because it may take away the mystique. I don't know. I'm just guessing. Also I think there are some who think you may catch on that they really don't know much more about it than you do. (Anne)

Findings From the Focus Group Interview

A focus group interview was held for approximately 1½ hours with six doctoral candidates who were not part of the study sample, but who met all of the criteria for participation. The focus group participants were assured that all of their comments would be held in strict confidence and that each would be identified by a pseudonym. Prior to the session, the researcher contacted the six participants individually by phone to schedule a convenient time to hold the session. Following that conversation, the six participants were sent the same consent form given to all interviewees and were asked to sign and return it in an enclosed stamped and self-addressed envelope to the researcher. Before the session began, the participants were told that the session would be audio recorded and subsequently transcribed by the researcher.

The researcher described her role as facilitator, monitoring the process and advising that the discussion would largely be in control of the participants. Participants were told that there would be two parts to the discussion. In the first part, they were asked to think about their experience in the research process and share with one another their perceptions of factors that helped them during that process. The facilitator indicted she would let them know when to turn their attention to the second part of the discussion. In the last part of the discussion, participants were asked to share with one another those factors they perceived might have stood in the way of their progress. Specifically, what, if any, obstacles and challenges did participants face that they believe may have impeded their ability to move forward in their research and what, if any, action did they take to overcome those challenges and/or obstacles?

It was interesting to see how the discussion by the six focus group participants parallels the findings that emanated from the interviews. All six participants indicated that they relied largely on themselves and a few classmates to help them when they got stuck. Michele said: "I really wanted to get through this process and I was determined to find out what I needed, no matter what. As an extravert, I wasn't shy about asking my classmates for help or advice; heck, they were in the same boat so I didn't have to impress them." Jacob followed up quickly by adding: "I was the opposite, Michele, I was and still am a real introvert—you know I like to figure things out on my own—but this process is so beyond that—so beyond my experience. I had no choice. I had to learn to become more like you, an extravert, not afraid to ask for help, and I mostly went to my peers because my advisor was, let us say, not often available!"

Jacob's comments precipitated a discussion of the access and availability of advisors. Two other members, Kent and Lauren, were almost talking over each other in recounting their experiences with advisement. The following captures a part of what Kent said: "I mustn't have been one of her favorites, I had to wait so long for feedback—it was frustrating as hell—it made me feel disregarded." Lauren added: "I know what you mean about waiting and waiting for feedback and then when you finally get something, it was let's say vague—to be kind. I really needed more direction." Another member chimed in: "Yeah, at a time like this who wants to be self-directed." The group laughed. Much like the descriptions from the interviews, the discussion continued, mostly centering on the frustration the six members had with the accessibility and timeliness of the advisement they received. Only one participant tied lack of advisement to financial difficulties. Beth said: "The tuition we pay—at least at my university is outrageous and goes up every semester it seems and to think you are paying these absorbent sums in tuition and you're not getting your money's worth—something is

wrong." Nods of acknowledgment led to the close of the discussion.

Both parts of the focus group discussion confirm perceptions of lack of advisement as an impediment to their moving more quickly through the process. The six members' discussions of what they perceived helped them also were consistent with data from the interviews. The focus group members indicated that they largely relied on themselves and their own resourcefulness while seeking the help of their colleagues and peers.

Chapter Summary

This chapter presented the five findings uncovered by this study. Findings were organized according to the research questions. Data from individual interviews, critical incidents, and a focus group revealed research participants' perceptions vis-à-vis their experiences of the dissertation process. As is typical of qualitative research, extensive samples of quotations from participants are included in the report. By using participants' own words, the researchers aim to build the confidence of readers by accurately representing the reality of the persons and situations studied.

The primary finding of this study is that the coursework did not prepare participants to conduct research or write the dissertations. This finding emanated from the expressed descriptions of 95% of the participants as they discussed their perceptions of what they needed to successfully conduct research and write their dissertations. In discussing why they felt unprepared after they completed the coursework, several participants talked about the lack of connection between the coursework and conducting and writing up the research. Although most participants appreciated the theoretical foundation the coursework provided, they expressed the need for more focus on the practical aspects of conducting research. A few said they knew what they were supposed to do with regard to the research, but were not sure about how to carry it out.

The second finding was that all 20 participants expressed the need to know the content and understand the process involved in conducting research and writing their dissertations. Some participants described the difficulty they had, and are having, in selecting a good, researchable problem. Others spoke about needing help in developing their proposal. Some had completed their proposals, but found themselves stuck in the beginning stages of the research process. In addition to needing to understand the process, two students also spoke about the need to be assertive, and a few others talked about learning to carry out the research process on their own or, as several put it, "the hard way."

The third finding was that the majority of participants attempted to learn what they needed to know by reaching out in dialogue with colleagues and others, rather than through more formal means. Half of all participants spoke of their experiences reaching out to other students. In addition to reaching out to others, a number of participants also described how they went about learning informally, in self-directed ways, through reading and research. A quarter of all the participants said they found the post-coursework dissertation seminars offered at their universities of help in understanding the practical aspects of doing research, and a quarter also mentioned that they got the direction they needed from their advisors.

The fourth finding was that the majority of participants relied on their own personal characteristics to facilitate their progress. More than half of these same participants also said colleagues were instrumental in helping them. A few participants said they received help from faculty other than their advisors.

The fifth finding was that the majority of participants cited lack of good, timely, and consistent advisement as a major barrier standing in the way of their progress. Some also mentioned lack of faculty and administration support and the rigidity of the process. In addition to these structural impediments, participants also described personal factors that impeded their progress, including professional work demands, personal and family issues, financial constraints, and lack of confidence in ability.

Findings from the focus group corroborated the findings from the interviews. All six participants indicated that they relied largely on themselves, and that they called on classmates to help them when they got stuck. Focus group participants discussed their frustration regarding accessibility and timeliness of the advisement they received, confirming interview perceptions of lack of advisement as a major impediment to moving more quickly through the dissertation process.

SUMMARY DISCUSSION FOR CHAPTER 4

Qualitative data analysis is an attempt to summarize the data collected from multiple data sources in a dependable and accurate manner. When analyzing qualitative data, you need to challenge yourself to explore every possible angle to find patterns and relationships among the data. The amount of data that needs to be transcribed, organized, and reduced can indeed be overwhelming. This chapter explains how to go about organizing and preparing the data for analysis and includes discussion around data reduction and data display. Organizing, preparing, and presenting the findings of your research is, as described in this chapter, a somewhat objective exercise; the researcher is, in this instance, a reporter of information.

Although the mechanics of data analysis vary greatly and are undertaken differently depending on genre and theoretical framework, some general guidelines can be useful. Although the guidelines we provide described the analytic process as if it were a series of separate sequential steps, it must be remembered that qualitative data analysis is an interactive and recursive process, rather than a linear one. The steps are repeated several times until the researcher feels that there has been sufficient immersion in the data, that sufficient information has been extracted from the data, and that the research questions have been adequately addressed. It is important to recognize that in qualitative research, data collection and data analysis are intimately interconnected processes. Having said that, our view is that for purposes of a dissertation, although it might seem a little contrived, it is most effective to present the findings (an objective exercise) and the analysis of those findings (a subjective exercise) as two separate chapters.

Qualitative research is typically reported in a narrative manner. Although the overall intent is not to quantify qualitative data, tallies and frequencies in qualitative research are essentially a supplement to the narrative. Essentially, you are forming a record of frequently occurring phenomena or patterns of behavior. Once you have established patterns, these need to be explained. You have to consult the literature and consider your pattern findings in light of previous research and existing theory. Do your findings confirm similar research? Do they contradict previous studies? How can you explain these differences or similarities? As you begin to consider answers to these sorts of questions and provide convincing explanations, you are interpreting and synthesizing. This is the stuff of chapter 5.

Chapter Checklist

✓ Do you have a clear introduction to this chapter that includes your purpose statement (if required), as well as an explanation of how the chapter will be organized?

✓ In your introduction, do you tell the reader how you have laid out the chapter?

✓ Are your data analysis steps clearly identified?

✓ Is it evident how you have managed and organized your data for analysis?

✓ Was your coding process adequately described in the introduction?

✓ Did you create data summary tables as you were coding data so that no information was missed?

✓ Is your roadmap clear and precise?

✓ Do the headings of your roadmap correspond with the headings in your narrative?

✓ Are your findings statements clearly and precisely stated?

✓ Are the findings presented in relation to the research questions?

✓ Are the findings presented in a logical sequence?

✓ Are the findings clearly organized and easy to follow?

✓ Are the findings directly responsive to the problem raised by the study? That is, do the findings answer the research questions?

✓ Is this chapter free from interpretation? That is, are your findings reported accurately and objectively?

✓ Are there appropriate lead-in sentences and clues?

✓ Have you selected the strongest and most appropriate quotations to support your points?

✓ Have you trimmed your quotations, eliminating all unnecessary wording?

✓ Is there a culminating summary of key findings?

✓ Does your summary paragraph offer some logical link to the next chapter?

✓ If tables and figures are used, are these well organized, self-explanatory, and easy to understand?

✓ Are the data presented in each table described in the text that either follows or precedes it?

✓ Have you tightened up your writing, resulting in short, crisp sentences?

✓ Have you refined and revised your initial drafts of this chapter to produce a polished final version?

✓ Have you checked for institutional and/or program-related differences regarding the content and structure of chapter 4?

✓ Have you checked for institutional and/or program-related differences regarding the appropriate use of qualitative language and terminology?

ANNOTATED BIBLIOGRAPHY

Boyatzis, R. E. (1998). *Transforming qualitative information: Thematic analysis and code development*. Thousand Oaks, CA: Sage.

As this author illustrates, thematic analysis—a process for encoding qualitative information—can be thought of as a bridge between qualitative and quantitative research. As such, the discussion in the book confronts the debate between positivist and postmodernist takes on the research act in an innovative and fresh way. More than that, and in a practical sense, however, this book helps the reader understand the concept of thematic analysis and provides clear guidelines about learning to develop techniques to apply to one's own research. This book shows how to sense themes—the first step in analyzing information—as well as how to develop the various types of codes. This book is useful for researchers across a broad spectrum of disciplines.

Creswell, J. W. (1998). *Qualitative inquiry and research design: Choosing among five traditions*. Thousand Oaks, CA: Sage.

Written in an easy-to-read way, this book examines the five most common traditions or genres in qualitative inquiry—biography, phenomenology, grounded theory, ethnography, and case study—at each phase of the research process. Chapter 8 focuses on data analysis and representation, beginning with a generic approach to analysis as provided by various leading authors in the field. Creswell then goes on to explore in greater detail each tradition of inquiry, examining the specific data analysis procedures within each tradition and discussing the differences and similarities among the traditions. The chapter concludes with a critical overview of the use of computers in qualitative analysis.

Huck, S. W. (2000). *Reading statistics and research* (3rd ed.). New York: Longman.

This book is useful for the qualitative researcher whose study includes a quantitative component. It provides the reader with an understanding of statistical terms, the ability to make sense of and set up statistical tables and figures, knowledge of what specific research questions can be answered by each of a variety of statistical procedures, and a better understanding of how to decipher and critically evaluate statistically based findings. Tables, figures, and passages of text from published research reports are used as examples.

Merriam, S. B. (1998). *Qualitative research and case study applications in education*. San Francisco: Jossey-Bass.

Many texts on qualitative research devote much space to theoretical discussions of methodology and data collection and relatively little to the management and analysis of data once they are collected. This book redresses that imbalance, devoting two chapters to data analysis. Chapter 8 reviews various strategies for analyzing qualitative data and addresses the increasing role and function of computers in qualitative data management and analysis. The chapter stresses the iterative nature of data collection and data analysis, recommending that these two processes be conducted concurrently. Chapter 9 explains the different levels of analysis possible—ranging from developing a descriptive account of the findings to constructing categories and themes to interpreting the meaning of the data. The chapter also speaks to within- and cross-case analysis, which is a common feature of case study analysis.

Miles, M. B., & Huberman, A. M. (1994). *Qualitative data analysis* (2nd ed.). Thousand Oaks, CA: Sage.

The classic on qualitative data analysis, this book takes the reader through a series of steps that illustrate how to approach and conduct the analytic process. The approach of these authors to data analysis is basically a systematic, deductive one, with the authors reflecting a somewhat formal, positivistic approach. Although those with a more interpretive/inductive outlook might be critical, these authors' goal is to make the qualitative research process manageable and doable. They focus on bounding data collection, developing a coding structure, and building a logical chain of evidence to support research conclusions. A useful and concise discussion regarding purposeful sampling procedure is offered on pages 27–34. The sections on coding are useful too as the authors provide a variety of ideas for analytical approaches, offering examples and addressing potential pitfalls. Particularly useful for the dissertation writer is the strong visual emphasis throughout this book; there are the many examples of ways of reducing and displaying qualitative data, including tables, charts, matrices, graphs, maps, networks, and figures. As the authors emphasize, graphic representation allows the reader to "see what's happening." Each of more than 60 methods of data display and analysis is described and illustrated in detail, with practical hands-on suggestions for adaptation and use.

Morse, J. M., & Richards, L. (2002). *Read me first for a user's guide to qualitative methods*. Thousand Oaks, CA: Sage.

These authors provide a framework for understanding the decision-making processes that underlie the making of data. Part II, "Inside Analysis," helps a researcher to think more clearly about what qualitative data actually are (and what they are not), how to record and manage appropriate data, and how to prepare data for analysis. Chapter 6 deals with the coding process and includes discussion of what coding is, the different ways of coding data, and managing and monitoring codes. What is useful is their notion of using codes to develop themes or, as they call it, "theme-ing." Chapter 7 deals with the ability to think abstractly to transform data so as to understand it. Chapter 8 offers useful distinctions among phenomenological, ethnographic, and grounded theory approaches to analysis. As these authors rightfully point out, each tradition is sensitive to particular analytic methods and strategies, demanding that the researcher think about analysis is a particular way.

Rea, L. M., & Parker, R. A. (1997). *Designing and conducting survey research: A comprehensive guide* (2nd ed.). San Francisco: Jossey-Bass.

Survey instruments are often included in qualitative research, and this book is useful in terms of designing and conducting survey research. The practical, step-by-step details help the researcher to more clearly understand the nuances involved in survey research and how to best analyze and present results. The exercises and examples that are included span a multitude of subjects, thereby appealing to a broad-based audience in the social and behavioral sciences.

Robson, C. (2002). *Real world research* (2nd ed.). Malden, MA: Blackwell.

This book offers some useful guidelines for qualitative data analysis. Chapter 14 deals primarily with the various approaches to the systematic analysis of qualitative data, stressing the central role of human as researcher and the tensions inherent in that role, and also discussing the advantages and disadvantages of computer-aided software. The author offers a detailed discussion regarding the different approaches vis-à-vis different research traditions, with a particular focus on case study, ethnography, and grounded theory. There is a focus throughout on ideas for data management and organization, as well as the use of matrices and data display. The author also provides useful discussion around content analysis for analyzing documentation, including computer aids to content analysis (pp. 351–359), discourse analysis (p. 365), and meta-analysis (p. 368). At the end of each of the relevant chapters are further reading options for those who seek more detailed information.

Rubin, H. J., & Rubin, I. S. (2005). *Qualitative interviewing: The art of hearing data* (2nd ed.). Thousand Oaks, CA: Sage.

Written in user-friendly language and incorporating many useful examples, this book explains in great detail how to obtain rich, detailed, and evocative information through interviews—the primary method of data collection in qualitative research. The book does well in striking a balance among the different qualitative traditions, addressing many of their criteria, issues, and concerns. Aside from the earlier chapters, which take the reader though all the steps involved in interviewing, extremely useful are chapter 11, "Analyzing Coded Data," and chapter 12, "Presenting the Results." In both of these chapters, the authors offer clear explanations and suggestions regarding different ways to clarify and summarize concepts and themes, group and sort information, search for patterns and linkages, and produce a rich, descriptive narrative.

Silverman, D. (2000). *Doing qualitative research: A practical handbook*. Thousand Oaks, CA: Sage.

Part III of this book presents a practical guide to analyzing data. As the author writes, "After the first year of research, people have varying degrees of uncertainty about the future. . . . The uncertain one asks: 'I've collected all these data, now what should I do?'" Using various examples, the author offers various strategies for beginning the data analysis process, including how to deal with interview transcripts and field notes. He then goes on to explain in more detail the actual process of analysis, including data reduction (by way of coding procedures), data display (assembling data by way of matrices, graphs, and charts), and drawing conclusions (noting patterns and themes). Chapter 12 discusses the use of computers to analyze qualitative data (CAQDAS). The author provides a thorough overview of the most commonly used analytic software packages available and offers the reader some useful insights regarding the advantages and disadvantages of this method of analysis.

CHAPTER 5

Analyzing and Interpreting Findings

OVERVIEW

Qualitative research begins with questions, and its ultimate purpose is learning. To inform the questions, the researcher collects *data*. Data are like building blocks that, when grouped into patterns, become *information*, which in turn, when applied or used, becomes *knowledge* (Rossman & Rallis, 2003). The challenge of qualitative analysis lies in making sense of large amounts of data—reducing raw data, identifying what is significant, and constructing a framework for communicating the essence of what the data reveal. This was the task of chapter 4. The challenge now becomes one of digging into the findings to develop some understanding of what lies beneath them; that is, what information we now have and what this really means. Analysis, in this sense, is about deconstructing the findings—an essentially postmodern concept.

Your goal in conducting analysis is to figure out the deeper meaning of what you have found, and that analysis began when you assigned codes to chunks of raw data. Now that you have a well-laid-out set of findings, you go to a second level. You scrutinize what you have found in the hope of discovering what it means or, more precisely, what meaning you can make of it. You are seeking ways to understand what you have found by comparing your findings both within and across groups, and by comparing your study's findings with those of other studies.

In qualitative research, we are open to different ways of seeing the world. We make assumptions about how things work. We strive to be open to the reality of others and understand different realities. We must listen before we can understand. Analysis of the findings begins with careful listening to what others have to say. Begin by asking yourself: Given what I have found, what does this mean? What does this tell me about the phenomenon under study? What is really going on here? In asking these questions, you are working back and forth between the findings of your research and your own perspectives and understandings to make sense and meaning. Meaning can come from looking at differences and similarities, from inquiring into and interpreting causes, consequences, and relationships.

Data analysis in qualitative research remains somewhat mysterious (Marshall & Rossman, 2006; Merriam, 1998). The problem lies in the fact that there are few agreed-on canons for qualitative analysis in the sense of shared ground rules. There are no formulas for determining the significance of findings or for interpreting them, and there are no ways of perfectly replicating a researcher's analytical thinking. In this chapter, we do not purport to offer a recipe, but rather some guidance for navigating the analytical process. Applying guidelines requires judgment, sensibility, and creativity. Because each study is unique, each analytical approach used is unique as well. As Patton (2002) puts it: "In short, no absolute rules exist except perhaps this: Do your very best with your full intellect to fairly represent the data and communicate what the data reveal given the purpose of the study" (p. 432). Indeed, because qualitative research depends on the skills, training, capabilities, and insights of the researcher, qualitative analysis and interpretation ultimately depends on the analytical intellect and style of each individual analyst.

As with all previous chapters, we present two sections: Section I, "Instruction," talks about (a) thinking about, (b) planning, and (c) presenting your analysis. Section II, "Application," presents what an analysis chapter might look like. By using the example carried throughout this book, we analyze and interpret the findings of the research that we have conducted.

It must be stressed that analyzing and interpreting are highly intuitive processes; they are certainly not mechanical or technical. The process of qualitative data analysis and synthesis is an ongoing one, involving continual reflection about the findings and asking analytical questions. As such, there is no clear and accepted single set of conventions for the analysis and interpretation of qualitative data. Indeed many qualitative researchers would resist this were it to come about, viewing the enterprise as more an art than a science. Therefore, the term *instructions* for this chapter might be somewhat misleading. Reducing the data and presenting findings can be explained in a stepwise and somewhat mechanical fashion. Analysis, synthesis, and interpretation of qualitative data, in contrast, is a far more nebulous endeavor—hence the clear paucity of published literature on how to actually do it (and hence the limited annotated bibliography that we offer for this section). Rather than instructions, what we provide in this chapter

are essentially guidelines for how to think about analysis and principles to use in selecting appropriate procedures that will organically unfold and become revealed as you become immersed in your own study.

Please be aware too that the guidelines and principles that we provide are essentially generic and can be applicable across a broad range of qualitative genres or traditions. Each tradition is sensitive to particular analytical methods and strategies. As such, each tradition requires that the researcher think about analysis in a particular way. For more details and nuances regarding analysis for pure qualitative traditions such as phenomenology, grounded theory, ethnography, and hermeneutics, we suggest that you consult with your advisor and also seek the relevant available literature related to your specific tradition.

CHAPTER OBJECTIVES

Chapter 5 Objectives

Section I: Instruction

- Explain the concept of qualitative analysis.
- Explain how to analyze and interpret the findings of your research.
- Explain the concept of synthesis as an ongoing process.
- Describe how to go about presenting a final synthesis.

Section II: Application

- Presentation of a completed analysis and interpretation chapter based on the content and process as described earlier.

The previous chapter discussed how to present the findings of your research by organizing data from various sources into categories to produce a readable narrative. The purpose of this chapter is to provide interpretative insights into these findings. This point in the process is where you shift from being an objective reporter to becoming an informed and insightful commentator. No one has been closer to the focus of the study, its data, and its progress than you have. You have done the interviewing, studied the transcripts, and read the related literature. You have lived with and wrestled with the data. You now have an opportunity to communicate to others what you think your findings mean and integrate your findings with literature, research, and practice. This process requires a good deal of careful thinking and reflection.

SECTION I: INSTRUCTION

Thinking About Your Analysis

Taking time to reflect on your findings and what these might possibly mean requires some serious mind work—so do not try and rush this phase. Spend a few days away from your research, giving careful thought to the findings, trying to put them in perspective, and trying to gain some deeper insights. To begin facilitating the kind of thinking process required, we have developed what we call an interpretation outline tool—a mechanism that enables you to consider the findings in a deeper way than you have had to do up until now; to "peel back" all the possible reasons regarding how else a finding can be explained, thereby fleshing out the meanings that underlie each finding. Findings should not be taken at face value.

Essentially, this simple but effective tool prompts and prods you to question each of your findings (and all the various aspects of each finding) by asking "Why?" and "Why not?" over and again, allowing you to brainstorm and exhaust all the possibilities that might explain that finding. In effect, those

explanations become the basis of your interpretations. This tool propels you to develop and strengthen your critical thinking and reflection on all the issues surrounding your findings. This process is essentially "problem posing"—an inductive questioning process rooted in the works of Lindeman, Dewey, and Piaget, who were advocates of an experiential and dialogical education. Freire (1970) and Mezirow (1981, 1985) used problem-posing dialogue as a means to develop critical inquiry and understanding of experience.

Figure 5.1 gives some idea of how such a tool can be developed. A sample completed interpretation outline tool is included as Appendix Y. We suggest that a completed version of an interpretation outline be included in your dissertation's appendix to illustrate to your readers the logical development and overview of your interpretive thought processes.

Planning the Analysis of Your Findings

In thinking about the analysis, you might ask yourself what this chapter is really all about and what it should constitute. How does one go about seeking the deeper meanings behind the findings? How does one get started? What is really involved? We asked ourselves these questions as we set about writing this chapter. We sought the answers by way of structuring our discussion according to three interrelated activities: (a) seeking significant patterns among the findings, (b) making use of description and interpretation, and (c) providing some sort of synthesis or integration. Keeping your findings in context and thinking holistically are among the cardinal principles of qualitative analysis.

Seeking Patterns/Themes

Analysis is essentially about searching for patterns and themes; that is, the trends that

STEP 1:

State Analytic Category 1: This category directly relates to your research questions. Describe the corresponding findings.

Ask "Why?" and "Why Not?"

"Think critically. Brainstorm all possible reasons. Continue to probe "Why?" and "Why Not?"

Ask: What is happening and why it is happening? *How else* can this be explained? Look (a) within findings, (b) across findings, and (c) across cases/individuals. State all linkages that can be made to the relevant literature.

STEP 2:

State Analytic Category 2: This category directly relates to your research questions. Describe the corresponding findings.

Ask "Why?" and "Why Not?"

Think critically. Brainstorm all possible reasons. Continue to probe "Why?" and "Why Not?"

Ask: What is happening and why it is happening? *How else* can this be explained? Look (a) within findings, (b) across findings, and (c) across cases/individuals. State all linkages that can be made to the relevant literature.

Instruction: Continue in the same manner for each analytic category, exhausting all possible interpretations.

Figure 5.1   Interpretation Outline Tool

you see emerging from among your findings. After having spent many hours interviewing (and/or observing) people, you are likely to come away with some possible explanations of how and why people are saying what they are saying. Having immersed yourself in your data and lived with them for an extended period of time, you have most likely reflected on emergent patterns and themes that run through your findings. You also have probably made conjectures and can offer hypotheses about the significance of certain outcomes, consequences, interconnections, and interrelationships that you see appearing.

A few words on significance are necessary at this point. Quantitative researchers utilize statistical tests of significance to research the frequency of responses. Typically these tests of significance are reported with preestablished levels of confidence. Data are numerically analyzed by determining means, modes, medians, rank orderings, and percentages. In qualitative research, we do not seek statistical significance that characterizes quantitative

research. In qualitative research, what we mean by significance is that something is important, meaningful, or potentially useful given what we are trying to find out. Qualitative findings are judged by their substantive significance (Patton, 2002). As Patton explains, in determining substantive significance, the qualitative analyst must address the following issues:

1. How solid and consistent are your findings?

2. To what extent and in what ways do your findings increase understanding of the phenomenon under study?

3. To what extent are your findings consistent with the existing body of knowledge? That is, do they support or confirm what is already known about the phenomenon? Do they refute what is already known? Do they break new ground in discovering or illuminating something?

4. To what extent are the findings useful in terms of contributing to theory-building, informing policy, or informing practice?

You need to establish some system for representing participants' perspectives on the most significant events or activities by describing the procedures that you have adopted in analyzing your findings. Patterns, as we have come to see them, include both quantitative and qualitative elements. At this point in the process, your data summary tables (see Appendices R through V for completed examples) and participant demographic charts (discussed in chapter 3) become useful for analysis. In the findings chapter, the purpose of the data summary tables was merely to report numbers and percentages of responses. In the analysis chapter, the data summary tables become useful vis-à-vis the significance of your findings. In the analysis of qualitative data, we are interested in the concentration of responses across individuals. Although not really a finding in itself, having a large number of data in a particular area or under a particular descriptor or criterion does suggest where to look for patterns.

Readers need to understand different degrees of significance of your various findings. In this regard, you need to be specific when patterns are clear and strongly supported by the data or when patterns are merely suggestive. Ultimately, readers arrive at their own decisions based on the evidence that you have provided, but your opinions and speculations hold weight and are of interest to the reader because you have obviously struggled with the data and know them more intimately than anybody else.

Looking for emergent patterns among your findings can be considered a first round of analysis. It is important to also look across findings and across dimensions of each finding—the subsets within each finding. This second round of searching for patterns can often generate new insights and usually uncovers patterns that may not immediately have been obvious or apparent in the initial round of analysis. Creating cross-case classification matrices is an exercise in logic. This involves moving back and forth between your findings and crossing one dimension (subset) with another in search of what might be meaningful or significant. Beyond identifying themes and patterns, you now build additional layers of complexity by interconnecting your themes or patterns into a story-line. Matrices can certainly push linkages. In creating matrices, however, be careful not to manipulate the data in any way or force the data to make cross-classification fit.

Finding patterns and themes is one result of analysis, whereas finding ambiguities and inconsistencies is another. You certainly want to determine how useful the findings are in illuminating the research questions being explored and how central they are to the story that is unfolding about the phenomenon under study. However, you also should challenge your understanding by searching for discrepancies and negative instances in the patterns. Seek all possible and plausible explanations other than those that are most apparent. Alternative explanations always exist. As is characteristic of qualitative research, you must be willing to tolerate some ambiguity. As such, look at issues from all angles to demonstrate the most plausible explanations. This step enables readers to assess the persuasiveness of your argument.

Once you have established patterns, they need to be explained. In this regard, you need to draw on your own experience and intuition. In addition, you have to once again consult the literature and consider your pattern findings in light of previous research and existing theory. Do your findings confirm similar research? Do your findings contradict previous studies? How can you explain these differences or similarities? As you begin to consider answers to these sorts of questions, you begin to describe and interpret your material.

Description and Interpretation

As Patton (2002) explains: "An interesting and readable report provides sufficient description to allow the reader to understand the basis for an interpretation, and sufficient interpretation to allow the reader to appreciate the description" (p. 503). The details in the description are your evidence, your logic; they build your argument. Therefore, description must necessarily precede interpretation. At the same time, the explanation and linkages revealed in the explanation serve to clarify the description and illuminate the details. Description is intended to convey the rich complexity of the research. Interpretation involves attaching significance to what was found, making sense of findings, considering different meanings, and offering potential explanations and conclusions.

An interpretive reading of your data involves constructing a version of what you think the data mean or represent or what you think you can infer from the data. You may be wondering why you should even bother with interpretation especially because interpretation involves taking risks and making educated guesses that might be off base. Wolcott (1994) argues for the importance of interpretation in qualitative research not only because interpretation adds a new dimension of understanding, but because the process of interpretation challenges qualitative researchers' taken-for-granted assumptions and beliefs about the processes and phenomena they have investigated—an important aspect of a researcher's personal and professional development.

Interpretation essentially involves reading through or beyond the findings (i.e., making sense of the findings). It is about answering the "why?" and "why not?" questions around the findings. Interpretation requires more conceptual and integrative thinking than data analysis alone because it involves identifying and abstracting important understandings from the detail and complexity of the findings. Interpretation in effect moves the whole analytic process to a higher level. You (the researcher) arrive at new understandings, finding meaning beyond the specifics of your data. What you have seen in the field and what you have heard participants say all come together into an account that has meaning for the participants, for you, and for the reader. As with qualitative analysis in general, there are no hard-and-fast rules for how to go about the task of interpreting the meaning of the findings. One way to facilitate the process of interpretation is to begin by asking the following questions: What is really going on here? What is the story these findings tell? Why is this important? What can be learned here?

Lincoln and Guba (1985) capture well the essence of interpretation when they ask: What were the lessons learned? Lessons learned are in the form of the researcher's understanding and insight that she or he brings to the study based on her or his personal and/or professional experience, history, and culture. But it is more than this: It is about the meaning derived from a comparison of the findings of your study with information gleaned from the related literature and previous research. Making connections between your study's findings and the relevant literature provides you with a way to share with colleagues the existing knowledge base on a research problem and acknowledge the unique contribution your study has made to understanding the phenomenon studied.

Searching the literature to see whether it corresponds, contradicts, and/or deepens your interpretations thus constitutes a second layer of interpretation. Interpretation, therefore, is not just a conglomeration of personal ideas. It is the subtle combination of your ideas in tandem with what has already been reported in the literature. The findings of your study will either confirm what is already known about the subject area surrounding your research problem or diverge from it. Therefore, it is imperative that you relate your analysis to the available literature on the subject.

Your integrity and credibility as a researcher are given credence by your inclusion of all information, even that which challenges your inferences and assumptions. You are building an argument about what you have learned in the field—an argument that is more compelling than other alternatives. As you put forward your interpretations, you should not forget to challenge the patterns that seem so apparent. Qualitative research is not about uncovering any single interpretive truth. Alternative understandings always exist; to demonstrate the soundness of your interpretation, you should be sure to search for, identify, and describe a variety of plausible explanations.

One barrier to credible interpretation stems from the suspicion that the analysis has been shaped according to the predispositions, assumptions, and biases of the researcher. Whether this happens unconsciously or inadvertently is not the issue. Rather, the issue is that you counter such a suspicion in the mind of the reader by reporting that you have engaged in a systematic search for alternative patterns and themes and rival or competing explanations and interpretations. This means thinking carefully, and with an open mind, about other logical possibilities and then seeing whether those possibilities can be supported by the findings and the literature. Failure to find strong supporting evidence for contrary explanations helps increase readers' confidence in the interpretations that you have generated.

As you guide the reader through your discussion, you attempt to create a compelling argument for interpreting your data in a specific way. Your reader should have some sense that your interpretations represent an exhaustive search for meaning from all your findings. Your explanations of the meaning drawn from the data should be multidimensional. The reader should get the sense that you have looked at your findings from different angles, that you have taken into account all the information relevant to the analysis, that you have identified and discussed the most important themes, and that your argument is systematically constructed. In the defense, you must be prepared to clarify your interpretations and defend your thinking while listening to alternative perspectives.

Your effort to uncover patterns and themes among your findings, as well as provide a variety of interpretations, involves both creativity and critical thinking. You need to make creative but also careful judgments about what you see as significant and meaningful. In this regard, you rely on your own experience, knowledge, and skills. However, analysis need not be a solitary endeavor—indeed it should not be. Although you are certainly the closest person to your study, discussion, dialogue, and debate with critical colleagues and advisors will certainly be helpful as you look at the findings from a variety of angles and vantage points. Analysis is all about learning what emerges from the findings of your research, and sharing perspectives through dialogue lies at the heart of learning.

Synthesis

Qualitative research involves the move from a holistic perspective to individual parts (analysis) and then back to a holistic look at the data (synthesis). Whereas the findings chapters split apart and separated out pieces and chunks of data to tell the "story of the research," the analysis chapter is an attempt to reconstruct a holistic understanding of your study. Analysis is intended to ultimately depict an integrated picture. What should emerge from your discussion is a layered synthesis. Synthesis is the process of pulling everything together—that is, (a) how the research questions are answered by the findings (b) to what extent the findings emanating from your data-collection methods can be interpreted in the same way, (c) how your findings relate to the literature, and (d) how the findings relate to the researcher's prior assumptions about the study. Synthesis is not, however, a linear process.

As you move toward interpretations about causes, consequences, connections, and relationships, you must be careful to avoid the simplistic linear thinking that characterizes quantitative analysis, which deals with variables that are mechanically linked out of context. Qualitative analysis is about portraying a holistic picture of the phenomenon under study to understand the nature of the phenomenon—which is usually extremely complex—within a given specific context. As such, synthesis becomes key.

Synthesis is ongoing throughout the analytical process. Synthesis is about combining the individual units of analysis into a more integrated whole. You need to account for all the major dimensions that you have studied. From your intimate familiarity with your data, you create a cohesive whole from the isolated bits and pieces. You also need to lead your reader to focus on the larger issues—the broader context. Analysis is ultimately about capturing the meaning or essence of the phenomenon and expressing it so that it fits into a larger picture. One problem that tends to occur is that we become so immersed in a highly specific research topic that we are unable to step back and think about more general and fundamental disciplinary frameworks. Give your research a broader perspective by thinking about how what you have discovered may relate to issues that are broader than your original research topic. Narrowly defined research problems are related to broader social issues. As Coffey and Atkinson (1996) argue:

> Qualitative data, analyzed with close attention to detail, understood in terms of their internal patterns and forms, should be used to develop theoretical ideas about social processes and cultural forms that have relevance beyond these data themselves. (p. 63)

As we have stressed throughout, there is no one "right" way to analyze your findings. You will not be judged on your analysis per se, but rather on your synthesis—that is, the way in which you have organized your discussion around major themes, issues, or topics, and the ways in which you have woven these together. What is of importance is the logic and coherence of your argument, how effectively you have tied your argument to the literature and prior research, and your ability to sweep your discussion into some broad and relevant discourse.

A final word on analysis: Qualitative analysis and interpretation are both an art and a science, and herein lies the tension. Qualitative inquiry draws on a critical as well as a creative attitude. The scientific part demands a systematic, rigorous, and disciplined approach and an intellectually critical perspective. The artistic dimension invites exploration, discovery, insight, innovation, and creativity to generate new possibilities and new ideas. The technical, procedural, and scientific side of analysis is easier to present and teach. Creativity is more difficult to distill and describe. Remember that each analysis is a unique expression of the researcher's skill and creativity. As you approach the analysis of your findings, remain open to new and unexpected possibilities. Be prepared to tolerate ambiguity. Have faith and trust in yourself as a thinker. Spend much time brainstorming. Also take the time to dialogue with others.

Presenting Your Analysis and Synthesis

Overview

In qualitative research, the emphasis is on understanding. You are not seeking to determine any single causal explanation, to predict, or to generalize. Your aim is to tell a richly detailed story that takes into account and respects a context and that connects participants, events, processes, activities, and experiences to larger issues or phenomena. As the researcher, it is your responsibility to explain in great detail what you have found—what you have discovered from your data, the sense you make of it, and what new insights you now have about the phenomenon under discussion. In this chapter, you serve as a guide to your readers, helping them to understand the findings of your study based on your intensive and careful analysis. The chapter is essentially a well-thought-out conversation that integrates your findings with literature, research, and practice.

Just as there is no one correct way to analyze findings, there is no one correct way to organize this chapter. The structure varies depending on your methodology, the findings, and your advisor's preferences. With the process being a highly intuitive one, and with the real learning taking place in the doing, what we offer is a set of guidelines, a way to proceed based on some strategies that have worked for us in our own research. Our hope is that these guidelines are useful to you in stimulating further thinking and ideas of how you might go about presenting this chapter of your dissertation.

A Set of Guidelines

Begin with a brief introductory paragraph that includes your research purpose statement as you have identified it in chapter 1, as well as a preview of how the chapter is organized so that the reader knows what to expect. Include a summary of the major findings and some explanation of how you have gone about analyzing and synthesizing your data. Exemplary dissertations provide sufficient information that enables the reader to envision all the steps that the researcher undertook in preparing and organizing the data. By providing a window into your procedures for analyzing the data, you assure the reader of your attempt to provide an impartial analysis. Moreover, you allow others who might want to follow the same procedures to do so, thereby establishing an audit trail, which contributes to the validity of your study. When professional colleagues are able to follow your line of reasoning, they have a more solid basis for determining the credibility of your study.

To offer this explicit documentation of your analytical procedures, both in the dissertation as well as at the oral defense, you have to make careful and detailed notes of all the steps you have gone though in the process of analysis, including even the ones that subsequently turned out to be dead ends or unsuccessful. Your explanation of all the decisions and choices that you made along the way conveys a sense of care about how you conducted your research and will promote the credibility of your interpretations.

Once you have introduced your reader to the chapter and given some indication of how the chapter is organized, you need to pull apart all the areas and discuss each one separately. Always remember to make one point at a time and fully flesh it out before moving on to the next point. This rule applies to all writing, especially to writing your analysis. Discuss each point from different perspectives, but stay on target. Avoid redundancy or repetition. Some material might need to be cut, placed in other sections, or saved until later. It is crucial that the reader be able to follow the logic of your argument and grasp what it is that you are trying to communicate. Do not distract the reader by too many arguments and/or ideas at once. Applying too many concepts at once can make your analysis confusing. Achieving a high-level product requires careful thinking on your part; therefore, revisions and redrafting are to be expected.

Analysis is a multilayered approach. When writing this chapter, keep in mind various key aspects:

- Establish the story line based on your findings. Based on that story, what do you think may really be going on? Think deeper as you go through all of the following levels:

  1. Level 1 means looking at each individual finding (i.e., going finding by finding). Ask yourself what each of the findings mean. What are all the possible explanations for what is being said by your participants?

  2. Level 2 means looking across your findings. Ask yourself how the findings are related and/or interconnected with each other? To what extent do the findings impact each other?

  3. Level 3 means looking across cases (i.e., cross-case analysis). Remember, each person is a "case." Here we look for similarities and differences among participants. You can address these issues by way of your interpretation outline tool (see Appendix Y).

- Structure your discussion by using headings. For example, you may choose to use your research questions or the analytic categories of your conceptual framework. Think carefully of how you can most logically and interestingly set up your discussion.

- When discussing your findings, carefully choose your words. Use qualifiers such as *seems, appears, possible, probable, likely, unlikely,* and so on. In your discussion, you offer ideas, suggest explanations, and/or identify reasons; you do not state facts. You speculate, and therefore you cannot come across as definitive or dogmatic.

- In the course of the discussion, identify any qualifications and/or limitations of factors, such as age, gender, and context, with respect to your findings. Make sure to mention that you have done extensive cross-case analysis, which enables readers to follow your interpretation and judge whether it is plausible. It also enables you to review your own thinking and perhaps find weaknesses or limitations within your discussion, which will then have to be addressed and remedied.

- Analysis is not just a naïve list of findings. In your discussion, you need to weave together the findings from the various data-collection methods that you have used. You do this to demonstrate that each of the methods you have used contributes similarly to the same analysis.

- It is your responsibility to convince your readers of the accuracy of your analysis by providing sufficient descriptive information for them to make independent judgments. Be sure to discuss the findings of your study with respect to the literature and prior research. The intent is that the inferences that you are making from your findings in combination with what the literature says will make a compelling argument. Overall, it is important for the reader to know the ways in which your study contributes to the current knowledge base. What are the differences between your study and the findings of previous studies? How do your findings compare with what the literature says? Do your findings help clarify contradictions in the literature? Do your findings go beyond the literature, breaking new ground? Are there any surprises? Surprises are the unanticipated outcomes of your study that may in some way contradict current thinking.

- Aside from including the relevant literature citations, also be sure to weave into your discussion direct participant quotations. The more support you can provide for your discussion, the more likely your readers will be to concur with your analysis.

Your interpretations, that is, your conjectures as to what the findings really mean should be clear, logical, relevant, and credible:

- *Clear* interpretations are easy to follow. If the reader has difficulty following your train of thought, you run the risk of losing the reader. Information must be presented systematically, and sufficient details must be provided to enable the reader to understand the issues as presented. Information that is presented in tables should always be preceded by a narrative that describes the table.

- Readers will consider your interpretation *logical* if you have presented your discussion in a systematic and thoughtful way. Based on your own understanding of your findings, you should decide which issues need to be addressed first and how the remainder of the discussion will flow naturally from those issues (your interpretation outline tool is your sketch of the order in which you will discuss your findings). Your presentation should lead your readers to understand your findings as clearly as you do.

- Your interpretation must be *relevant*; that is, it must be directly related to the research problem, purpose, and research questions that have guided your research. It also must relate to the literature and/or theoretical base within which your study is situated. Make sure to keep your interpretation tight and focused. Whereas your findings chapter includes a multitude of elements, you now need to focus only on the most important and relevant issues and highlight and address the most prominent findings of your research. Determining the major issues may be viewed as a judgment call on your part. However, you are the person most familiar with your data, and thus you are in a position to help the reader recognize and accept your focus. A good idea is to run your ideas by others, thereby remaining open to different understandings and acknowledging different perspectives.

- Establishing *credibility* in qualitative research means that you have engaged in the systematic search for rival or competing explanations and interpretations. Think carefully about other logical possibilities and see whether those can be supported by the findings and the literature. In doing this, you should not be focused on attempting to disprove alternatives. You are not looking for clear-cut "yes" or "no" answers. Rather, you are searching for the best fit. As such, seek support for alternative ways of seeing things. Also keep track of and report alternative classification systems, patterns/themes, and explanations that you have considered during your analysis, which

demonstrates intellectual integrity and lends credibility to your study.

In thinking carefully about what meaning may lie behind the findings—that is, what is really driving your findings—researchers frequently create visual displays—figures and tables. These displays organize the findings diagrammatically and illustrate the relationships among identified topics, categories, and patterns. Visuals are useful for demonstrating linkages and connections as well as differences within each case, across cases, across categories, as well as by demographics or other dimensions. The information enables the reader to clearly see and understand issues and concepts discussed in the narrative. In addition to augmenting your discussion, constructing diagrams or charts can help you with your analytical thinking. Displays often help you "see" some aspect of your findings in new ways. Through displays you might notice emergent trends, discover new connections or relationships, or even recognize the significance of certain pieces of information or lack thereof.

If you choose to include visuals, give careful thought to the most logical place to insert them so as not to interrupt the flow of the discussion. If the diagrams are working tools, they are typically included as appendices. There are different ways of constructing diagrams, charts, and graphs in the analysis of qualitative data. In this regard, Miles and Huberman (1994) and Booth et al. (2003) offer excellent suggestions. Make sure that all information presented in tables is consistent with information presented in the narrative.

Finally, tie together the various threads of the discussion. As such, there should be a strong culminating paragraph that provides a summary of the whole chapter. This summary should include the key points made, as well as some form of reflection on the analytic process. You also might choose now to revisit your initial assumptions (stated in your first chapter) and comment on these in light of your findings. The researcher-as-instrument is an inquirer, writer, analyst, and interpreter. We have to leave open the possibility that other researchers might have told a different story given the same set of data. What we learn from our research, how we understand what we find, and how we report it is but one view. Some acknowledgment that there are multiple ways of interpreting data will serve to show that you fully understand the subjective nature of qualitative research. Such an acknowledgment further enhances your study's credibility in the eye of the reader.

There are many subtleties involved in the kind of detailed analysis that is required for a qualitative dissertation. As such, it is unlikely that you will achieve a well-argued, reader-friendly analysis chapter in one go. Writing this chapter takes many hours of thinking and rethinking, and much tightening up is involved to ensure the logic, depth, and breadth of your argument. Based on your advisor's feedback, you usually have to write and rewrite drafts of this chapter, revising and/or expanding sections of it accordingly. In most cases, this step may occur more frequently than you anticipated, as you work toward organizing the sections into a cohesive and powerful chapter that explains your findings. If your interpretation is thoughtful, logical, and reasonable, it is more likely to be compelling to your readers. In addition, it will provide the opportunity for an informed discussion, making a worthwhile contribution to your academic discipline.

Following is the application section, which demonstrates the salient features of an analysis chapter in terms of how it should be structured and the interpretive style it should take on. However, please be aware that what we present in Section II is a sketch of what an analysis chapter might look like, rather than a full-blown analysis of the findings. In a real dissertation, the discussion would be further elaborated to achieve deeper and richer levels of analysis and synthesis.

SECTION II: APPLICATION

CHAPTER V
Analysis, Interpretation, and Synthesis of Findings

The purpose of this multicase study was to explore with a sample group of ABDs their perceptions of why they had not managed to complete their dissertations. It was hoped that a better understanding of the perceptions of students struggling at various stages of the dissertations process, as well as those students who have become inactive, would provide insight about how to encourage and support other current and future students to successfully conduct their research, write the dissertation, and obtain the desired doctoral degree.

This research used naturalistic inquiry to collect qualitative data by conducting in-depth interviews and collecting supportive data by use of critical incidents and a focus group discussion. Participants in the study included 20 current and former doctoral candidates. The data were coded, analyzed, and organized first by research question and then by categories and subcategories guided by the conceptual framework, as depicted in chapter 2. The study was based on the following five research questions:

1. Upon completion of the coursework, to what extent did participants perceive they were prepared to conduct research and write the dissertations?

2. What did participants perceive they needed to learn to complete their dissertations?

3. How did participants acquire the knowledge, skills, and attitudes they perceived were necessary to complete their dissertations?

4. What factors did participants perceive might help them to complete their dissertations?

5. What factors did participants perceive have impeded and/or continue to impede their progress in working toward completing their dissertations?

These five research questions were largely satisfied by the findings presented in chapter 4. The overriding finding in this study revealed that students perceived the coursework did not prepare them for the dissertation process. This perceived disconnect between the coursework and understanding and knowing how to carry out the research was compounded by the fact that students perceived lack of timely, consistent, and helpful advisement as a further impediment to their progress. As a consequence, students were left to rely on themselves, their self-directed activities, and the help they received from colleagues and other faculty and experts.

This chapter analyzes, interprets, and synthesizes the findings. The chapter is organized by the following analytic categories:

1. The relationship between coursework and students' ability to complete their dissertations. (*Research Question 1*)

2. Perceptions of what students needed to learn and how they acquired the learning they needed. (*Research Questions 2 and 3*)

3. Supports and barriers influencing students' progress. (*Research Questions 4 and 5*)

The prior analytic categories are directly aligned with each of this study's research questions. These same analytic categories were used to code the data and present the findings in the previous chapter. In the analysis, the researcher searches primarily for connecting patterns within the analytic categories, as well as the connections or themes that may emerge among the various categories. As a secondary level of analysis, the relevant theory and research is tied in, as these themes are compared and contrasted to issues raised by the literature.

The previous chapter presented the findings of this study by organizing data from various sources into categories to produce a readable narrative. The purpose of this chapter is to provide interpretative insights into these findings. Whereas the findings chapter split apart and separated out pieces and chunks of data to tell the "story of the research," this chapter is an attempt to reconstruct a more holistic understanding. Analysis is intended to depict a more integrated picture, and what emerges is a layered synthesis. Throughout the process, the elements that continued to frame the analysis were (a) connective threads among the experiences of the research participants, (b) ways in which participants understand and explain these connections, (c) unexpected as well as anticipated relationships and connections, (d) consistency or inconsistency with the literature, and (e) ways in which the data go beyond the literature.

The discussion takes into consideration the literature on higher education and doctoral programs and adult learning. The implications of these findings are intended to augment the understanding of the perceptions of why some students are unable to manage completion of their research and the resultant dissertation. The chapter concludes with a reexamination of the researcher's assumptions, which were identified in the first chapter, and a summary that incorporates a note regarding the effect of possible researcher bias in interpreting the findings.

Analytic Category 1: The Relationship Between Coursework and Students' Ability to Complete Their Dissertations

The first research question sought to determine how well participants understood what they needed to know, and what they needed to be able to do to successfully conduct research and write the dissertations once they completed the coursework. Participants indicated that there was a disassociation between the first part of the doctoral program, the coursework, and what follows as doctoral candidates engaged in the research and dissertation writing process. One of the participants, Morris, reflected this view when he said: "I didn't get the information during the coursework. I didn't pick up what I needed to know about actually doing research and what's worse, I didn't know how to find it out." Sternberg, author and professor emeritus at John Jay College, gives credence to this perspective when he says:

> ...the real issues are sociological and structural in the formation, the way the whole doctoral process is shaped. And then linked to that, of course, is that after you have finished your comprehensives, you just fall off the cliff, there is no linkage at all in that sense. You know the dissertation is seen as a trial by fire, you have got to do it yourself. (personal communication, September 14, 2006)

At the same time, casting the onus for not being able to complete the dissertation solely on the design and structure of particular doctoral programs may be misplaced. Such an assertion might be warranted because a number of studies dealing with possible causes of high attrition rates among doctoral students identify not only issues of program design, but factors directly related to students' idiosyncrasies (Bourner, Bowden, & Laing, 2001; Hawlery, 2003; Hockey, 1994; Lewis, Ginsberg, Davies, & Smith, 2004).

Let us consider the implications of both perspectives—that of doctoral programs and the students enrolled in those programs. It can be argued that the primary purpose of institutions of higher education is to foster critical thinking by exposing students to philosophical and theoretical concepts, and to the various bodies of literature that inform theory. Therefore, the focus of doctoral programs is not so much to demonstrate the practical application of theory, but rather to expand and build on existing theory and/or to fill gaps that may exist in the literature.

Hawlery (2003) expands on the purpose of doctoral programs as the development of academic scholarship, rather than the training and development of practitioners. The author points out that new psychological and intellectual demands are placed on doctoral students. The author describes the implications of both demands in this way:

> In most disciplines, the Ph.D. is considered a research degree and means that its primary purpose is not to prepare practitioners, clinicians and teachers but to produce scholars. If you want to be considered a scholar, you must do research. This calls for a major transition in how you think and what you do. (p. 21)

Although attrition in doctoral programs is high (estimated at 50% nationwide; Berg, 2007; Lazerson, 2003; Lovitts & Nelson, 2000; Smallwood, 2004), it also can be said that another 50% of students, exposed to the same coursework, are successful in completing their dissertations and subsequently earn their doctoral degrees. This finding suggests that there may be innate or idiosyncratic student characteristics that cause some to succeed in attaining their degrees—despite the fact that coursework does not prepare them in the practical application of research—while others remain unable to complete their dissertations. In addition to possible personal characteristics, there also may be environmental factors that contribute to students' success.

Taking on doctoral work can be overwhelming and can place a psychological burden on some students, for which they are unprepared. Karen, one of the participants who commented on this, said: "It (the dissertation) is an overwhelming task and one doesn't have experience with it and so it can be very anxiety provoking."

Lovitts (2001) explains the dissertation process as complex, long, and daunting, and one in which students have little or no experience. The author notes:

> These are complex processes with which most students have little familiarity or prior experience. Students who reach this stage know (or discover) that they must conduct research that distinguishes them from their peers. Most feel inadequately prepared to do this type of research and find themselves unprepared for the writing in the style required for a dissertation. (p. 72)

Although lack of experience can lead to confusion and even debilitation, and although the coursework has not adequately prepared students, this impasse may only be temporary as students begin learning by doing. Meloy (1994) found that, for novice qualitative researchers, developing a sense of the project's coherence was dictated by the project, rather than any suggested a priori plan or program structure. As she explains:

> One of the most common ways we have of learning to do something is *by doing it.* But unlike fastening our shoes or baking a cake, "doing research" is becoming more complex and controversial. Although qualitative researchers are making substantial contributions to scholarship by describing not only how research is conceptualized but also how its products are finally presented and understood, there is for novice researchers, and traditionally trained faculty members across the wide array of disciplines, a down side. As the number of methodological options and alternative presentations increases, so does the ambiguity. (p. xi)

In terms of her own research, Meloy (1994) acknowledges that her coursework did not fully prepare her to do qualitative research, and she recounts her experience by saying:

> In spite of my coursework, I had no idea of what it felt like to do research. Writing the dissertation was an experience in itself. Adding qualitative research on top of that made for an especially interesting time of learning, reflection, and practice. (p. 2)

Indeed, unlike quantitative research, qualitative research is not structured, systematic, and procedural. As such, coursework cannot fully prepare the student for the experience of actually doing it; that is, conducting the research and writing the dissertation. Moreover, aside from the necessary research skills, the level of writing skill required in a dissertation is something that is not easily taught. Thus, it can be reasonably argued that coursework cannot be expected to prepare the student for academic writing of a project as intense and complex as a dissertation.

Although some faculty and administrators view lack of progress or even attrition as a function of students' academic ability, motivation, or commitment, Lovitts (2001) and other researchers

suggest it is a constellation of psychological/personal and structural factors that explains why some students are not able to complete their dissertations while others succeed. Thus, it appears to the researcher that ABD status and attrition rates cannot be placed solely at the doorstep of the institution or squarely on the shoulders of students. Rather, students' progress in doctoral programs might be better understood as the dynamic interaction of students and the institutional context.

Being unprepared may mean, in a sense, that students are unsocialized as to the scope and meaning of a doctoral dissertation (Bauer & Green, 1994; Sternberg, 1981). This notion brings into play the idea of a doctoral dissertation as an institution in itself; that is, the traditional model of a dissertation and all the expectations that go along with it. This theory includes the political aspects involved with faculty, the university system, institutional protocol (ambiguities, nuances, rules, regulations), and working with committee members who often have differing and sometimes even competing requirements. Students often do not have a clear grasp of the policies and procedures involved. The system of dissertation work and all the expectations surrounding that system are unfamiliar to them—hence the general feeling of unpreparedness.

The above notwithstanding, there are still some doctoral faculty who feel the main reason that students do not progress and some even drop out of doctoral programs is because of some aspect of the student's background. Hawlery (2003) raises this perspective in her book about the doctoral experiences and feelings of graduating students when she says:

> ...standing behind each smiling graduate is the shadow of another person who also expected to be there on the auspicious occasion, but dropped out somewhere along the way. Are these "shadow people" intellectually inferior to those who stayed the course and received their PhD? Is the graduation ceremony portrayed here simply an example of Social Darwinism in which only the fittest (brightest) survive? (p. 3)

To address their perspective, doctoral faculty in some programs have tried to tighten up the admission requirements for enrollment into their programs so as to admit only those students who are able to withstand the pressures of doctoral work (Lovitts, 2001). However, it is interesting to note that more stringent admission requirements in a number of doctoral programs have not affected the dropout rates, which continue to be high (Lovitts & Nelson, 2000) According to Lovitts (2001), those who enter doctoral programs are high achievers in the base case; they are people who have prior academic experience that often includes numerous honors and academic awards, and yet they are among the best and brightest who drop out of doctoral programs. Having taken the onus solely off the students, Lovitts (2001) identifies three reasons for the stagnation and/or dropout rates within doctoral programs, which the author sees more as a function of the interaction of students and the institution. She describes these as:

1. It is not the background characteristics that students bring with them to the university that affects their persistence outcomes; it is what happens to them after they arrive.

2. Graduate student attrition is a function of the distribution of structures and opportunities for integration and cognitive map development.

3. The causes of attrition are deeply embedded in the organizational culture of graduate school and the structure and process of graduate education. (p. 2)

Azad and Kohun (2006) attribute feelings of isolation among doctoral students as a major factor affecting their progress. The authors point out that, "...despite this recognition, the feeling of isolation has yet to be addressed fully in the design of some doctoral programs" (p. 21). The authors find support from others in the academic community that most doctoral programs are not designed to specifically address the emotional needs, social feelings of estrangement, and/or inadequacy experienced by matriculating doctoral students. In other words, the design of most doctoral programs does not provide a supportive environment for students to successfully complete their dissertations and obtain their degrees (Azad & Kohun, 2006; Berg, 2007; Hawley, 2003; Lovitts, 2001; Lovitts & Nelson, 2000).

Lack of progress in a doctoral program also may be a function of mutually exclusive expectations on the part of program faculty and the students they enroll. One of the participants in this study wrote the following in his critical incident:

> It was the constantly changing expectations among the committee members themselves about what I was expected to do and how I was expected to do it. I was writing various chapters and I had constant and conflicting messages about what I was supposed to write and how I was supposed to write it and that was very frustrating. (Hank)

As one of the participants who said that her expectations were not met described:

> While I found the coursework intellectually stimulating, I was learning a lot, the language, the terminology, the theory. But once I was on my own I had this expectation that I would be given some guidance around actually doing the research, writing the dissertation—and it just wasn't there. Then I started to think it's a matter of learning along the way and it is up to me to figure it out— but somehow I keep thinking it shouldn't be that way. (Jane)

Brause's (2004) study lends support to the expectations of some doctoral students with regard to the dissertation process and what they believed were the obstacles that stood in their way. One participant in Brause's study described it this way: "I sought assistance in understanding a process which has seemingly been cloaked in 'darkness and secrecy'" (p. 143). Lovitts (1996) also reports that doctoral students understand formal program requirements, but often do not have a good understanding of the informal expectations vis-à-vis carrying out the work. From the perspective of the doctoral program faculty, there may well be an unspoken expectation that the rigors of producing a dissertation require students to be highly self-directed given their view that the doctorate is a terminal degree of intellectual import and of the highest prestige. Hawlery (2003) explains this perception of doctoral faculty in this way:

> It is understandable that academics view the cognitive realm as their primary domain and intellectual accomplishment as their primary mission. Few would argue with this focus. Nevertheless, there are vast differences among faculty in the degree to which they recognize the psychological components implicit in an understanding of this kind. It is subjectively painful experiences that underlie most students' decision to quit, yet many doctoral faculties refuse to concern themselves with that they see as non-cognitive matters. (p. 24)

With regard to the differing expectations, research studies have shown that when students are given timely, relevant information about the program and, as importantly, the doctoral process, they are better able to develop good working relationships and are able to maintain their commitment to the program (Bauer & Green, 1994). This sentiment was expressed by many participants in this study and was best reflected by one, who said:

> I think at the beginning of the course work there needs to be some additional assistance as to how to get people to begin thinking about their dissertation, because indirectly everything is associated, in my opinion, with the dissertation. So I think there could have been a better job done with an overview that keeps getting referred to as one goes through the coursework, so as one moves forward in the classes one can see the relevancy. And there should be more about what's expected, you know what lies ahead. More direction would have been very helpful to me. (Debbie)

In summary, it has been argued in the foregoing that the lack of student progress and even student departure cannot be attributed solely to the fact that coursework does not typically prepare students to conduct research and write their dissertations. This view is posited because the intent of coursework is primarily designed to provide a sound theoretical foundation for subsequent research and not to address the practical application of theory. At the same time, there are significant psychological and social aspects that affect students' ability to carry out this work, most notably issues of self-efficacy and feelings of isolation.

In many cases, psychological symptoms and social feelings of estrangement and/or isolation experienced by students may be a function of the ambiguity within which the academy portrays the research process during the coursework. Participants characterized this phenomenon as "shrouded in mystery." Therefore, it appears there should be opportunities in the design of doctoral programs to demystify the research process without sacrificing the intellectual rigor intended to escalate higher-order thinking among students. The following comments reflect participants' strong reactions when what is expected is not made explicit by the faculty:

> I think it's [the dissertation] a terrifying process, I really do. And, I don't know that faculty really wants to disarm anybody of what it's all about because it may take away their mystique....I don't know. I'm just guessing. So you are left with this feeling of loneliness—like you are hanging out in the wind, and it's overwhelming. (Anne)

> What I have come to realize as I get further involved in this work is that there is something of a mechanical process to putting this dissertation together. And you know if they had explained how these pieces all fit when I was taking classes, it didn't have to be such a mystery, and it doesn't have to be so difficult. And I wonder sometimes if the field—doctoral programs in general—if they just try to make if difficult for students . . . you know, a rite of passage or whatever! (Doris)

The prior comments illustrate the sense of isolation that students experience in the absence of not knowing what is expected and what lies ahead. Research suggests that the more students are informed about the process, the more they are integrated into the academic community, and the more they feel part of its social life, the less likely it is that students will feel isolated and the more likely it is that they will persist in the program (Lovitts, 2001; Tinto, 1993). In light of this notion, it appears that mechanisms need to be put in place to clarify expectations that faculty have of students and what students can reasonably expect of faculty; it is really a question of shared responsibility.

Analytic Category 2: Students' Perceptions of What They Needed to Learn and How They Acquired the Learning They Needed

The perception of the overwhelming majority of participants in this study that the coursework did not prepare them to do research may explain why they also reported they were left to rely on their own resources and the help of colleagues to identify what they needed to learn. The findings revealed that all participants in this study indicated they needed to either (a) acquire knowledge about the *content* involved in doing research, and/or (b) understand what they actually had to do to carry out the *process* of conducting research.

On the surface, it appears obvious that if students felt the coursework did not prepare them to carry out research and write their dissertations, they would seek that information and knowledge elsewhere. However, this may not necessarily be attributed to a failure of the coursework. It may likely be that students were more focused on meeting the demands of the coursework and not looking beyond to the potential relevancy of the theories to which they were being exposed and how those theories might subsequently inform their future research. Knowles (1980) provides support for this likelihood when he says:

> Adults . . . tend to have a perspective of immediacy of application toward most of their learning. They engage in learning largely in response to pressures they feel from their current life situation. To adults, education is a process of improving their ability to cope with life problems they face now. They tend, therefore, to enter an educational activity in a problem-centered or performance-centered frame of mind. (p. 53)

This may well be the "frame of mind" of many participants in this study, who were focused on the demands of the coursework and not the application of what they were learning to subsequent practice. One of the participants expressed it this way:

> As I was going through the coursework I was paying a lot of attention to other papers and things. And the research stuff got very much pushed aside for me in my own mind. And it was, well, you know what, I don't have to deal with that right now. I'm going to have to do that at the end of it. But I've really got to get this paper done, and I really have to do well in this class. And I know that when the research stuff was presented, there was something in my unconscious that was saying "you know what, you can learn this later." (Mollie)

This idea may be further understood in light of what Knowles (1980) describes as having a "readiness to learn" and the associated "timing of the learning." Knowles reminds us that adults must be ready to receive the learning, and this readiness constitutes what he calls a "teachable moment." In other words, presentation of the learning must be timed or in step with a particular stage of development. In this case, development can be understood as students' maturation within the doctoral program.

The majority of participants in this study completed the coursework with content knowledge relative to theory, but not content knowledge relative to the practical aspects of what to research and how to conduct the research. The work of Beeler (1991) may provide some further insights. Beeler describes four stages he says students experience as they move through the doctoral journey: (a) unconscious incompetence, (b) conscious incompetence, (c) unconscious competence, and (d) conscious competence. These stages may explain why students in this study were not ready to relate the theories to which they were being exposed to the practical application of research.

The essence of good research is its content; it must be sound, authentic, and researchable. In other words, the subject of inquiry, the problem or phenomenon, must be one that warrants investigation. Several participants in this study described their struggle after the coursework to identify a problem about which meaningful research could be conducted. One participant framed the dilemma in this way:

> It's a year later (after the coursework) and I am still at this impasse, as the problem really was/is how to develop a problem and purpose that is concrete and one that I can stick with, and I still seem to be having this problem. I'm also not sure what will get me over this impasse and what is at the source of it. (Shana)

Participants reported struggling throughout the process to understand *how* they should go about carrying out the research. In reflecting on the process as a whole, Brad, one of the participants, summed up a prevailing view when he said: "If I had more of the *how,* I could have been further along sooner, but I try not to focus on what wasn't but what I have to do now." Another participant described her struggle and frustration with trying to understand what to do in a critical incident form:

> Looking back to the long process of the dissertation research, one critical stage for me started after my proposal defense when I had the pilot data when I needed guidance on how to code the data so as to pave the way for my later data analysis. When I asked for help, I didn't get the guidance or the direction I was looking for. I was just told—go read the works of so and so, and I struggled a long time with this trying to code every line before I had a breakthrough with the help of a colleague. (Jane)

The struggle of students who lacked the knowledge of what to do and how to do it also is reflected in Brause's (2004) study of the experiences of doctoral students as they engage in the dissertation process. In reporting the findings of her study, Brause notes that:

> The one constant theme was lack of knowledge. There was a clear desire to know as much as possible about the process so that they [students] could predict what was going to happen, allocate time and money wisely, and understand their roles in that process. . . . Explicit information, respondents believed, would make it easier to manage their responsibilities within and beyond their doctoral program, as well as enabling them to feel more knowledgeable about their progress. (p. 149)

In addition to the perception of the majority of participants that the coursework did not prepare them to conduct research and write their dissertations, they also had little confidence that they would learn what they needed from faculty and/or their advisors post-coursework. This perspective is best illustrated by a participant who explained it this way:

> For me, it comes down to how the dissertation process is handled, and how much support you get from faculty once you get to that point because that's where they lost me. I just couldn't get off square one for doing a dissertation, and I did three proposals with an advisor who kept saying: "well that's not it yet; I'll know it when I see it." So, it was that kind of response. They gave me no guidelines. My guess is that this advisor didn't have a clue himself. I think when he said he'd know it when he saw it, he really did look to the student to try and figure it out on their own or get help from someplace else on campus. (Anne)

Further, it might be that some students were simply unmotivated to move forward with the dissertation work. Having spent many years at this point in the doctoral program, it might simply be that they lacked the necessary energy to continue; that they were, in effect, running out of steam. As one of the participants stated:

At this point [following completion of course-work] I was simply exhausted. I had just about come to the end of my tether.... Yes, I badly wanted the doctorate—otherwise why would I have enrolled in the first place? But let's face it, I had a life too, and many commitments, including a family who needed me. I weighed the pros and cons and the toll the doctoral work had taken on my life so far, and I started to question whether I really wanted this thing [the doctorate] so badly after all. (Frank)

It cannot be assumed that students who enroll in doctoral program will necessarily be motivated. Motivation is indeed a factor that cannot be taken for granted in terms of adults' participation in learning experiences and in their subsequent learning success (Houle, 1988; Knowles, 1998; Merriam & Caffarella, 1999; Wlodkowski, 1985; Wlodkowski & Ginsberg, 1995). Knowing why some doctoral students do not progress and what deters their progress is a function of the extent to which intrinsic and/or extrinsic motivating factors are compelling. In the present study, when participants were asked what prompted them to enroll in a doctoral program, almost equal numbers cited extrinsic and intrinsic motivating factors. Therefore, one can surmise that, in this case, motivation was not determined by any one particular motivating factor—either extrinsic or intrinsic—but rather by the *intensity* of the factors at play.

In light of the lack of formal preparation during coursework and formal guidance post-course work, as cited earlier, participants went about learning informally by relying primarily on themselves and their colleagues—those others who were, in their view, "in the same boat." This mode of learning is not so much an anomaly, but rather is consistent with the concept in the literature that says adults learn largely through informal means. In fact, it is in the informal domain that most learning occurs. Marsick and Volpe (1999) define *informal learning* as "learning that is predominantly unstructured, experiential and non-institutional. Informal learning takes place as people go about their daily activities at work or in other spheres of life" (p. 4). As such, the authors

view informal learning as integral to daily life and say, further, that its value comes from the fact that " it occurs 'just in time' as people face a challenge, problem or unanticipated need. By its nature, such learning cannot be fully preprogrammed; it arises spontaneously within the context of real work" (p. 4).

Learning informally requires individuals to engage in self-directed activities, either through interactions with others or independent of others. Candy (1991) characterizes self-directed learners as individuals who take responsibility for their own learning and do not rely on others to tell them what they need to learn. Nor do they rely on structured programs for their learning. Therefore, it was not surprising to see that the participants in this study sought to learn what they needed primarily by engaging in dialogue with colleagues and, to a lesser extent, by other solitary activities, such as reading relevant texts and completed dissertations and conducting literature searches for the kinds of information they needed.

Some participants expressed a clear preference for finding things out on their own. For example, in reflecting on the advice she might give to new doctoral students, Debbie commented: "I would tell someone they really need to read, read, read—get a hold of as many dissertations as you can, and examine how they are structured. It helped me a lot, and this was the main way that I figured things out." Other participants, like Lin, talked about "losing themselves for hours in the online library." Angela talked about how invaluable the Internet was in helping her find the information she needed.

The following comment describes the value that most participants in this study placed on having colleagues to talk to and with whom they could brainstorm:

I just started reaching out to my some of my peers and I found they would listen, they understood and a lot of the time, I would walk away just a little bit clearer. You know, you get another perspective, another way of looking at things when you talk it over with someone or with other people. I tried to be there for others when they needed to talk, to discuss ideas or even just listen when they needed to vent; after all they had done that for me. And I don't think I would still be in the program if it weren't for some of my classmates. (Karen)

Many participants maintained consistent communication with colleagues, as one participant, Fay, noted: "After the coursework, we formed a small group and we kept in touch and still do—there's a lot of caring, and we continue to help one another and we share information." The value that participants in this study placed on their interactions with colleagues finds support generally in the adult learning literature, which places an emphasis on how collaboration, dialogue, and reflection are vehicles for learning (Brookfield, 1986, 1987; Merriam & Caffarella, 1999; Mezirow, 1991; Mezirow & Associates, 1990, 2000; Taylor, Marienau, & Fiddler, 2000). Learning from and with colleagues specifically within the context of doctoral work also finds support in the work of Meloy (1994) and Piantanida and Garman (1999). These researchers found that study groups with colleagues were a strong support factor for students in doctoral programs. Study groups, according to these researchers, were found to encourage scholarly development, generate thought-provoking issues with respect to qualitative research, provide opportunities for dialogue and reflection, and engender emotional support.

Although most participants were involved in self-directed activities to help them learn what they needed to progress in their work, some also mentioned that they received some help in the post-coursework seminars they attended. These seminars were described by participants as "less structured than typical coursework classes." Although students were provided with contextual material vis-à-vis research, the "discussions were largely informal." Interestingly, participants reported that students who attended these seminars were, in the words of Dexter, "not held accountable for producing work."

Lack of accountability may indeed promote a sense of complacency and allow students unspoken permission to avoid the real work of doing research and writing a dissertation. In contrast, having students set objectives and commit to producing a particular piece of work within a certain given time frame would create momentum for the students' progress. In this regard, lack of accountability may well have contributed to the high "time-to-completion" rate of participants in this study.

A further explanation as to why students did not find these seminars helpful may be due to the fact that they were not involved in setting objectives and planning. Indeed, one of the distinguishing characteristics of many adult learning programs is the shared control of program planning and facilitation (Knowles, 1998). Even when the learning content is, to a large extent, prescribed, sharing control over the learning strategies is believed to make learning more effective. Engaging adult students as collaborative partners satisfies their "need to know," as well as appeals to their self-concept as independent learners.

In summary, although working and learning through others is the primary way that adults learn, in the context of knowing what to do and how to complete research and write a dissertation may require the "others" to be informed experts. In other words, although it is important to have empathetic and supportive colleagues, in the absence of some form of formal, structured guidance and/or the accessibility of informed experts, collegial support may well be insufficient and actually slow down the process of completing arduous dissertation work. Further, although a fair amount of self-directed activities is necessary, such as reading other dissertations and searching the literature, time expended on these activities should be content-specific; that is, searching out information related specifically to the subject of inquiry at hand.

Analytic Category 3: Supports and Barriers Influencing Students' Progress

The perception of participants was that—in the absence of formal help either through coursework, faculty, or advisement—they had to rely on themselves and their colleagues to understand and carry out their research. In light of this perception, it is not surprising that participants would cite their own personal attributes or qualities as well as the help of colleagues as primary supports to them in their doctoral work. At the same time, participants cited access and availability of advisors and, in some cases, the quality of advisement as the single most significant impediment to their post-coursework progress. This perception raises a serious point of contention that warrants closer examination, especially given the pivotal role advisors play in doctoral programs. Lovitts (2001) sheds light on the importance of the advisor in this way:

> The advisor influences how the student comes to understand the discipline and roles and responsibilities of academic professionals, their socialization as a teacher and researcher, the selection of a dissertation topic, the quality of the dissertation and subsequent job placement. (p. 131)

Given the importance of advisement in the dissertation process, painting all advisors with the same brush may well be an unfair and unwarranted assumption. As previously mentioned, approximately half of the students who enroll in doctoral programs succeed in obtaining the degree. Thus, in light of the success of roughly half the population of doctoral students, it is likely that those students who completed their dissertations and obtained their doctoral degrees did receive the kind of guidance and support from advisors that is required. However, the fact that more than half of the participants in this study viewed the advisor relationship as an impediment does suggest the advisement that students received may not have been adequate. There may be several reasons that so many students in this study held this perspective. In many cases, the workload and professional demands placed on faculty can be daunting; hence, they may not always be able to meet students' expectations by providing timely and consistent guidance. Sternberg (1981) sheds light on why faculty members are not always consistently helpful to students. He says:

> From a sociological perspective, dissertation advising rates low as a career promoting activity. People are promoted, given tenure, receive more attractive offers from other universities principally in terms of what they publish themselves, certainly not for editing and advising the writing and publications of graduate students. (p. 17)

Consider as well that not all faculty members who provide advisement have the same level of commitment or the same degree of interest in the various research topics of all their advisees. Further, it also is conceivable that advisors can and do become frustrated by the lack of initiative and lack of progress of the part of some students despite the prodding, encouragement, and direction the advisor provides. Given these considerations, one explanation may be that it is easier and even more comfortable for students to blame their lack of progress on their advisors rather than on their own competencies, level of motivation, or even habits of laziness. Another explanation to consider is that conducting research and writing a dissertation is new terrain for most students, one for which most have little or no prior experience on which to draw. As such, it is difficult for students to have the confidence in their ability to carry out such a large-scale scholarly project without the support, encouragement, and direction of advisors who have traversed this terrain and, therefore, are content experts.

At the same time, it should be noted that two participants in this study did comment favorably on their relationship with their advisors. Sal, one of the two, said: "I am a very lucky person; my advisor gives me a lot of feedback, a lot of personal care, and a lot of dedication. I know that is not the case for everyone." Further, given that one-fourth of the participants did not mention advisement at all—either positively or negatively—may suggest that other personal and overriding issues impeded progress in addition to or beyond the student–advisor relationship.

Doctoral students face all the life issues and demands typical of adulthood. Therefore, it was not surprising that, in addition to lack of support from their advisors, participants also cited professional/work demands and personal family issues as significant challenges that stood in the way of their progress. As is the case in most doctoral programs, the participants in this study are working adults who have to manage the demands of both work and school.

In all cases, the participants in this study have to maintain employment to support themselves and their families as well as pay the "not insignificant" tuition. Maintaining balance between work and academic life is not easy; when the demands in one domain increase, productivity in the other may be affected. Maintaining this balance can be stressful, thus producing anxiety and even debilitation that threatens effectiveness in one domain or the other. The level of individual stress placed on students, as with many other adults, is often compounded by concern and worry about other personal, family, and/or health issues.

Because participants in this study perceived that they were not getting the formal help they needed from the coursework, the faculty, or their own advisors, they said they had to rely on themselves and their colleagues to get through the research process. Therefore, it is understandable that those participants who persist in the program would describe themselves as being resourceful and used terms such as *dedicated*, *committed*, *motivated*, and *self-directed* as personal characteristics that keep them going. It is likely that the kind of perseverance, and even tenacity, that these characteristics encapsulate are important elements contributing ultimately to a student's ability to successfully complete their dissertation.

In summary, why some students do not progress more quickly and why others abandon the process altogether is more likely the result of a complex set of factors. In other words, it does not appear to be a function of coursework not preparing students, advisors not providing guidance, students not being able to handle the pressures of daily life, or students not being sufficiently motivated or self-directed. Some or all of these factors impinge, to a lesser or greater extent, on the lives of all students. Despite these challenges, some students in doctoral programs persist and prevail, whereas others do not.

Revisiting Assumptions From Chapter 1

It is useful to revisit the five assumptions underlying this study that were stated in chapter 1. These assumptions were presented at the inception of this study and were based on the researchers' backgrounds and professional experiences. The five basic assumptions identified at the outset are discussed next in light of the analysis of this study's findings.

The first assumption underlying the research was that coursework does not prepare doctoral candidates to conduct research and write their dissertations. This assumption held true according to the first finding (chap. 4). The sample of students in this study expressly stated that the coursework did not prepare them to carry out the practical aspects of conducting research and writing their dissertations.

A second assumption posited by the researchers was that, because doctoral students are mature adults, they will be sufficiently self-reliant and self-directed and that will enable them to carry out research and write their dissertations. This assumption turned out to be partially true. Initially, students appeared to be dependent on the coursework and were not prepared to be self-directed. It was only when they had completed the coursework and realized they did not know the steps involved or how to proceed that they became self-reliant and were self-directed as they reached out to colleagues for help. This notion was illustrated in the third finding uncovered in this study.

The third assumption was that, because students were successful in completing all the course requirements, they would be able to achieve success in doing research. This assumption did not hold to be true. Judging by the slow progress and, in some cases, lack of progress of the sample students in this study, past academic success is not always or necessarily a predictor of future academic success.

The fourth assumption is that doctoral candidates do not always receive the direction and guidance they need from their advisors. This assumption held true given that the majority of participants cited the lack of good, timely, and consistent advisement as a major barrier standing in the way of their progress.

The fifth and final assumption is that people who enroll in doctoral programs are strongly motivated to obtain the doctoral degree and are thus likely to complete the dissertation. This assumption did not hold true given that motivation alone is insufficient to carry out doctoral work. This idea was illustrated in Finding 2, which revealed that students needed to understand the content and process involved in research and have the knowledge and skills required to complete their dissertations.

Summary of Interpretation of Findings

This chapter portrayed the dissertation experiences of a sample of doctoral candidates. In summary, the prior discussion illustrates the multifaceted and complex nature of the dissertation experience. The discussion reveals various reasons that students might feel unprepared following coursework. It offers an explanation as to what students feel they really need to know to conduct research and write a dissertation, why they then go about learning the way they do, and why certain factors are seen either as supports or barriers to their progress.

The endeavor of analyzing the findings was to produce a nuanced and multitiered, but holistic and integrated, synthesis. The challenge throughout data collection and data analysis, which were not separate but rather interlocking phases of this research, was to make sense of large amounts of data, reduce the volume of information, identify significant patterns, and construct a framework for communicating the essence of what the data reveal given the purpose of the study. In addition, the researchers performed extensive within- and across-case analyses and did not find any significant relationships between any of the demographic factors (age, gender, ethnicity, discipline/field of practice) in explaining the findings one way or another.

Presenting an analysis of the findings uncovered in this study warrants a degree of caution. First, the research sample was small, comprising interview data from only 20 interviews with doctoral students involved in qualitative research. Second, the focus of the study was on those who are either struggling at some stage of the dissertation process or who have withdrawn from their doctoral studies entirely. Thus, the perceptions of those students who persist in the process and those who complete the process and obtain the doctorate are not represented. For these reasons, it must be stressed that the implications that can be drawn are specific to the experiences of the sample group under study.

Remembering that the human factor is both the greatest strength and the fundamental weakness of qualitative inquiry and analysis, the researcher recognizes the subjective nature of the claims he or she makes regarding the meaning of the data. Aside from the potential biases involved in researcher as instrument, as is typical of qualitative research, the researcher acknowledges possible additional bias in analyzing the findings because they are faculty members teaching in a doctoral program. Toward this end, and to help minimize this limitation, throughout the process of data collection and data analysis, the researchers engaged in ongoing critical reflection through journaling and discussions with critical colleagues. Remaining open to the possibility that others might have told a different story, this chapter is essentially, and ultimately, a presentation of how *these* researchers understand and make sense and meaning of the material and the connections they see in it.

SUMMARY DISCUSSION
FOR CHAPTER 5

As pointed out previously, analysis of data begins to occur before you can present your findings; by coding and sorting, you are in effect analyzing your raw data. Having organized and prepared mounds of raw data so you could present an accurate and objective account of the findings of your research (Chapter 4), you are now ready to move on to the final step of the analytic process: to provide an interpretation and synthesis of those findings. Both in the previous chapter as well as in this one, we emphasized the distinction between reporting and presenting findings and interpreting them. These are two distinct processes.

We covered some difficult ground in this chapter. Qualitative analysis is not a simple task, and is therefore not simple to explain. Because the concepts of analysis, interpretation, and synthesis are difficult to explicitly articulate, thinking about how to compose a chapter describing these processes is somewhat challenging. Therefore, the suggestions we have made in this chapter should be viewed more in the nature of guides to possible approaches and combinations of approaches, rather than as tight prescriptions.

In the previous chapter, you presented the analysis of your raw data, which were your findings. In this chapter, you presented the analysis, interpretation, and synthesis of your findings. You moved beyond *data* to *information*. In the findings chapter, you stood back and remained objective. Your task was to offer as accurate an account of the findings as possible. In the analysis chapter, you moved from the objective to the subjective. Your voice and opinion, in conjunction with the literature, now take center stage. Findings cannot be taken at face value. Your aim in writing the analysis chapter is to tell a richly detailed story that takes into account a specific context that connects participants, processes, activities, and experiences to larger issues or phenomena.

First, you seek to identify significant patterns or themes. Then you move on to provide some sense of understanding; that is, you attempt to explain these patterns and themes—possibly the most creative part of the dissertation. Findings need careful teasing out. As a researcher, you must ask yourself what you have learned from conducting the research and studying the findings. What connective threads are there among the experiences of your study's participants? How do you understand and explain these connections? What new insights and understanding do you have as a result of conducting your study? What surprises have there been? What confirmation of previous instincts and hunches have there been? Are your findings consistent with the literature? Have they perhaps gone beyond the literature? The answers to these questions add another dimension of understanding to your findings.

Providing careful step-by-step documentation of your analysis offers other researchers access to your procedures. In this way, your study can become a model for other studies—a contribution to the research community and an implicit affirmation of the value of your work. Readers of dissertations also are drawn to visual representations of information, which typically compare and contrast key findings of the study. Displaying data visually makes things clear and also can facilitate your seeing findings in new and striking ways.

The central requirement in qualitative analysis and interpretation is clear and logical thinking. You need to examine your findings critically so as to produce credible and meaningful interpretations. Interpretation of qualitative data precludes reducing the task to any single defined formula or fixed blueprint. Moreover, we must appreciate that, in dealing with interpretation, we are unavoidably dealing with human subjectivity, and, as such, there are differences in the ways we make meaning.

Be sure to acknowledge that there are multiple ways of interpreting findings, that you have sought rival explanations, and that your interpretations are but one perspective. The human as instrument in qualitative inquiry is both its greatest strength and its greatest weakness. Nowhere does this ring more true than in analysis.

Chapter Checklist

✓ Do you have an introductory paragraph that includes purpose statement (if required) as well as a brief explanation of how you went about analyzing and synthesizing the findings?

✓ Does your argument flow logically and coherently?

✓ Do you make one point at a time?

✓ Are your interpretations clear, thoughtful, and reasonable?

✓ Are your interpretations relevant to the research problem, purpose, and research questions?

✓ Are the major themes interrelated to show a higher level of analysis and abstraction?

✓ Is your analysis positioned and discussed in terms of the related bodies of literature and previous research?

✓ Have you included relevant participant quotations to support your argument, making sure that these same quotations did not appear in previous chapters?

✓ Have you made appropriate use of tables and other displays to augment and support the discussion?

✓ Have you made sure that all information presented in tables is consistent with information that is presented in the narrative?

✓ Have you checked throughout your discussion for unclear/ambiguous language?

✓ Have you eliminated any needless repetition?

✓ Have you checked for insufficient detail and areas that are "unfinished"?

✓ Have you acknowledged that there are multiple ways of interpreting findings and that you remain open to other interpretive possibilities?

✓ Do you offer a comprehensive overview summary?

✓ If you have chosen to revisit and reflect on your initial assumptions as stated in your opening chapter, do you flesh these out sufficiently in terms of your study's findings?

✓ Have you kept track of and reported on alternative classification systems, patterns/themes, and explanations that you have considered during your analysis?

✓ Have you engaged in discussion with critical colleagues throughout the analysis process to hear and acknowledge different perspectives and points of view and to be open to a variety of possible interpretations?

ANNOTATED BIBLIOGRAPHY

Coffey, A., & Atkinson, P. (1996). *Making sense of qualitative data: Complementary research strategies*. Thousand Oaks, CA: Sage.

This book provides insight into understanding the complexities of the analytic process and the strategies involved in transforming data into something meaningful. As the authors explain, data analysis is based on the identification of key themes and patterns. This process begins with coding, which the authors describe in great detail in chapter 2. The discussion moves to a further level—from coding toward interpretation— that is, the transformation of the coded data into meaningful data. Chapter 5 focuses on writing and representation; that is, creating accounts of and interpreting what we have found. As the authors stress, qualitative researchers convey messages, explicit and implicit, about the social world of others. Thus, it is incumbent on social science researchers not only to acknowledge that they are accountable for their own acts of interpretation and representation, but also to do so carefully, responsibly, and explicitly.

Mason, J. (1996). *Qualitative researching*. Thousand Oaks, CA: Sage.

This book provides novice researchers with a clear and accessible introduction to the practice of qualitative research, identifying the many steps in the process and helping the researcher develop the needed skills. This book also highlights the difficult questions that researchers should get in the habit of asking themselves in the course of doing qualitative research and outlines the different ways of resolving challenges and issues. In chapter 6, the author explores ways in which qualitative researchers can begin to sort and analyze their data and offers some suggestions about the types of analysis or explanation building that the different methods might support. Chapter 7 examines in greater detail the kinds of analyses and explanations that are required in qualitative research. The authors pose questions as to how one can determine whether explanations are sufficiently convincing and credible. They also tackle some of the key issues regarding the ethics and politics of qualitative data analysis and presentation.

Patton, M. Q. (2002). *Qualitative research and evaluation methods* (3rd ed.). Thousand Oaks, CA: Sage.

Part III of Patton's book is possibly the best text that we have come across with regard to explaining qualitative analysis, and it is a must read for those interested in getting a better handle on what is essentially an extremely elusive and ambiguous endeavor. Chapter 8 deals with analysis, interpretation, and reporting of the findings, explaining in great detail the challenges and complexities involved. Especially useful are the sections dealing with thick description, case study analyses, pattern, theme, content analysis, and interpretation of findings. Aside from looking at generic approaches to qualitative analysis, Patton also provides suggestions for what he calls "theory-based analysis approaches." Here he examines the theoretical and philosophical perspectives of phenomenology and grounded theory and offers detailed guidelines for how a qualitative researcher would approach data analysis within each of these traditions. Chapter 9 deals with enhancing the quality and credibility of qualitative analysis. The author details how to determine the criteria for truth and provides insight into some of the current debates about establishing the trustworthiness of qualitative analysis.

Drawing Sound Conclusions and Presenting Actionable Recommendations

OVERVIEW

We know how exhausted you are at this point. But you are almost at the end of the process, so keep up the energy for just a short while longer! This final chapter of your dissertation is much more than just a cursory summary of findings. It is your chance to have the last word about your study, and it should help the reader decide what to make of your work. It also should stimulate your readers to think more deeply about the findings of your study and the implications thereof. Please note that some institutions require that the chapter presenting conclusions and recommendations must stand alone as a separate final chapter. In other institutions, conclusions and recommendations are incorporated into the analysis chapter. As we have emphasized throughout this book, in the interests of conforming to structural requirements, we advise that you check with your own program and/or institution. As with all previous chapters, we present this chapter in two sections: Section I, "Instruction," and Section II, "Application."

As you were writing your findings, you may have begun to think about various interpretations and draw tentative conclusions. Remember that interpretation and conclusions in qualitative data analysis are always open to revision. In essence, you are building an argument based on your data and attempting to develop explanations that fit the data—a process of inductive reasoning. This process is unlike quantitative analysis, where you collect data to test a hypothesis or deductive reasoning.

CHAPTER OBJECTIVES

Chapter 6 Objectives

Section I: Instruction

- Demonstrate how to think about and write sound conclusions.
- Demonstrate how to think about and write actionable recommendations.
- Offer ideas for a final reflection statement.

Section II: Application

- Presentation of a completed concluding chapter based on the content and process as described earlier.

SECTION I: INSTRUCTION

Let us hearken back for a moment to Table 1.1. The simple but useful matrix in the bottom right corner of the table (reproduced as Table 6.1) explains the essence of how to think about the conclusions that you will draw from your findings and the actionable recommendations you will be able to make based on those conclusions.

Presenting Sound Conclusions

Thinking About Your Conclusions

The interpretation outline tool (see Fig. 5.1) was helpful in stimulating critical thinking and reflection about all the potential deeper meanings behind your findings. Findings should not be taken at face value, and so you probed and dug deeper beneath the surface of your findings by asking over and again, "Why?" and "Why not?" As such, you were able to brainstorm a number of possible interpretations that explained your findings; that is, you developed some ideas of what you thought the findings really meant.

In thinking about how you were going to interpret your findings, you were in effect saying to yourself: "If I find this . . . then I think this means. . . ." In generating conclusions, you need to go back to your findings and interpretations once again and ask yourself, "I found . . . and I think this means . . . therefore I know the following to be true. . . ."

Conclusions flow directly from your findings. In effect, the conclusions are assertions based on your findings, and must therefore be warranted by the findings. With respect to each finding, you are asking yourself: Knowing what I now know, what conclusion can I draw? Although your conclusions will be backed up by your findings, do not confuse conclusions with findings. Conclusions are not a restatement of your research findings; they represent a higher level of abstraction. Drawing conclusions from your findings pushes you to consider broader issues and make new connections among ideas. In effect, by doing this, you are expanding on the significance of your findings.

Just as your conclusions are not the same as findings, neither are conclusions the same as interpretations. Rather, conclusions are essentially conclusive statements of what you now know, having done this research, that you did not know before. As in the case of providing interpretations, writing conclusions draws on your ability to be a critical and, at the same time, a creative thinker. In writing up the conclusions, you are in effect evaluating, analyzing, and synthesizing information.

Table 6.1   If/Then/Therefore/Thus Matrix

Findings Through Recommendations:			
Findings	*Interpretations*	*Conclusions*	*Recommendations*
"If I find this. . . ."	*"Then I think this means . . . "*	*"Therefore I conclude, or what I know to be true is . . ."*	*"Thus I recommend that . . ."*

Remember that your study's research questions, right from the beginning, formed the backbone of your research. Remember too that the findings of your research must provide answers to these questions. To check your thinking and ensure consistency among the research questions and all that follows from them, it is recommended that you develop a matrix—what we refer to as a "consistency chart," presented as Table 6.2. This chart tracks the findings through the interpretations to conclusions, making certain that these components are all aligned. A sample consistency chart is presented as Appendix Z. Note that each finding relates to its same numbered research question so the research question is not repeated in the table.

It is important to bear in mind, when thinking about and formulating each of your conclusions, that they must be logically tied to one another. That is, there should be some sort of consistency among your conclusions; none of them should be at odds with any of the others. This type of consistency among your conclusions goes without saying; it is a nonsequitor. If your study's research questions are tied together or interconnected, as they necessarily should be, and because your findings are the answers to the research questions, then your findings statements also will be interconnected with one another. Hence, your conclusions should "fit" with each other and not contradict each other. Your findings, in effect, tell the initial "story of the research." Your interpretations then add another dimension, bringing the story to a deeper level of understanding. Your conclusions, in terms of what you now know to be true, become the beginning of a new story. By way of the conclusions, the story of your research is wrapped up, bringing it to its logical finale.

Writing Your Conclusions

As a general rule of thumb, you should provide at least one conclusion for each finding. However, the process is not altogether linear. As such, one conclusion can (but does not always) cut across more than one finding. Each conclusion should be clearly and crisply stated in a few sentences. Following this notion, you need to expand on and amplify your main idea in a paragraph or two. This amplification provides further support for your conclusion. Because your conclusions must be concise, the discussion should be relevant, organized, and tight. Avoid repetition and ambiguity. Be sure that what you want to say comes across just as you intend.

Table 6.2   Consistency of Findings, Interpretations, and Conclusions

Findings	Interpretations	Conclusions
Write Finding Statement 1 here.	List all possible interpretations in summarized form.	Identify conclusions you draw from your first finding.
Write Finding Statement 2 here.	List all possible interpretations in summarized form.	Identify conclusions you draw from your second finding.
(*Continue in the same manner with your other findings.*)		

Presenting Actionable Recommendations

Thinking About Your Recommendations

Recommendations follow your findings and conclusions. In thinking about conclusions, you asked yourself, "I found . . . therefore I know the following to be true. . . ." Recommendations are the application of those conclusions. In other words, you are now saying to yourself: "Knowing what I now know to be true, I recommend that. . . ." Therefore, recommendations are the final stage of a logical thought process. In your recommendations, your research findings now have a springboard for action.

In chapter 1 of your dissertation, you discussed the significance of your study. In that discussion, you mentioned who would be likely to benefit from your study, what they would learn from it, and what they would gain from this knowledge. That section in chapter 1 now becomes the basis for thinking about your recommendations. Be aware that recommendations must move away from the theoretical to the actionable and doable. In other words, what are the *actions* that you would recommend and for whom?

The reasonableness of a recommendation depends on it (a) being logically and clearly derived from the findings, (b) being both content- as well as context-specific, and, most important, (c) being practical; that is, it is capable of implementation. Whereas your interpretations and conclusions are speculative, and may be the subject of dispute, your recommendations, although a set of opinions, should be firmly grounded in the findings and must be doable.

Recommendations have implications for policy and practice, as well as for further research. Based solidly on your findings, think of all the possible ways that people could and should now do things differently. As a result of your findings, how might

practice change? As a result of your findings, what new ideas can now be explored and researched further? How might your study be improved on and how might future studies in other contexts expand on your own and contribute to the field? In offering practical recommendations, you can and should make recommendations for your own program/organization, as well as for others that are similar. With regard to research recommendations, you might think about implications of your study's limitations and include the appropriate suggestions for further research. In this regard, ask yourself: In light of what I have learned, what more can be done? What can be done differently now? Here you might suggest studies designed to replicate your study in other contexts or settings. You might also suggest next-step studies designed to investigate another dimension of your study's research problem.

Writing Your Recommendations

Your findings will have implications for both professional practice as well as further research. You make recommendations based on your own experiences in conducting the research, as well as in any other professional capacity. In writing up your recommendations, it is important that you describe exactly how you envisage each recommendation being implemented. Be specific about identifying who will be responsible for implementation and who will monitor the ongoing implementation.

In offering recommendations, you are free to make a range of suggestions for the usefulness of the findings. Although the liberty to make suggestions is appealing, you should restrict your suggestions to only those that you think will make an important impact and that, to the best of your knowledge, are doable and actionable. Remember that fewer, stronger, and more focused recommendations will make more of an impact than a long list.

Researcher's Final Reflections

Stake (1995) writes:

> Qualitative case study is highly personal research. Persons studied are studied in depth. Researchers are encouraged to include their own personal perspectives in the interpretation. . . . The quality and utility of the research is not based on its reproducibility, but on whether or not the meanings generated, by the researcher or the reader, are valued. Thus a personal valuing of the work is expected. (p. 135)

Having come to the close of your study, you might be asking yourself: How do you personally value your work? How do you personally value the research experience? In this final section of the final chapter of your dissertation, you have an opportunity (but are not always required) to offer your own thoughts on the experience of conducting the research and writing the dissertation. Here you can describe how you came to your research. You also can reflect on the research experience and what it means to you. What are the lessons learned from conducting the study? What insights and inspirations have you derived from conducting your study? Think about your role as a researcher and what new learning—both personal and professional—you have had as a result of the qualitative research experience. There is cause for celebration! You are now writing your closing paragraphs!

SECTION II: APPLICATION

CHAPTER VI
Conclusions and Recommendations

The purpose of this multicase study was to explore with a sample of doctoral candidates their perceptions of why they have not managed to complete their dissertations. The conclusions from this study follow the research questions and the findings and therefore address four areas: (a) perceptions that the coursework would prepare students to conduct research and write a dissertation; (b) students' uncertainty about what they need to do and how to go about doing what is needed to complete the dissertation; (c) acquiring information, learning the skills, and developing the attitudes needed to complete the dissertation; and (d) what helps or hinders students' learning. Following is a discussion of the major findings and conclusions drawn from this research. This discussion is followed by the researcher's recommendations and a final reflection on this study.

Perceptions That Coursework Would Prepare Students

The first major finding of this research is that the majority of students in this study indicated that the coursework did not prepare them to conduct research and write their dissertations. A conclusion to be drawn from this finding is that students who enroll in doctoral programs should not expect that coursework alone will or can fully prepare them to conduct research and write their dissertations. Completion of a good dissertation is a content-specific journey taken by the student and, as such, becomes a process of discovery. Although research classes during the coursework can provide a general understanding of research methods and strategies for conducting research, it may be difficult for students to relate those methods or strategies to some future and often not-yet-identified research problem. In this regard, it also can be concluded that the primary purpose of coursework is to provide students with a sound theoretical foundation required for intellectually rigorous research and not to provide the nuts and bolts of application. A further and related conclusion that can be drawn is that, although doctoral programs do include courses on research, in some cases such courses may be inadequate in providing a basic and rudimentary understanding of qualitative research methods and the approaches and strategies to carryout those methods.

Uncertainty About What to Do and How to Do It

The second major finding was that all participants expressed the need to gain knowledge about the content and to understand the process involved in conducting research and writing their dissertations. During the first 2 years, students are often more preoccupied with understanding theoretical concepts and meeting the demands of the coursework than relating theoretical concepts to knowing what is involved in carrying out future research. A conclusion that can be drawn from this finding is that being grounded in theory alone is insufficient. Inexperienced student researchers also need the "know-how" (i.e., practical information about what to do and how to do it) to conduct research and write their dissertations, and they need to acquire this competency through more informal means. A related conclusion is that, in the absence of formal preparation, students need to be open to learning, be able to tolerate ambiguity, and have a compelling and fierce desire to succeed regardless of their circumstances.

Acquiring Information, Learning the Skills, and Developing the Attitudes Needed

The study's third major finding was that the majority of participants attempted to learn what they perceived they needed to learn by reaching out in dialogue with colleagues, rather than through more formal channels (i.e., advisement, other faculty, or post-coursework seminars). A conclusion to be drawn from this finding is that (in the absence of formal preparation) dialogue with colleagues in a similar situation can serve as a catalyst for reflection and action, and at the very least can provide a source of support to ameliorate feelings of isolation. Students may desire autonomy, but may not have the skills or even the motivation to learn the same material in isolation. Through dialogue, students have the opportunity to share information, exchange perspectives, challenge assumptions, test ideas, and play devil's advocate for one another, and all of these

collaborative opportunities hold the potential for the development of new understanding, new learning, and the ability to take constructive action.

What Helps or Hinders Learning

The sample of students identified different factors that they perceived helped or hindered their learning. This study's fourth finding was that the majority of students indicated that, in the process of attempting to do their dissertation, they relied on themselves. More than half of these same participants also said that colleagues were instrumental in facilitating their progress. *There are two primary conclusions that can be drawn from this finding.* First, adults have a need to be self-sufficient and self-reliant, and most adult students have a preference for directing their own learning. Second, whether students progress well in the dissertation process is largely a function of their own personal characteristics and their motivation and drive to succeed.

The fifth finding was that the majority of students cited the lack of good, timely, and consistent advisement as a major barrier standing in the way of their progress. The primary conclusion that can be drawn from this finding is that, although students want to be self-reliant, good and consistent advisement must be an integral part of the doctoral experience. Dissertation work cannot and should not be a solitary endeavor. To move forward in the dissertation process, students need support, feedback, and guidance from advisors; without it, the ability to progress, in most cases, is limited.

Recommendations

The researcher offers recommendations based on the findings, analysis, and conclusions of this study. The recommendations that follow are for: (a) doctoral program administrators and faculty, (b) current and prospective doctoral students, and (c) recommendations for further research.

Recommendations for
Doctoral Programs and Faculty

Given that there are multiple factors that affect attrition rates and acknowledging that these vary across universities, the recommendations put forth here for doctoral program administrators and faculty should be considered for their appropriateness on an individual basis. At the same time, it should be noted that there are many excellent university programs where the completion rate has steadily been improving. Therefore, some of the following recommendations may already be in place.

Recommendations for Doctoral
Program Administration and Faculty

Administrators of doctoral programs should consider:

1. Revisiting the reward and recognition system for faculty involved in advising and mentoring doctoral students by bringing forward to university leaders and decision makers any enhancements to the system that would create further incentives for faculty who provide advisement.

2. At the same time, administrators should consider the development and implementation of formal training programs in mentoring for faculty.

3. Administrators and faculty should review on an ongoing basis the criteria for acceptance of students into the university's doctoral programs. In addition, once students are enrolled in the program, guidelines and benchmarks should be put into place to monitor students' progress.

4. Ongoing assessments of students' status should take place to uncover on a timely basis any problems, issues, and/or challenges that may be blocking student progress, and resources should be identified to help students with such issues.

Recommendations for Current
and Prospective Doctoral Students

Individuals contemplating enrolling in a doctoral program should:

1. Take sufficient time to find out as much about not only criteria for acceptance and course requirements, but equally as important the kind of support, direction, and guidance they can rightfully expect to receive during the entire time they are in the program.

2. Have realistic expectations about the investment in time and money involved in completing a dissertation.

3. Become knowledgeable about what recourse they have if they find they are not receiving the guidance and direction they require. For those students already involved at some stage of the dissertation process, they should be aware that, if they do not have a satisfactory relationship with their advisor, it is legitimate and appropriate to seek another advisor. Further, students should be aware that there should be neither a penalty nor any political implications for changing advisors.

Recommendations for Further Research

The researcher recommends further studies be conducted to develop a larger database of information to gain a more comprehensive understanding of why some students who complete the required coursework do not go on to complete their dissertations.

In light of this, the following should be considered:

1. Based on the limitations of the current study and to correct for researchers' bias, a survey of a large sample of active and inactive doctoral students should be conducted to assess the extent to which the same or similar findings would be uncovered.

2. A further similar study using the same criteria should be undertaken among students who successfully completed their dissertations and obtained their doctoral degrees to compare and contrast the experiences of students who graduate with those in this study who remain at ABD status.

3. A comparison and analysis of research should be undertaken to assess the recent experiences

of doctoral program administrators and faculty, and students who have obtained doctoral degrees and those who remain ABDs. This research should be undertaken to uncover similarities and/or differences in perspectives as well as the implications for success or failure in doctoral programs.

Researcher Reflections

"There are two ways of spreading light: to be the candle or the mirror that reflects it."

—Edith Wharton

As we come to the close of this study, we want to pause for a moment and reflect on the journey that we have undertaken with you. We hope we have been like the candle guiding those students struggling at various stages of the process, rekindling the flame of possibility for those who have abandoned this work and shedding some light on what lies ahead for those who are contemplating taking up this work. This was our intention and sincere hope from the moment we began this project. But as with everything in life, the more we attempted to give, the more we received in return, and we came to understand how prophetic are the words of Jourbert, who reminds us that: "To teach is to learn twice." This study was a collaborative effort among ourselves, and it was greatly enhanced by the insight and feedback of the research participants who willingly gave of their time to share their experiences with us. Our fondest hope is that we lit the candle that may help demystify the process for you and that you have come to see this work, although difficult, as achievable. At the same time, by mirroring the process, we are grateful for all that we have learned and continue to learn as researchers, academics, and doctoral advisors.

SUMMARY DISCUSSION FOR CHAPTER 6

The process of generating solid conclusions and actionable recommendations takes time and should be carefully thought out. In planning how to articulate and present your conclusions and recommendations, you should be sure to discuss provisional ideas with advisors and critical colleagues. Also be sure to complete your own consistency chart because this will help you focus and maintain the necessary alignment between your research questions—the core of your research—and the key elements that follow: findings, interpretations, conclusions, and recommendations.

Chapter Checklist

✓ Have you made sure whether conclusions and recommendations are required to stand alone as a final chapter or whether these should be incorporated into the analysis chapter?

✓ If this is your dissertation's final chapter, have you included a brief but informative introduction?

✓ Are your conclusions clearly derived from your study's findings? In other words, is it clear to the reader that your conclusions are warranted by the findings?

✓ Do you offer at least one conclusion per finding? In other words, although conclusions can cut across findings, is each finding tied to at least one conclusion?

✓ Are your conclusions logical and clearly explained?

✓ Are you sure that your conclusions are not restatements of the findings?

✓ Are you sure that your conclusions are not interpretations, but rather strong conclusive statements?

✓ Are your conclusions consistent with each other? Do they flow logically from each other and not contradict each other?

✓ Can your conclusions be challenged? If so, can you think of any flaws or limitations in the way in which you have stated and explained each conclusion?

✓ Are all your recommendations justified by the findings?

✓ Are all your recommendations doable and actionable or are they theoretical and esoteric?

✓ Have you discussed applications for practice?

✓ Have you discussed applications for policy?

✓ Have you offered suggestions for further research?

✓ Have you selected some strong recommendations under each of the prior sections?

✓ If you have included a final reflective piece, does this make a statement regarding your role as a qualitative researcher and/or your experience in writing the dissertation?

✓ If you step back and review this, your chapter, do you think that it offers the reader a completed picture of your research?

✓ As the writer, would your readers be likely to walk away with a good understanding of the study and with a general feeling of finality and closure?

Nearing Completion:
Some Final Considerations

OVERVIEW

Finally, you have reached the "almost-completion" stage of the dissertation process. We know how much time and effort you have invested up until now, and for this you certainly deserve to give yourself much credit. Indeed, take a moment to reflect on the many varied activities you have engaged in to reach this point. This work has been no small accomplishment. Part III of this book addresses the final stages of the dissertation process. We offer advice and suggestions regarding checking on the alignment of all the key elements that constitute your study, selecting the most appropriate title for your study, writing the abstract, assembling your manuscript and making sure that all the necessary components of the dissertation's layout are addressed, proofreading and editing the manuscript, selecting a defense committee, preparing for a successful defense, as well as thinking about possible avenues for postdissertation career development.

OBJECTIVES

- Explain all the activities that need to take place as you near completion of your dissertation.
- Provide guidelines regarding how to most effectively engage in these final activities.
- Bring a sense of closure to the dissertation process.
- Offer some suggestions for moving beyond the dissertation.

REVISITING THE IMPORTANCE OF ALIGNMENT

Part I of this book started out by indicating the elements that would need to be included in a completed dissertation. In chapter 1, Table 1.1 provided a visual outline of the contents of an entire dissertation. The table was a prelude to the steps involved in each of the chapters that were described and demonstrated in Part II. In addition, Figure 1.1 illustrated the importance of alignment among the first three core critical elements: problem, purpose, and research questions.

At this juncture, as you reach the final stages of writing your dissertation, it is crucial that you once again make certain that all the necessary elements that constitute a dissertation are aligned with one another. In this regard, it is important to revisit the chapters of your dissertation, as if in detective mode, and check that the elements are all tied together—that they are aligned with one another. Check specifically that each element (a) flows sequentially from the elements prior to it, and (b) leads logically to the elements that succeed it. In particular, make sure of the following:

- Problem statement defines the subject of inquiry.
- Specific research problem is situated within a broader context.
- Purpose addresses the research problem.
- Research questions together shed light on purpose.
- Conceptual framework is based on research questions.
- Conceptual framework is the repository for the findings.
- Findings, which are objective, are the basis for interpretation, which are subjective.
- Findings and interpretations together are the basis for drawing conclusions.
- Conclusions are the springboard for actionable/doable recommendations.

Ensuring that you have achieved all of these steps means that your study is tight and you have taken an important step in ensuring methodological integrity. This process is extremely important for the defense when, among other things, the methodological integrity of your research is finely scrutinized. Table III.1 is based on Table 1.1, which is, in effect, the final "dissertation picture," illustrating clearly the alignment that is required among the qualitative dissertation's key elements.

CRAFTING A TITLE

The title of your dissertation should catch the readers' attention while properly informing them of the main focus of your study. From the beginning of your research, and certainly from the initial proposal stage, you will have had some kind of guiding working title. You have most likely revised and re-revised the title as you proceeded. Now, at the end of the study, you hone that title so that it is crystal clear, interesting, and appropriately worded. Most important, it should accurately reflect your work.

A title serves various functions. The first function is to identify the content of your study. The title is the first contact that your readers have with your research. It generates some anticipation of what is to follow and, as such, must communicate a concise, thorough, and unambiguous picture of the content of your dissertation. The second function of a title is for retrieval purposes. By including the most applicable key words, you enable another researcher doing a literature search to locate your study. Therefore, a title becomes an important factor in sharing research.

A well-crafted title conveys the essence of what is under study and the mode of inquiry. In composing a title, be sure to include the central phenomenon of your study, as well as the research approach you have used. The title should describe as accurately as possible the main elements of your study. Although such accuracy demands the use of specific language, the title should be clear (i.e., free of obscure technical terms, highly specialized language, and jargon). Mechanically, the title should be concise, to the point, and free of elaborate constructions, alliteration, and other literary devices that detract from the content of the title. Excessive length should be avoided, too, because that dilutes the impact of the key elements presented.

Generally, a two-part title structure offers you the scope to specify the key elements of

Table III.1   Alignment Flowchart

Chapter 1: Introduction	Chapter 2: Literature Review	Chapter 3: Research Methodology	Chapter 4: Presentation of Findings OBJECTIVE	Chapter 5: Analysis & Interpretation of Findings SUBJECTIVE	Chapter 6: Conclusions & Recommendations
• Research problem must be situated within a broader context • Purpose statement must be formulated in such a way that it will shed light on the problem • Research questions must address the purpose	• Each body of literature that is reviewed must be tied to and address some aspect of the problem • Conceptual framework: —Categories emanate from research questions —Descriptors/ subcategories emanate from "hunches" as well as from the literature • Conceptual framework becomes the repository for findings • Based on the findings and interpretations, make sure that all areas of literature reviewed are relevant and appropriate. Eliminate unnecessary sections, and add in what might still be needed.	• Check that all data-collection and data-analysis methods have actually been done in the way that you have described • Be sure to eliminate any unnecessary material	• Findings are answers to the research questions • Each finding must be tied to a research question • Findings are basis for interpretation	• Interpretation is about what you think the findings really *mean* • Final synthesis includes findings from all data collection methods, integrated with the literature	• Each conclusion that is drawn should be tied to respective findings and interpretations • There should be at least one conclusion per finding • Conclusions are the springboard for actionable recommendations • Typically there are recommendations for (a) the organization or institution; (b) people in the particular discipline under study; and (c) for further research
			"If I find this. . ."	*"then I think this means. . ."*	*"therefore I conclude, or what I now know to be true is. . ."* *"thus I recommend that. . ."*

your report: a few words capturing the essence of your study, followed by a colon that introduces a more specific and descriptive subtitle. One way to begin constructing an effective title is to list all the elements that seem appropriate for inclusion and then weave them in various ways until you are satisfied with the title both aesthetically and technically. As you do this, make a list of all possible two-part titles. Reverse the order. See which works best. Try to obtain feedback from advisors and critical colleagues, and revise accordingly.

In qualitative research, the title provides the researcher with a conceptual frame of reference for continuous reflection. As you immerse yourself in the context of your study, you become increasingly attuned to the key issues of your research—issues you may have been unaware of before starting your research. This process may lead you to shift the focus of your study and, as a result, to change the title to more accurately reflect the new focus. It is a good idea to keep notes of how your title evolves, and we suggest that you keep all ideas of titles as memos. If systematically monitored, your changing title can become a means to track the evolution of your perspective as a researcher, as well as the ways in which the focus and direction of your study have shifted over time.

WRITING THE ABSTRACT

You are required to write an abstract—a carefully worded summary that precedes the main body of the report and that tells readers what to expect. The information included in your abstract influences whether readers proceed to look at your total study. In addition, your abstract is the means through which other researchers, searching for studies on your topic, will be able to evaluate whether your study is useful to them. Therefore, the abstract offers a valuable opportunity for

your study to inform a wide audience. It is the means with which to capture potential readers' interests, thereby expanding your professional opportunities within the research community. As in the case of the title, focusing on the most significant elements and using precise wording are key.

Abstracts can differ in terms of style and word count. We suggest that you consult with your advisor, departmental regulations, and the relevant style manual regarding abstract requirements. In the social sciences, abstracts are usually published in the *Dissertation Abstract International*, and for this there is a 350-word restriction. The content of an abstract typically includes the following elements:

- Title of your study
- Research problem or issue that was addressed
- Qualitative research tradition or genre
- Theoretical basis that guided the study
- Data sources that informed your study
- Methods and procedures of data collection and data analysis
- Key findings, conclusions, and recommendations

Within the specified word limit, try to make your research summary as informative and comprehensive as possible. To achieve a final, solid version, go through various drafts. Usually you will start off by writing an extended abstract, and this is followed by various iterations in which you pare down the words so that the key elements are expressed concisely within the imposed limits. A sample abstract is included as Appendix AA.

ASSEMBLING THE MANUSCRIPT

Although format and style is a function of individual taste and institutional and/or departmental regulations, several general rules can be adopted in design and layout:

1. Pages must be numbered consecutively throughout. Page numbers are usually centered at the bottom of the page or placed at the top right. Roman numerals (i, ii, iii, iv) are used for the preliminary pages or front matter (abstract, dedication, acknowledgments, list of tables and figures, table of contents). Note that the title page is always the first page (i), but it is not numbered. Arabic numbers (1, 2, 3, 4) are used throughout the rest of the manuscript.

2. The entire document, including page numbers and table captions, must be typed in the same typeface/font and size. The most common usage is 12-point type Times New Roman.

3. The body of the dissertation should be double spaced. Single spacing is permitted in the following text: (a) footnotes, (b) block quotations, (c) tables and figures and their captions, and (d) bibliography entries. (If single spaced, you must still have double space between entries.)

4. Don't "justify" (square off) on the right margin. This style is for published articles only.

5. It is customary to use 1-inch margins all round. In some cases, the margin on the left side may be required to be 1.5 inches for binding purposes.

6. Regarding headings and subheadings, refer to the standards set by your department's choice of style manual. Regardless of style, all heading and subheading format must be consistent throughout.

7. Paragraphs are distinguished by indentation. Make sure there are no skipped lines or extra spaces between paragraphs.

8. The reference list must include all sources that were directly used in writing your dissertation. Every source that you have cited should be included in the reference list, and every entry listed in the reference list must appear in the manuscript. Because it is critical that the reference list is precise and accurate, we suggest that you carefully check all your citations.

9. Footnotes can be used for explanatory purposes where necessary.

10. Figures and tables must be consecutively numbered throughout. Alternatively, you may make use of combination chapter and figure/table number designations (e.g., Table 1.1, 1.2, 1.3, 2.1, 2.2, etc.). The number and caption of the table is placed above the table and must appear in the same typeface and size of the dissertation text. The number and caption of a figure is placed below the figure and must appear in the same typeface and size of the dissertation text. All tables that are working tools should be included as appendices, rather than in the main body of the text.

11. Appendices provide information that is pertinent to the study, but that is either too lengthy or not important enough to be included in the main body of the text. This information includes materials especially developed for the study, such as cover letters, data-collection instruments, tables containing raw data, and tabulated data analysis. Appendices are lettered, not numbered (Appendix A, Appendix B, etc.).

12. The final element to check is the table of contents, which must be clearly and logically organized. The function of the table of contents is to guide your readers, allowing them to follow a long and involved story. It should enable them to find their way easily around the different parts of your dissertation and quickly pinpoint those sections that they are most interested in reading. Therefore, it is essential that every heading and subheading that you use must appear in the table of contents. Your style manual will indicate specified differences regarding the levels of subheadings and how these should be numbered. The list of tables and figures is presented on a separate page. This list must give the number and title of each table and figure and the page on which it can be found. A sample table of contents is presented as Appendix BB.

PROOFREADING AND EDITING

Getting the dissertation ready for submission refers to both the form as well as the content of the document. Although some revisions are required following the defense, what you present at the defense cannot be incomplete in any way, nor should it contain any grammatical and/or typographical errors. Although you anticipate some changes and alterations following the defense, you should consider your dissertation a polished final version, not a work in progress.

At this point, go back and, if necessary, adjust chapters 1 through 3. Make sure all text elements are necessary and relevant. Check for items that need to be expanded. Also be aware that the literature review was an important early task. You now need to reread it and ensure that everything in your review is directly relevant to your study. If not, it needs to be eliminated. Equally important, if a section of literature review is missing, it needs to be added. Check throughout your document for correct tenses. In the proposal, you used the future tense because you were writing about what you were intending to do. In the dissertation, you are reporting on research that you have already completed, so you should change to past tense.

All manuscripts require editing and proofreading. Especially if English is not your native language, you might need editing assistance in this regard. A word of advice: After you complete your final draft, it is often helpful to set your manuscript aside for several days. Stepping back in this way creates the distance needed to change roles from "writer" to "reader," which is a way to approach and review your work with fresh eyes.

PRE-DEFENSE PREPARATION[1]

Submitting Necessary Information

To stay within required time frames, you should plan ahead accordingly. When you approach your defense, you should generally keep in regular contact with your institution's Registrar and Office of Doctoral Studies for their calendar of deadline dates and requirements for submissions of all the necessary documentation. Check dates carefully because your degree may be delayed if you have not complied with all the necessary submissions. Especially make sure whether you need to file the "intent to defend" form and do not exceed the required deadline. This form declares that you and your advisor believe that you can meet all the institutional demands for defense; this stage usually requires advisor approval.

As you near completion of your dissertation, you also should check that all your required courses have been completed in accordance with your approved program plan, that all necessary credits are entered on your transcript, that your proposal is on file, and that all your records are in proper order. If there are any discrepancies or concerns, you should bring these matters to the immediate attention of your program administrator and/or dissertation secretary in the Office of Doctoral Studies. You certainly want no unwelcome surprises at this point.

Selecting and Forming Your Committee

As mentioned in Part I, each university has a different system regarding dissertation committee structure and the process of preparing for that structure. You need to find out what system is adopted in your particular institution; your advisor/sponsor and/or departmental chair are likely to be in the best position to inform you of these matters. A dissertation committee typically consists of four to six faculty members. In some instances, all committee members are from within the department of the student's major. At other times, the committee is multidisciplinary, with members representing various academic departments. In some cases, a dissertation committee consists of three faculty members who guide the development and completion of the dissertation. In these cases, a final oral panel is convened, consisting of the dissertation committee plus two outside readers selected by the Graduate Office.

In some universities, the doctoral committee structure is based on an apprenticeship model and is used as a vehicle to guide the student from coursework through the defense. The dissertation committee is the group of faculty responsible for the student's progress right from the beginning, with all those involved contributing to the development of an acceptable dissertation. The committee is a hierarchical organization, with each member of the committee having a different responsibility vis-à-vis the student's research. Ideally, the doctoral committee is composed of faculty with different areas of expertise whose resources the student will be able to tap into during the dissertation process. Sometimes the same committee will stay with the student from the outset, guiding the apprenticeship. In other cases, this committee will evolve during the course of conducting research and writing the dissertation as the necessary expertise becomes evident based on the developing project.

At some universities, the student will be required to work with an advisor (sponsor) and second reader from the proposal stage onward; it is only when the student has almost completed the dissertation that a dissertation committee needs to be formed. In this instance, you can usually select your committee from among those in your own and related departments, those whose courses you have taken, and/or those whose work bears some relation to the focus of your dissertation. Some of these faculty members may be involved in other programs or schools within your university. In some rare cases, experts beyond your university can be chosen. In most instances, faculty has the choice to accept or decline to serve on a doctoral committee. Given the voluntary nature

of serving on a dissertation committee, faculty typically elects to work with those candidates whom they perceive to be academically strong and/or easy to work with. Faculty frequently seek those students who demonstrate these characteristics in their coursework. If you have difficulty in securing a committee, you might want to seek assistance from your sponsor/advisor and/or from your departmental chair.

The more information you have about potential committee members, the easier it will be for you to make decisions regarding which individuals may be best suited in helping you achieve your goals. You certainly want your committee to enhance the quality of your academic work and to be supportive of your progress. Therefore, you need to identify the best match between your own learning style and the faculty who are available to work with you. In addition, because progress is, to a large extent, the function of a collaborative team effort, you also need to give careful consideration as to how faculty members get along with each other. We suggest that you seek faculty who can meet the following criteria:

- They are knowledgeable in your discipline and have an interest in your research topic.
- They are familiar with the procedures of your university.
- They are respectful of each other and value collegial relationships.
- They are cooperative and supportive of students' progress.
- They have the time available and are accessible based on their own busy schedules and time constraints.

In the process of selecting members for your committee, you want to remain cautious of offending others in the department—those who will become your professional colleagues once you graduate and/or those who may ultimately participate in the process of evaluating your dissertation. One never knows which committee members will need to be replaced, for a variety of reasons, and which colleagues might participate in your defense as the fourth reader. Academic institutions, by their nature, are highly political arenas. Therefore, selection of the committee requires careful planning, with an emphasis on maintaining respectful professional relationships at all stages of the dissertation process.

Once you have filed your intent to defend and your sponsor and second committee member have approved your defense, you should secure the necessary additional committee members. This process usually includes selecting the third reader and arranging for the assignment of a fourth reader. Each institution has its own way of going about setting up the defense meeting, and we suggest that you consult with your institution's Office of Doctoral Studies with regard to the correct procedures and protocol. Usually it is the student's responsibility to contact all committee members to find a mutually agreeable time that all four members can be available for the defense. The defense is usually scheduled for a 2- to 3-hour block of time.

Preparing for the Defense

Generally, it is a safe rule of thumb to figure out that a complete draft of the dissertation should be in the advisor's hands within the first weeks of the semester in which you intend your defense to take place. This allows your primary advisor sufficient time to review your material and make recommendations, forward to the second reader for approval and recommendations, and secure third and fourth readers and comply with the institutions' scheduling procedures regarding the defense committee. You need to make sure that you have the necessary information regarding all required deadlines by consulting with your advisors as well as contacting your institution's Office of Doctoral Studies for guidelines and rules.

The purpose of the dissertation defense is twofold: (a) To publicly discuss what you have researched and what you have discovered in the process; and (b) evaluate the acceptability of the study as a scholarly piece of research in your area of specialization, and to make a collective decision that will determine the recommendations for revisions.

The defense, in effect, moves your dissertation from the private domain into the arena of public discourse, providing you with some sense of closure. Actual procedures for conducting the meeting and the formalities involved are likely to vary, not only among universities, but also among departments. Your advisor will most likely outline the proceedings of the defense, as well as explain to you the roles of the various committee members. As such, although each experience will certainly be unique, you should be well prepared as to what to expect in the session.

Each institution is concerned with maintaining an implicit academic standard for acceptable scholarship. You have just completed a rigorous piece of research, and so your research apprenticeship is ending. The defense marks this transition as you are invited to sit at the table and talk about your research as a peer with your professors. With your knowledge from your just-completed research study, you are expected to provide authoritative insight into previously uncharted or contested issues. Your ideas are as highly valued as your committee members,' and you have an equal place at that table.

In our view, no student should be allowed to schedule the defense if the dissertation is not regarded as complete and worthy of examination. Your advisor will no doubt have had the opportunity to review the final document prior to its official distribution to committee members and will already have determined that the document meets the necessary academic standards, thereby qualifying for formal review. Consequently, part of the function of the defense is a formal induction of the doctoral candidate into a scholarly community—the celebration of a major scholarly achievement and a symbolic rite of passage to the awarding of the doctorate.

Being the culminating aspect of a rigorous, traditional, and long-standing ritual, we understand that, like we ourselves did, you will likely approach the defense with some anxiety. The more you can frame the defense as an opportunity to present your research publicly and the more you take a proactive and nondefensive position, the better the experience is likely to be. View the defense as an opportunity to think about your study more deeply and creatively and to articulate the implications of your work. Your months of concentrated reading and research have contributed to unique knowledge on your topic that few possess. Display confidence in your own knowledge and experience. Think of the meeting essentially as an academic conversation among colleagues that involves the exchange of ideas and the sharing of knowledge—an opportunity to extend your thinking in new directions.

You can certainly prepare to make the defense a positive experience. Therefore, being fully conversant about all aspects of your study is crucial. By the time you have completed your study, you are likely an authority on your particular topic. The more familiar you are with the details of your study, including the relevant literature and research, the more you will appear as the expert. You have lived with your study for an extended length of time and have been totally immersed in it. The role that the committee can rightfully play is to provide some new lenses with which to review your work and to offer you some new perspectives.

Usually, at the defense, as the researcher you are given an opportunity to set the stage by presenting an overview of your study to the committee. Typically students are given anywhere from 10 to 45 minutes to do this. Although you can use your discretion in making the choice as to what points you want to get across in the time available, you should think carefully about this task beforehand. Rather than just summarizing the salient points of your study, you should think of that part of your research that is most critical, interesting, unique, and/or controversial. Committee members have read your study (or at least certain parts of it). Therefore, they are not expecting to hear from you what they already know, but rather to learn something new.

Think about whether there is anything that is deserving of further discussion. What regarding the content or process might require additional emphasis, illustration, explanation, elaboration, and/or clarification? What might committee members not know that they might need or want to know more about? Also think about what predictable concerns or needs that committee members might have regarding your study. In what ways might the limitations of your study deserve special mention? What broader or more pressing social issues does your study connect with? Having completed the study and lived with your findings, are there any ways your work might be revised and/or extended so that it would make a useful contribution either theoretically and/or practically?

Try to remain as specific and focused as possible, rather than crowding too much detail into this opening discussion. An interesting, concise, topical, and meaningful researcher presentation usually lays the ground for the discussion to follow. Maintaining the close attention of committee members allows you to maintain some degree of control over what will be given attention in the conversation that ensues. Remember that you have only limited time available to make your presentation. Note your beginning and ending times. Inform the committee of what is to come and for how long you intend to speak. This, for them, is a sign of careful planning and will be appreciated.

In planning your presentation, prepare an outline of what you want to talk about, laid out in sequence. You also might want to prepare some graphic aids to organize, illustrate, and support your oral presentation, including flowcharts, diagrams, audiotape segments, or even photographs or video clips. Audiovisual materials can provide focus and heighten impact. However, in light of the limited time that you have available, if you do decide to use visuals, be selective; use only what is highly pertinent to your discussion. Be sure that these are *used* and not simply displayed. Present them, explain their significance, and allow readers the time to digest these materials and ask questions. Visuals should feel like an integral and relevant aspect of the conversation, rather than an interruption. Although visual materials can certainly be used effectively, an overreliance on handouts and visuals can be off-putting to faculty who come to the defense expecting to engage in substantive conversation with the candidate and each other.

Typically, the presentation of your study is followed by questions and comments from the various committee members, which usually generate a discussion of your study that can further establish your professional credibility. Part of the expertise of being an acknowledged specialist is the ability to explain your work logically and intelligently. In the days prior to your defense, read over your dissertation carefully so you can respond authoritatively to the questions asked. Be able to succinctly summarize your research problem as well as your key findings. Be prepared to defend your choice of research tradition (or combination of traditions), choice of data-collection methods, sample selection procedures, as well as methods of data analysis. If there are any concerns over the quality of the inquiry or the document, these obviously will be a major focus of deliberation. Know that you can provide elaborate explanations on all aspects of your work and offer a rationale for your decision making. Also be ready to explain any figures and tables that you have included.

In the days leading up to your defense, reflect on the value of your dissertation. Recall the relevant literature in your field and bring yourself up to date with the most recent work. Think carefully about how your study contributes to the current knowledge base. Probe yourself about how your work relates to the literature, both theoretically and practically. Try to anticipate all possible questions that the committee members might ask. In this regard, play "devil's advocate" with yourself and try to identify as many of your study's strengths and weaknesses as possible. Following are some of the specific questions that examiners might predictably raise:

- What do you see as the main contributions of your research for your discipline, practitioners, and/or policymakers?
- In what ways, if at all, does your study contribute to the existing literature and/or prior research in the field? In what ways does it extend the literature? Contradict the literature? Fill gaps in the literature? Clarify contradictions in the literature?
- In planning and conducting this study, which major theorists influenced your thinking?
- What are the conflicting issues in your field (every field has conflicts—hence, the research problem), and what contributed most to your understanding of these issues?
- In what ways do you expect that your work will clarify the conflicting issues in your field?
- What motivated you to conduct this study? In other words, what brought you to explore this particular topic?
- What new learning about qualitative research have you come away with as a result of conducting this study?
- What, if any, are the unanticipated outcomes of your study? What surprises have you come away with?
- What new learning about yourself have you come away with having conducted this

study? What additional insights has the dissertation experience afforded you?

- What were the high and/or low points for you in the dissertation experience?
- If you were to redo this study, how might you conduct this study differently? How might you change your research methodology? Why?
- How could you build on or extend this research in the future?
- What are the major strengths and/or limitations of your research design/methodology?
- What might further strengthen this study?
- Why did you analyze the data in the way that you did? How might you have analyzed your data differently?
- What suggestions might you offer somebody about to conduct a study of this nature?

The discussion during the defense can evolve in many directions and on many levels. It pays to be prepared for all the prior potential questions, as well as any that your advisor and other critics might have raised with you over the course of discussions about your research. You are certainly free to refer as needed to your dissertation as you respond to questions. Be sure that you understand what is being asked of you before attempting to answer questions. If you are uncertain as to any question that is posed to you, ask that the question be rephrased or restated. Try at all times to provide clear, logical answers. Present your reasoning carefully. Avoid overlong and verbose answers that might take you off course. Count on being asked a few questions that you may not have anticipated. If you do not have an answer to a particular question, acknowledge that you need more time to think about the issue.

As the defense meeting draws to a close, you will be asked to leave the room, affording the committee members privacy in their final deliberations regarding your dissertation. Having heard each other's perspectives, they collectively assess the extent to which their individual views are congruent. Depending on the quality of the dissertation, the meeting can conclude with one of several outcomes. What everybody hopes for, of course, is approval. What everybody dreads—and which is hardly likely to occur—are substantive revisions that might necessitate another meeting. Typically, some revisions are necessary, and the committee arrives at agreement as to what changes they would recommend. Usually the primary advisor is charged with ensuring that these requests are addressed in the finally approved document.

POST-DEFENSE PREPARATION

Making Revisions to Your Manuscript

On the basis of the committee members' discussion, there are likely to be a number of suggestions, additions, and/or corrections. In a few cases, substantive or major alterations may be required. The most likely outcome, however, is a pass with the request for minor revisions. These revisions can include some further analyses, expansions to the literature review, additional methodological details, and additional conclusions and/or recommendations. You might be required to reorder parts or sections of the text, clarify and/or elaborate some discussion points, rewrite or omit sections that seem confusing, as well as attend to various technical, grammatical, and/or editorial details.

Generally a post-defense meeting is held with your advisor to discuss the necessary changes, reconcile any contradictory feedback, and make sure that you understand what needs to be done. We strongly suggest that, within a few days, with the defense discussion still fresh in your mind, you make a point of processing all the feedback you received. Be sure you understand what needs to be changed and how to proceed. Most minor revisions can usually be completed within a week or two. The sooner you tackle the required revisions, the sooner you will be able to submit a final copy of the document to your Office of Doctoral Studies for a final round of proofreading. Allowing sufficient time for possible redrafting is especially important if you hope to graduate in the same semester in which the dissertation was completed and defended. Filing the final dissertation means that the approval of any revisions as indicated by your advisor is complete.

Although you have revised and refined your manuscript many times prior to the defense, following the required revisions, you need to carefully and meticulously edit your manuscript one final time. The purpose for this final review is to check accuracy regarding content as well as mechanics and style. There is no substitute for painstaking proofreading, preferably by somebody else. This is not simply because it is a tedious task, but because your familiarity with the text is likely to impede your effectiveness at the task.

In doing a final check of your manuscript, look for the following requirements:

- Have you addressed all issues that were raised by the committee members?
- Have you added the necessary sections in the most logical places so as not to interrupt the flow of the discussion?
- Regarding any added material, have you checked with your style manual regarding mechanics, style, and consistency?
- Are all headings and subheadings formatted in accordance with the guidelines specified in the style manual?
- If necessary, have you added and/or deleted any citations?
- Have you adjusted your reference list according to all additions and/or deletions of citations?
- Have you adjusted your abstract according to any changes that were made?
- Have you added your acknowledgments and/or dedication? This appears after the abstract and is an opportunity to express appreciation to those who have contributed significantly to the completion of your dissertation.
- Have you checked that your table of contents corresponds with all headings, subheadings, and pagination? This check is especially important if you have adjusted your margins for binding purposes.
- Have you checked that all tables and figures are correctly numbered and labeled throughout?
- Have you reread and edited your manuscript one final time?
- Have you performed a final spell-check on the entire manuscript?

The instructions for preparing final copies of your dissertation can be quite complex, and these differ from university to university. As such, we recommend that you consult with your institution's Office of Doctoral Studies regarding format and style details, as well as the number of copies of the dissertation and abstract that you are required to submit and to whom. Generally, you can rely on your advisor to clarify procedures regarding your university's protocol for completion of the dissertation process, including final approval and sign-off.

Presenting and Publishing Your Research

The dissertation process comes to a definitive end when the final document is submitted and the doctoral degree is awarded. You have undoubtedly devoted an extensive amount of time and energy to your research. Finally, having reached the end of the trail, you should feel a well-deserved sense of accomplishment. This is a time to bring closure to your doctoral program. It is also a time to move forward and celebrate your enhanced knowledge and expertise. Completion of the dissertation is a significant milestone of an ongoing journey. As is usually the case, as one door closes, another door opens.

At this juncture, you might consider looking beyond the dissertation and contemplating new projects, particularly those you may have deferred while working on your dissertation. Think especially of how you can more fully share what you have researched with a broader audience than the academic community. Following your immersion in your research, you will certainly want to disseminate your findings to others, enabling others to have access to cutting-edge information as well as extending your own professional network. Presenting and/or publishing your findings is a way to contribute to the ongoing knowledge base and work toward advancing your professional career.

Students have often launched their careers by distilling their dissertations into one or more promising publications, including appropriate scholarly journal articles and book chapters. In preparing a piece for submission, find a focus that interests you and that you think might be of value and interest to others. In doing so, you also might consider redefining your audience (lay, practitioner, and/or policymaking). In addition to review pieces, you also might consider developing and publishing materials such as manuals, handbooks, and/or programs. These could be based on your recommendations—a practical outgrowth of your dissertation work and certainly a valuable contribution to your field of practice.

In addition to publications, completion of the dissertation provides you with an opportunity to present your study in other academic settings and research forums, such as graduate seminars and professional associations. Presentations can be made at regional, state, national, and international conferences. Being the "expert" (i.e., knowledgeable about the specific area that you have studied) means that you are undoubtedly well prepared to present this information persuasively and articulately.

SUMMARY AND DISCUSSION

Part III of this book addresses the final stages of the dissertation process, and we offer suggestions regarding the various activities involved.

It is crucial that all the necessary elements that constitute a dissertation are aligned with one another. At the end of the process, it is necessary that you revisit the chapters of your dissertation and check that each element flows sequentially from the elements prior to it, and also that each element leads logically to the elements that succeed it.

The first thing your readers will read, and something you will need to revise following the completion of your study, is the title of your dissertation. Therefore, the wording of your title deserves careful consideration. By conveying the key concepts of your study, the title attracts the attention of interested readers. The title also enables your work to be correctly catalogued, and effective wording is essential for retrieval purposes.

You want your study's abstract to be an accurate representation of all the hard work you have devoted to this project. More important, you want people who are studying issues related to yours to find your study among all the others. Therefore, in your abstract, careful wording and attention to key elements are essential. An abstract should generally state the research problem, describe the research approach, and announce key findings, conclusions, and recommendations. There is usually a specified word limit. Within that word limit, try to make your abstract as comprehensive and informative as possible.

Although format and style are a function of individual taste and institutional and/or departmental regulations, some general rules can be adopted in designing the layout of your manuscript. We offer various ideas on what to check in assembling your manuscript.

In preparing for your defense, check that all necessary documentation is completed in a timely manner. You do not want any unnecessary delays at this point. Customs and routines surrounding the number of faculty who attend a dissertation defense vary among institutions and programs. Make sure that you are familiar with the system adopted by your university regarding the dissertation committee structure as well as the process for preparing for that structure. At most universities, students have the opportunity to request specific faculty members to serve on their dissertation committee. If you have the freedom to exercise some choice, committee membership should be designed to maximize the support and assistance available.

The defense, in effect, moves your dissertation from the private domain into the arena of public discourse. As a result of your research, you are now considered a specialist in your topic area. Part of the expertise of being an acknowledged specialist is the ability to explain your work logically and intelligently. Under all imaginable circumstances, everybody on your committee wants you to do well. With a solid, thoughtful, and well-prepared presentation, you are highly likely to be successful.

Following the defense, there are almost always some revisions you will have to make. We strongly suggest that, within a few days, with the defense discussion still fresh in your mind, you make a point of processing all the feedback you received. The sooner you tackle the required revisions, the sooner you will be able to submit a final copy of your document to the Office of Doctoral Studies for a final round of proofreading. As you incorporate the necessary revisions, make sure that any and all additions conform to the style manual that you are using.

Note

1. The dissertation defense is variably referred to as "Orals," "Oral Examination," "Dissertation Hearing," or "Vivas."

Afterword

A dissertation is an extensive, challenging, and rigorous scholarly endeavor. As such, completing it represents the pinnacle of academic achievement. This book traces the path of the dissertation process from the time your research was the beginning of an idea to its final successful completion. We illustrated what is involved in moving from a broad topic to a researchable problem replete with research purpose and research questions. We explained how to operationalize those research questions by actually doing research; collecting, managing, and analyzing the data; presenting findings; and then analyzing and synthesizing those findings in light of your own interpretations as well as prior research. We also discussed how to think about and prepare sound conclusions as well as a set of actionable recommendations. Finally, we dealt with the dissertation defense and offered some suggestions regarding planning and preparing for the meeting.

Our intention is that this book provides the guidance and initiative for the careful and systematic planning, preparation, and management of what might at first seem to be a nebulous and seemingly impossible task. Hopefully, with this roadmap in hand, you are now better equipped for the challenges ahead and are on your way to graduating with your doctorate. The dissertation journey is about achieving several milestones, one at a time. Once you have made the decision to complete your dissertation, which is a significant milestone in itself, do not allow one day to go by without doing *something*. Certainly you can expect your initial projections to be revised. But keep a positive attitude, actively finding ways to *succeed*.

It is the philosophy of each of us adult educators that what matters ultimately in life is not only what one has learned, but also what one has taught. Our sincere hope is that if this book has given you some new knowledge, skills, and insight, you will pass these on to somebody else who is starting off on the qualitative dissertation process or who might be stuck along the way and attempting to move forward.

Our best wishes for your continued success.

—Linda and Marie

References

Anfara, V. A., & Mertz, N. T. (Eds.). (2006). *Theoretical frameworks in qualitative research.* Thousand Oaks, CA: Sage.

Argyris, C., & Schon, D. A. (1996). *Organizational learning: II. Theory, method and practice.* Reading, MA: Addison Wesley.

Azad, A., & Kohun, F. (2006). Dealing with isolation feelings in doctoral programs. *International Journal of Doctoral Studies, 1.*

Bair, C. R., & Haworth, J. G. (1999, November 18–21). *Doctoral student attrition and persistence: A metasynthesis of research.* Paper presented at the annual meeting of the Association for the Study of Higher Education, San Antonio, TX.

Bauer, T. N., & Green, S. G. (1994). Effect of newcomer in work-related activities: A longitudinal study of socialization. *Journal of Applied Psychology, 2,* 211–223.

Beeler, K. D. (1991). *Graduate student adjustment to academic life: A four-stage framework.* Retrieved November 27, 2006, from www.findarticles.com/p/articles/mi_mOPCR/is-2_38/ai_n6146820

Berg, B. L. (2004). *Qualitative research methods for the social sciences* (5th ed.). Boston: Pearson.

Berg, J. (October 3, 2007). "Exploring ways to shorten the asent to a PhD." *New York Times,* p. B9. Retrieved from http://www.nytimes.com/2007/10/03/education/03education.html?em&ex=1191556800&en=f96cc1319be46d7b&ei=5087%0A

Bloomberg, L. D. (2007). Revisiting research approaches. Unpublished manuscript.

Bogdan, R. C., & Biklen, S. K. (1998). *Qualitative research for education: An introduction to theory and methods.* Boston: Allyn & Bacon.

Boote, D. N., & Beile, P. (2005). Scholars before researchers: On the centrality of the dissertation literature review in research preparation. *Educational Researcher, 34*(6), 3–15.

Booth, W. C., Colomb, G. G., & Williams, J. M. (2003). *The craft of research* (2nd ed.). Chicago: University of Chicago Press.

Bourner, T., Bowden, R., & Laing, S. (2001). Professional doctorates in England. *Studies in Higher Education, 26*(1). Retrieved November 22, 2006, from EBSCOHost database.

Bowen, W. G., & Rudenstein, N. L. (1992). *In pursuit of the PhD.* Princeton, NJ: Princeton University Press.

Boyatzis, R. E. (1998). *Transforming qualitative information: Thematic analysis and code development.* Thousand Oaks, CA: Sage.

Brause, R. S. (2004). *Writing your doctoral dissertation: Invisible rules for success.* New York: Routledge Falmer.

Brookfield, S. D. (1986). *Understanding and facilitating adult learning.* San Francisco: Jossey-Bass.

Brookfield, S. D. (1987). *Developing critical thinkers.* San Francisco: Jossey-Bass.

Brookfield, S. D. (1991). Using critical incidents to explore assumptions. In J. Mezirow & Associates (Eds.), *Fostering critical reflection in adulthood* (pp. 177–193). San Francisco: Jossey-Bass.

Brookfield, S. D. (2005). *The power of critical theory: Liberating adult learning and teaching.* San Francisco: Jossey-Bass.

Candy, P. C. (1991). *Self-direction for lifelong learning: A comprehensive guide to theory and practice.* San Francisco: Jossey-Bass.

Charmaz, K. (2000). Grounded theory: Objectivist and constructivist methods. In N. K. Denzin & Y. S. Lincoln (Eds.), *Handbook of qualitative research* (2nd ed., pp. 509–535). Thousand Oaks, CA: Sage.

Chronicle of Higher Education. (2004, January 16). Washington, DC: Author.

Clandinin, D. J., & Connelly, F. M. (2000). *Narrative inquiry: Experience and story in qualitative research.* San Francisco: Jossey-Bass.

Coffey, A., & Atkinson, P. (1996). *Making sense of qualitative data: Complementary research strategies.* Thousand Oaks, CA: Sage.

Crabtree, B. F., & Miller, W. L. (Eds.). (1992). *Doing qualitative research: Multiple strategies.* Newbury Park, CA: Sage.

Creswell, J. W. (1994). *Research design: Qualitative and quantitative approaches.* Thousand Oaks, CA: Sage.

Creswell, J. W. (1998). *Qualitative inquiry and research design: Choosing among five traditions.* Thousand Oaks, CA: Sage.

Creswell, J. W. (2003). *Research design: Qualitative, quantitative, and mixed methods approaches* (2nd ed.). Thousand Oaks, CA: Sage.

Creswell, J. W. (2005). *Educational research: Planning, conducting, and evaluating quantitative and qualitative research* (2nd ed.). Upper Saddle River, NJ: Prentice Hall.

Creswell, J. W., & Miller, D. L. (2000). *Determining validity in qualitative inquiry. Theory into Practice, 39*(3), 124–130.

Denzin, N. K. (1989/2001). *Interpretive interactionism.* Newbury Park, CA: Sage.

Denzin, N. K., & Lincoln, Y. S. (Eds.). (1998). Competing paradigms in qualitative research. In N. K. Denzin & Y. S. Lincoln (Eds.), *The landscape of qualitative research: Theories and issues* (pp. 195–220). Thousand Oaks, CA: Sage.

Denzin, N. K., & Lincoln, Y. S. (Eds.). (2000). *Handbook of qualitative research* (2nd ed.). Thousand Oaks, CA: Sage.

Denzin, N. K., & Lincoln, Y. S. (Eds.). (2003). *Strategies of qualitative inquiry* (2nd ed.). Thousand Oaks, CA: Sage.

Dewey, J. (1916). Democracy and education. New York: MacMillan.

Ercikan, K., & Roth, W. (2006). What good is polarizing research into qualitative and quantitative? *Educational Researcher, 35*(5), 14–23.

Fanger, D. (1985, May). The dissertation from conception to delivery. *On Teaching and Learning: The Journal of the Harvard-Danforth Center, 1,* 26–33.

Flanagan, J. C. (1954). The critical incident technique. *Psychological Bulletin, 51*(4), 327–358.

Fontana, A., & Frey, J. H. (2003). The interview: From structured questions to negotiated text. In N. K. Denzin & Y. S. Lincoln (Eds.), *Collecting and interpreting qualitative materials* (pp. 61–106). Thousand Oaks, CA: Sage.

Fowler, F. J. (1993). Survey research methods (2nd ed.). Newbury Park, CA: Sage.

Freire, P. (1970). *Pedagogy of the oppressed.* New York: Seabury.

Gadamer, H. (1960). *Truth and method.* London: Sheed and Ward.

Galvan, J. L. (2004). *Writing literature reviews: A guide for students of the social and behavioral sciences.* Glendale, CA: Pyrczak.

Gay, L. R., Mills, G. E., & Airasian, P. (2006). *Educational research: Competencies for analysis and application* (8th ed.). Upper Saddle River, NJ: Pearson.

Glesne, C. (2005). *Becoming qualitative researchers: An introduction* (3rd ed.). Boston: Allyn & Bacon.

Green, K. E., & Kluever, R. C. (1996, April 8–12). *The Responsibility Scale.* Paper presented at the annual meeting of the American Education Research Association, New York.

Green, K. E., & Kluever, R. C. (1997, March 24–28). *The dissertation barrier scale.* Paper presented at the annual meeting of the American Education Research Association, Chicago, IL.

Guba, E. G., & Lincoln, Y. S. (1998). Competing paradigms in qualitative research. In N. K. Denzin & Y. S. Lincoln (Eds.), *Handbook of qualitative research* (pp. 105–117). Thousand Oaks, CA: Sage.

Hacker, D. (2003). *A writer's reference* (5th ed.). Boston: Bedford/St. Martin's.

Hart, C. (2005). *Doing a literature review: Releasing the social science research imagination.* Thousand Oaks, CA: Sage.

Hawley, P. (2003). *Being bright is not enough.* Springfield, IL: Charles C. Thomas.

Heinrich, K. T. (1991). Loving partnerships: Dealing with sexual attraction and power in doctoral advisement relationships. *Journal of Higher Education, 62*(5), 514–538.

Hockey, J. (1994). New territory: Problems of adjusting to the first year of a social science PhD. *Studies in Higher Education, 19*(2), 177–190.

Holloway, I. (1997). *Basic concepts for qualitative research.* Oxford, UK: Blackwell.

Houle, C. O. (1988). *The inquiring mind* (2nd ed.). Madison, WI: University of Wisconsin Press.

Huck, S. W. (2000). *Reading statistics and research* (3rd ed.). New York: Longman.

Hycner, R. H. (1985). Some guidelines for the phenomenological analysis of interview data. *Human Studies, 8,* 279–303.

Katz, E. (1995, April 18–22). *The dissertation: Academic interruptus.* Paper presented at the annual meeting of the American Education Research Association, San Francisco.

Kilbourn, B. (2006). The qualitative doctoral research proposal. *Teachers College Record, 108*(4), 529–576.

Knowles, M. S. (1980). *The modern practice of adult education.* New York: Cambridge University Press.

Knowles, M. S. (1998). *The adult learner* (5th ed.). Houston, TX: Gulf Publishing.

Krathwohl, D. R. (1998). *Methods of educational and social science research: An integrated approach* (2nd ed.). Reading, MA: Addison-Wesley.

Kreuger, R. A. (1988). *Focus groups: A practical guide for applied research.* Newbury Park, CA: Sage.

Kreuger, R. A., & Casey, M. A. (2000). *Focus groups: A practical guide for applied research* (3rd ed.). Thousand Oaks, CA: Sage.

Kvale, S. (1996). *Interviews: An introduction to qualitative research interviewing.* Thousand Oaks, CA: Sage.

Lazerson, M. (2003). *Navigating the journey: A case study of participants in a dissertation support program.* Unpublished doctoral dissertation, University of Pennsylvania.

Lenz, K. (1995, April 18–22). *Factors affecting the completion of the doctoral dissertation for non-traditional aged women.* Paper presented at the annual meeting of the American Education Research Association, San Francisco.

Lewin, K. (1935). *A dynamic theory of personality.* New York: McGraw-Hill.

Lewis, C. W, Ginsberg, R., Davies, T., & Smith, K. (2004). The experiences of African American Ph.D. students at a predominantly white Carnegie I research institution. *College Student Journal, 38*(2), 231–235.

Lincoln, Y. S., & Denzin, N. K. (2003). The seventh moment: Out of the past. In N. K. Denzin & Y. S. Lincoln (Eds.), *Strategies of qualitative inquiry* (2nd ed., pp. 1047–1065). Thousand Oaks, CA: Sage.

Lincoln, Y. S., & Guba, E. G. (1985). *Naturalistic inquiry.* Beverly Hills, CA: Sage.

Lincoln, Y. S., & Guba, E. G. (2000). Paradigmatic controversies, contradictions, and emerging confluences. In N. K. Denzin & Y. S. Lincoln (Eds.), *Handbook of qualitative research* (2nd ed., pp. 163–188). Thousand Oaks, CA: Sage.

Locke, L. F., Spirduso, S. J., & Silverman, S. J. (2000). *Proposals that work.* Thousand Oaks, CA: Sage.

Lovitts, B. E. (1996). *Leaving the ivory tower: A sociological analysis of the causes of departure from doctoral study.* Unpublished doctoral dissertation, University of Michigan, Ann Arbor, MI.

Lovitts, B. E. (2001). *Leaving the ivory tower: The causes and consequences of departure from doctoral study.* Lanham, MD: Rowman & Littlefield.

Lovitts, B. E., & Nelson, C. (2000). *The hidden crisis in graduate education: Attrition from Ph.D. programs.* Retrieved November 22, 2006, from www.aaup.org/publications/Academe/2000/00nd/ND00LOVI.HTM

Marshall, C., & Rossman, G. B. (2006). *Designing qualitative research* (4th ed.). Thousand Oaks, CA: Sage.

Marsick, V., & Volpe, M. (Eds.). (1999). Informal learning on the job. *Advances in Developing Human Resources. The Academy of Human Resource Development*, No. 3.

Mason, J. (1996). *Qualitative researching.* Thousand Oaks, CA: Sage.

Maxwell, J. A. (2005). *Qualitative research design: An interactive approach* (2nd ed.). Thousand Oaks, CA: Sage.

Meloy, J. (1992). *Writing the qualitative dissertation: Voices of experience.* Paper presented at the annual meeting of the American Education Research Association, San Francisco.

Meloy, J. (1994). *Writing the qualitative dissertation: Understanding by doing.* Hillsdale, NJ: Lawrence Erlbaum Associates.

Merriam, S. B. (1998). *Qualitative research and case study application in education.* San Francisco: Jossey-Bass.

Merriam, S. B., & Caffarella, R. S. (1999). *Learning in adulthood: A comprehensive guide.* San Francisco: Jossey-Bass.

Merriam, S. B., & Associates. (2002). *Qualitative research in practice.* San Francisco: Jossey-Bass.

Mezirow, J. (1981, Fall). A critical theory of adult education. *Adult Education, 31*, 3–24.

Mezirow, J. (1985). A critical theory of self-directed learning. In S. Brookfield (Ed.), *Self-directed learning from theory to practice* (pp. 17–30) San Francisco: Jossey-Bass.

Mezirow, J. (1991). *Transformative dimensions of adult learning.* San Francisco: Jossey-Bass.

Mezirow J., & Associates. (1990). *Fostering critical reflection in adulthood: A guide to transformative and emancipatory learning.* San Francisco: Jossey-Bass.

Mezirow, J., & Associates. (2000). *Learning as transformation: Critical perspectives on a theory in progress.* San Francisco: Jossey-Bass.

Miles, M. B., & Huberman, A. M. (1994). *Qualitative data analysis* (2nd ed.). Thousand Oaks, CA: Sage.

Miller, M. M. (1995, April 18–22). *ABD status and degree completion: A student's perspective.* Paper presented at the annual meeting of the American Education Research Association, San Francisco.

Morgan, D. L. (1997). *Focus groups as qualitative research* (2nd ed.). Newbury Park, CA: Sage.

Morse, J. M., Barrett, M., Mayan, M., Olson, K., & Spiers, J. (2002). Verification strategies for establishing reliability and validity in qualitative research. *International Journal of Qualitative Methods, 1*(2), 1–19. Retrieved June 12, 2006, from http://www.ualberta.ca/~ijqm/

Morse, J. M., & Richards, L. (2002). *Read me first for a user's guide to qualitative methods.* Thousand Oaks, CA: Sage.

Moustakas, C. (1994). *Phenomenological research methods.* Thousand Oaks, CA: Sage.

Neuman, W. L. (2000). *Social research methods: Qualitative and quantitative approaches* (4th ed.). Boston: Allyn & Bacon.

Patton, M. Q. (1990). *Qualitative evaluation and research methods* (2nd ed.). Newbury Park, CA: Sage.

Patton, M. Q. (2002). *Qualitative research and evaluation methods* (3rd ed.). Thousand Oaks, CA: Sage.

Pellegrino, V. C. (2003). *A writer's guide to powerful paragraphs.* Wailuku, HI: Maui'ar Thoughts Company.

Phillips, D. C., & Burbules, N. C. (2000). *Postpositivism and educational research.* Lanham, MD: Rowman & Littlefield.

Piantanida, M., & Garman, N. B. (1999). *The qualitative dissertation: A guide for students and faculty.* Thousand Oaks, CA: Corwin.

Polkinghorne, D. E. (1983). *Methodology for the human sciences: Systems of inquiry.* Albany: State of New York University Press.

Pring, R. (2000). *Philosophy of educational research.* London/New York: Continuum.

Punch, M. (1994). Politics and ethics in qualitative research. In N. K. Denzin & Y. S. Lincoln (Eds.), *Handbook of qualitative research* (pp. 83–97). Thousand Oaks, CA: Sage.

Rea, L. M., & Parker, R. A. (1997). *Designing and conducting survey research: A comprehensive guide* (2nd ed.). San Francisco: Jossey-Bass.

Reichardt, C. S., & Rallis, S. F. (1994). The qualitative quantitative debate: New perspectives. *New Directions for Program Evaluation, 61,* 5–11.

Robson, C. (2002). *Real world research: A resource for social scientists and practitioner-researchers.* Malden, MA: Blackwell.

Rossman, G. B., & Rallis, S. F. (2003). *Learning in the field: An introduction to qualitative research* (2nd ed.). Thousand Oaks, CA: Sage.

Rubin, H. J., & Rubin, I. S. (2005). *Qualitative interviewing: The art of hearing data* (2nd ed.). Thousand Oaks, CA: Sage.

Rudestam, K. E., & Newton, R. R. (2001). *Surviving your dissertation: A comprehensive guide to content and process* (2nd ed.). Thousand Oaks, CA: Sage.

Schram, T. H. (2003). *Conceptualizing qualitative inquiry.* Columbus, OH: Merrill Prentice Hall.

Schwandt, T. A. (1997). *Qualitative inquiry: A dictionary of terms.* Thousand Oaks, CA: Sage.

Schwandt, T. A. (2000). Three epistemological stances for qualitative inquiry. In N. K. Denzin & Y. S. Lincoln (Eds.), *Handbook of qualitative research* (2nd ed., pp. 189–213). Thousand Oaks, CA: Sage.

Seidman, I. E. (1998). *Interviewing as qualitative research* (2nd ed.). New York: Teachers College Press.

Silverman, D. (2000). *Doing qualitative research: A practical handbook.* Thousand Oaks, CA: Sage.

Smallwood, S. (2004). Survey points to mismatch in doctoral programs. *The Chronicle of Higher Education, 47*(20), A14–A15.

Stake, R. E. (1994). Case studies. In N. K. Denzin & Y. S. Lincoln (Eds.), *Handbook of qualitative research* (pp. 236–247). Thousand Oaks, CA: Sage.

Stake, R. E. (1995). *The art of case study research.* Thousand Oaks, CA: Sage.

Stake, R. E. (2000). Case studies. In N. K. Denzin & Y. S. Lincoln (Eds.), *Handbook of qualitative research* (2nd ed., pp. 235–254). Thousand Oaks, CA: Sage.

Stake, R. E. (2001). The case study method in social inquiry. In N. K. Denzin & Y. S. Lincoln (Eds.), *The American tradition in qualitative research* (Vol. II, pp. 131–138). Thousand Oaks, CA: Sage.

Sternberg, D. (1981). *How to complete and survive a doctoral dissertation.* New York: St. Martin's Griffin.

Strauss, A. (1987). *Qualitative analysis for social scientists.* New York: Cambridge University Press.

Strauss, A., & Corbin, J. (1990). *Basics of qualitative research: Grounded theory procedures and techniques.* Thousand Oaks, CA: Sage.

Strauss, A., & Corbin, J. (1998). *Basics of qualitative research: Grounded theory procedures and techniques* (2nd ed.). Thousand Oaks, CA: Sage.

Strunk, W., & White, E. B. (2000). *The elements of style* (4th ed.). New York: Longman.

Taylor, K., Marienau, C., & Fiddler, M. (2000). *Developing adult learners.* San Francisco: Jossey-Bass.

Tinto, V. (1993). *Leaving college: Rethinking the causes and cures of student attrition.* Chicago: University of Chicago Press.

Torraco, R. J. (2005). Writing integrative literature reviews: Guidelines and examples. *Human Resource Development Review, 4*(3), 356–367.

Van Maanen, J. (1988). *Tales of the field: On writing ethnography.* Chicago: University of Chicago Press.

Van Maanen, J. (Ed). (1995). *Representation in ethnography.* Thousand Oaks, CA: Sage.

Van Manen, M. (1990). *Researching lived experience: Human science for an action sensitive pedagogy.* New York: State University of New York Press.

Vaughn, S., Schumm, J. S., & Sinagub, J. (1996). *Focus group interviews in education and psychology.* Thousand Oaks, CA: Sage.

Weitzman, E. A., & Miles, M. B. (1995). *Computer programs for qualitative data analysis: A software sourcebook.* Thousand Oaks, CA: Sage.

Wlodkowski, R. J. (1985). *Enhancing adult motivation to learn.* San Francisco: Jossey-Bass.

Wlodkowski, R. J., & Ginsberg, M. G. (1995). *Diversity and motivation: Culturally responsive teaching.* San Francisco: Jossey-Bass.

Wolcott, H. (1994). *Transforming qualitative data: Description, analysis, and interpretation.* Thousand Oaks, CA: Sage.

Wolcott, H. (1995). *The art of fieldwork.* Walnut Creek, CA: AltaMira.

Yin, R. K. (2003). *Case study research: Design and methods* (3rd ed.). Thousand Oaks, CA: Sage.

Appendices

Appendix A. Commonly Used Electronic Library Databases

ABI INFORM

Provides access to business information in more than 800 journals. Excellent source of information on management, the corporate environment, and business conditions. Consists of bibliographic entries and abstracts.

Current Contents Search ®

Provides access to tables of contents and bibliographic data from more than 7,000 of the world's leading scientific and scholarly journals and more than 2,000 books. Offers full, up-to-date journal information, as well as reprint and research addresses.

Dissertation Abstracts International

Contains bibliographic citations and abstracts of doctoral dissertations in all subject areas submitted by more than 1,000 accredited colleges and universities worldwide. Going back to 1861, this database allows access to dissertations that address topics and research problems similar to your own. Once you identify the relevant dissertations, you can order full-version copies through interlibrary loan or through the University of Michigan Microfilm library. (University Microfilm Inc, Ann Arbor, Michigan [www.umi.com]).

Education Full Text

Includes journal articles, monographs, and yearbooks related to education. There is substantial overlap with ERIC, but it does cover 40 journals not indexed in ERIC.

Emerald Management Xtra 150

This is the largest, most comprehensive collection of peer-reviewed management journals. It features access to 150 full-text journals, with reviews from the top 300 management journals, including, among others, *Cross Cultural Management, Education and Training, Development and Learning in Organizations, European Journal of Innovation Management, Handbook of Business Strategy, International Journal of Sociology and Social Policy, International Journal of Sustainability in Higher Education, Journal of Educational Administration, Journal of Health Organization and Management, Journal of Knowledge Management, Leadership and Organization Development Journal, The Learning Organization, Multicultural Education and Technology Journal, Quality Assurance in Education,* and *Strategy and Leadership.*

ERIC (Educational Resources Information Center)

Provides access to approximately 1 million abstracts of documents and journal articles related to educational research and practice. These include conference papers, master's theses, doctoral dissertations, government reports, books, book chapters, reports, and unpublished documents. Most documents published by ERIC are available in full text and can be purchased from the ERIC Document Reproduction Service using the form and procedures found in the back of *Review of Research in Education.*

(Continued)

Appendix A (Continued)

JSTOR

An archive of important scholarly journals spanning both multidisciplinary and discipline-specific collections. The Arts & Sciences Collections represent more than 600 journals in the arts, humanities, and social sciences. Because of JSTOR's archival mission, it is not a current issues database.

MUSE

The foremost collection of more than 150 peer-reviewed interdisciplinary journals from leading university presses, not-for-profit publishers, and prestigious scholarly societies. It offers comprehensive coverage of journals in the humanities and social sciences, including education.

Political Science Abstracts

Important source for political science articles published since 1976. Contains abstracts of materials from professional journals, news magazines, and books. Useful resource for charting political issues and processes and public policy worldwide.

ProQuest

A database of journal articles, in many instances providing access to full text. Besides offering current periodicals and dissertations, ProQuest also offers access to archival material, including major newspapers dating back 100 to 150 years.

PsycINFO®

Comprehensive international database covering the academic, research, and practice literature on topics in psychology and related disciplines, including education, social work, medicine, psychiatry, criminology, and organizational behavior. This database indexes more than 850 journals under 16 different categories of information. It allows you to limit your search to reviews of literature or specific types of research studies, such as case studies or experimental research, and provides a link to more recent studies that have cited the study that is presented. PsycINFO® also provides indices to journals, dissertations, book chapters, books, technical reports, and other documents from 1887 to the present, with optional access to Historic PsycINFO®, an archival file database.

PAIS International (Public Affairs Information Service)

Index to political, economic, and social issues. This database covers the public and social policy literature of business, economics, finance, law, international relations, public administration, and political science, among others. Dating from 1972 to the present, PAIS contains abstracts of journal articles, books, statistical yearbooks, conference proceedings, research reports, and government documents from all over the world.

Social Work Abstracts

Contains information on the fields of social work and human services from 1977 to the present. Provides coverage of more than 450 journals in all professional areas, including theory and practice, areas of service, and social issues. Useful for research in the areas of social sciences, public health, criminology, and education.

Social Sciences Citation Index (SSCI)

Covers about 5,700 journals that represent virtually every discipline in the social sciences. Provides access to 300 major international periodicals in the social sciences and related disciplines: anthropology, environmental sciences, law and criminology, psychology, political science, public health, sociology, urban studies, and women's studies. Like PsychInfo®, it can be used to locate articles and authors who have conducted research on a topic. You can also trace all studies since the publication of the key study that have cited the work. Using this system, you can develop a chronological list of references that document the historical evolution of an idea or study.

Sociological Abstracts

This database contains abstracts to articles in more than 2,500 journals as well as book reviews and abstracts for dissertations and books.

Provides access to the most current worldwide findings in theoretical and applied sociology, social science, and policy science. Features journal citations and abstracts, book chapters, and software review citations. This database is useful for interdisciplinary research on social science issues and for practitioners seeking sociological perspectives on various disciplines.

Wilson Social Sciences Abstracts Full Text

Contains abstracting and indexing coverage for all 513 periodicals included in Social Sciences Index, as well as the full text of more than 150 periodicals. Subjects include anthropology, criminology, psychology, public administration, and sociology.

Appendix B. Sample Conceptual Framework

Preparedness for Dissertation Process
- Very prepared
- Unprepared
- Somewhat prepared

Knowledge, Skills, Attitudes/KSA (what they think they needed)
- Knowledge of content; knowing *what* they needed to do
- Understanding the process; knowing *how* to do what they needed to do
- Need to be assertive (be resourceful; find what you need on your own)

How They Learned

Formal Learning
- Coursework
- Post-coursework seminars
- Advisors and other faculty

Informal Learning
- Dialogue with colleagues
- Researching
- Reading

Perceptions of Facilitators
- Advisor
- Other faculty
- Colleagues/classmates
- Personal attributes

Perceptions of Impediments
- Advisor
- Faculty/administration
- Rigidity of the process
- Personal and family issues
- Professional work demands
- Financial constraints
- Lack of confidence in ability

Appendix C. Overview of Purposeful Sampling Strategies

Purposeful Sampling Strategy	*Explanation*
• Typical case sampling	Individuals are selected because they represent the norm and are in no way atypical, extreme, or very unusual.
• Critical case sampling	Researcher samples those individuals who can "make a point quite dramatically" (Patton, 2002, p. 236).
• Snowball, network, or chain sampling	A few participants who possess certain characteristics are selected, and they are asked to identify and refer others who are known to have the same or similar characteristics.
• Criterion sampling	All participants must meet one or more criteria as predetermined by the researcher.
• Extreme or deviant case sampling	Individuals are selected because they represent the extremes. The researcher seeks to learn from highly unusual manifestations of the phenomenon of interest.
• Maximum variation sampling	Individuals are selected because they represent the widest possible range of the characteristics being studied. Includes "a deliberate hunt for the negative" (Miles & Huberman, 1994). Diverse variations are included to identify patterns. This strategy was first identified by Glaser and Strauss (1967) in their presentation of grounded theory.
• Homogenous sampling	In contrast to maximum variation, individuals with only similar experiences are selected.
• Stratified purposeful sampling	Sampling in this way illustrates subgroups and facilitates comparisons among them.
• Theoretical or theory-based sampling	Selection is ongoing: Sampling begins purposefully. The researcher analyzes data, and as the theoretical framework emerges, the researcher decides from whom to collect more data next. Sampling is thus an evolving process guided by emerging theory. Strategy was popularized by Glaser and Strauss (1967).
• Intensity sampling	The researcher seeks information-rich cases that manifest the phenomenon intensely, but not extremely.
• Convenience sampling	This is the least desirable sampling strategy. Tendency is to rely on availability. Can save time and effort, but is at the expense of information and credibility. Can produce "information-poor" rather than "information-rich" cases (Patton, 1990, p. 183).
• Purposeful random sampling	One of the purposeful sampling procedures mentioned above is used, followed by a randomization procedure. This strategy supposedly adds credibility to the study, although the initial sample is based on purposeful selection.

*Note 1: The sample size in qualitative research is relatively small, but consists of "information-rich" cases. In-depth interviews and immersion in a culture make a large sample size unnecessary, particularly as qualitative researchers do not seek to generalize. It is generally recommended that researchers use their judgment regarding the numbers in the sample.

*Note 2: Samples in qualitative research do not consist merely of people, but also of texts, events, cultural phenomena, and artifacts.

Appendix D. Sample Participant Demographics Matrix

Participant Code	Pseudonym	Years in Doctoral Program	Program Concentration/ Discipline	Gender	Age	Ethnicity
1:EF106C	Mollie	6	Education	F	36	Hispanic
2:EF112G	Hank	Inactive	Political Sci.	M	51	White
3:EF114G	Morris	7	Org. Psy.	M	70	White
4:EF114C	Debbie	Inactive	Art Education	F	43	White
5:EF120G	Doris	Inactive	Ed-Admin	F	47	White
6:EF202w	Anthony	5	Education	M	38	White
7:EF207C	Anne	7	Education	F	54	White
8:EF210C	B.J.	6	Teacher-Ed.	F	35	Black
9: EF213C	Angela	Inactive	Political Sci.	F	49	White
10:A102G	Jane	8	Education	F	49	Asian
11:A201C	Brad	Inactive	Political Sci.	M	46	White
12:A210C	Dexter	5	Org. Psy.	M	37	Black
13:B01G	Frank	Inactive	Org. Psy.	M	49	Hispanic
14:C103G	Sal	5	Education	M	31	Hispanic
15:C104C	Shana	8	Nursing Ed.	F	52	Black
16:C113W	Lin	7	Education	F	46	Asian
17:D01C	Carin	9	Ed-Admin.	F	47	Black
18:D05G	Fay	8	Nursing Ed.	F	39	White
19:D07w	Connie	6	Psychology	F	41	White
20:G01C	Julia	Inactive	Psychology	F	49	White
TOTAL N = 20				F = 13 (%) M = 7 (%)		White = 11 Asian = 2 Black = 4 Hispanic = 3

Appendix E. Sample Overview of Information Needed

Research Questions	Information Needed *What the Researcher Wants to Know*	Method
1. To what extent do participants feel that the coursework prepared them to conduct research and write their dissertations?	- Participants' perceptions about whether the coursework prepared them for the dissertation process.	Interview
2. What did participants perceive they needed to learn to complete their degrees?	- The kinds of knowledge, skills, and attitudes participants felt were important to carry out and write their dissertations.	Interview
3. How did participants attempt to develop what they perceived they needed to complete their dissertations?	- What activities did participants engage in to help develop the knowledge, skills and attitudes to carry out the research and write their dissertations?	Interview Critical Incident
4. What factors did participants perceive helped them complete their dissertations?	- Who and what helped them; what kinds of supports enable them to progress?	Interview Critical Incidents Focus Group
5. What factors did participants perceive impeded and/ or continues to impede their progress in working toward completing their dissertations?	- The obstacles that stood in the way of the participants; the stumbling blocks encountered.	Interview Critical Incident Focus Group

Appendix F. Sample Flowchart of Research Design.

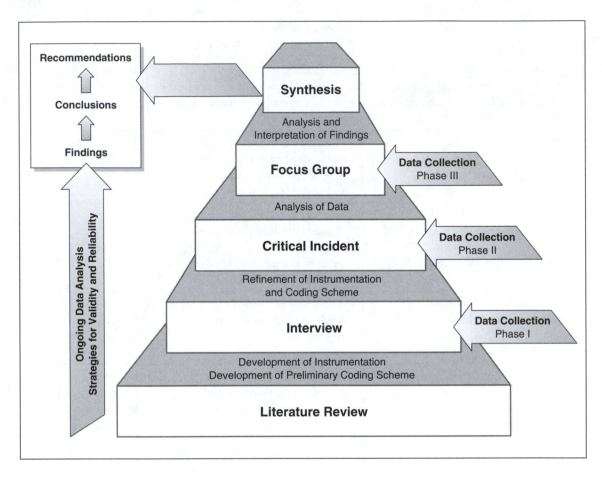

Appendix G. Qualitative Data Collection Methods*: A Summary Overview

Method	Function
Document review	*Data are collected in their natural setting *Records, documents, and artifacts provide contextual information and insights into "material culture" *Facilitates discovery of cultural nuances
Survey	*Provides demographic information *Provides contextual information *Provides perceptual information *Can include both quantitative (numerical) and qualitative (open-ended) elements
Interview	*Fosters interactivity with participants *Elicits in-depth, context-rich personal accounts, perceptions, and perspectives *Data are collected in their natural setting *Interviews can be unstructured, structured, or semistructured *Explains and describes complex interactions and processes *Facilitates discovery of nuances in culture *Notes or verbatim transcriptions are used to document the interview
Focus group	*Fosters interactivity and dialogue among participants *Describes complex interactions *Clarifies and extends findings yielded by other methods *Allows for increased richness of responses through synergy and interaction *Notes or verbatim transcriptions are used to document the interview
Observation	*Researcher observes and records behavior, but does not interact with participants *Provides data collected in their natural setting *Useful for describing complex processes and interactions *Runs the risk of observer effect and observer bias *Field notes are used to document observations
Participant observation	*Fosters face-to-face interaction with participants *Provides data collected in their natural setting *Facilitates insight into complex social and cultural nuances by allowing researcher to develop relationships with participants *Runs the risk of observer effect and the potential for the researcher to become emotionally involved *Field notes are used to document observations
Critical incidents	*Engages participants in the reflective process *Draws on the personal meaning of experience *Provides critical perceptual information
Life history	*Discovers retrospective information *Enhances participants' critical thinking, reflection, and depth of response *Encourages participants to extract meaning from their own experience *Enables participants become partners in the inquiry process

*Rather than relying on any one method, qualitative researchers typically triangulate a variety of data-collection methods.

Appendix H. Sample Interview Schedule/Protocol Based on Research Questions.

Interview Schedule

Upon completion of the coursework, to what extent did participants perceive they were prepared to conduct research and write their dissertations?

1. Think back to when your coursework was completed. You were on your own. How did you go about beginning the work that lay ahead of you?

2. When there were no more formal classes to attend and you had to begin your research, how did you know what to do and how to do it?

What did participants perceive they needed to learn to complete their dissertations? How did participants acquire the knowledge, skills, and attitudes they perceived are necessary to complete their dissertations?

3. Going into the program, what were some of the things you thought were important to know to successfully conduct and write your dissertation?

4. How did you get the information you needed?

5. After you completed the coursework, how did you know what you needed to do to conduct the research and complete the dissertation?

6. How did you go about finding out how to do what was needed?

7. Being at the point you are now, in what ways have your perceptions of what is needed to complete a dissertation changed?

8. What do you think are the important personal characteristics needed to carry out this kind of work?

9. How do these personal characteristics describe you?

10. If you were to advise someone entering a doctoral program on what they needed to do or know, what would you tell them?

What factors did participants perceive might help them to complete the dissertation?

11. Who or what would you say has been most helpful to you thus far in doing this work?

12. What else has been most helpful to you along the way?

What factors did participants perceive have impeded and/or continue to impede their progress in working toward completing their dissertation?

13. What are some of the things that you believe have stood in your way?

14. What do you think could have helped you in making more progress along the way?

Notes:

1. Research questions in bold followed by relevant and numbered interview questions.
2. Research questions are written in future tense in the proposal and in past tense in the dissertation.

Appendix I. Sample Coding Legend/Schema

1. Preparedness for Dissertation Process
   P1 Very prepared
   P2 Unprepared
   P3 Somewhat prepared

2. Knowledge, Skills, Attitudes/KSA (what they think they needed)
   KSA1 Understand the process; knowing how to do it
   KSA2 Knowledge of the content; knowing what was required
   KSA3 Assertiveness

3. How They Learned
   Formal Learning
   FORM1 Coursework
   FORM2 Post-coursework seminars
   FORM3 Advisors and other faculty
   Informal Learning
   INFORM1 Dialogue with colleagues
   INFORM2 Researching
   INFORM3 Reading

4. Perceptions of Facilitators
   FAC1 Advisor
   FAC2 Other faculty
   FAC3 Colleagues/classmates
   FAC4 Personal attributes

5. Perceptions of Impediments
   IMPED1 Adviser
   IMPED2 Faculty/Administration
   IMPED3 Rigidity of the process
   IMPED4 Personal and family issues
   IMPED5 Professional demands
   IMPED6 Financial constraints
   IMPED7 Lack of confidence in ability

Appendix J. Sample Coding Scheme Development Chart

Developmental Phases of Analytic Framework	Explanation and Description of Resulting Changes to Coding Scheme
(1) Coding scheme version 1: April 2005 After conducting the relevant literature reviews, the researcher developed an initial literature-based coding framework for the dissertation proposal.	This coding scheme, developed as part of the researcher's initial ideas about a conceptual framework, was based on Bogdan and Biklen's (1998) coding category system for organizing data. Based on this system, a simple two-level scheme was employed: a general etic level and a more specific emic level, close to the literature, but nested in the etic codes. At the outset, the original scheme includes 108 alphabetically ordered codes.
(2) Coding scheme version 2: August 2006 Based on discussions with colleagues, the researcher developed a revised conceptual framework and related coding scheme. Analytic categories directly relate to the study's five research questions.	This preliminary version of the coding scheme is a predefined approach to coding and is primarily developed from the literature review combined with personal experience. Five broad analytic categories as they relate to the study's three research questions are identified: (1a) "Preparedness"; (b) "Knowledge, skills, attitudes"; (c) "How learning occurred"; (d) "Facilitators of learning"; and (e) "Barriers to learning." The original scheme includes 34 numeric codes.
(3) Coding scheme version 3: October 2006 Descriptors are too abstract and theoretical and need to be tied more closely to what the researcher anticipated to be participants' actual responses. Based on this critique, a new coding scheme is developed, This is framed in terms of the literature in conjunction with anticipated participant responses.	An initial round of open coding yielded further ideas, and the coding scheme is refined. Some descriptors are split apart to make them more precise: Under Categories 3, 4, and 5, "advisors" and "other faculty" are added as opposed to just "advisors." Six new descriptors are added: "desire for continuous leaning," "knowledge of content," "draw on experience," "post-coursework seminars," "personal attributes," and "interest in topic." This scheme includes 39 alphanumerically ordered codes.
October 17, 2006 The researcher conducted three pilot interviews. Using coding scheme version 2, the transcript was open coded by the researcher and a doctoral candidate colleague.	The coding scheme is still cumbersome, and categories are overly detailed. Further descriptors are collapsed, and some are eliminated: In Category 1, "self-esteem" and "personal fulfillment" overlap, therefore "self-esteem" is eliminated. "Time constraints" is eliminated from Category 5 due to overlap with "personal/family issues" and "professional demands." "Promotion" and "compensation" are both eliminated from Category 1 because they both fall under "credentials." "Faith/confidence" and "realistic expectations" are eliminated from Category 2. "Trial and error" and "draw on experience" are removed from Category 3, and "faculty" and "advisors" becomes collapsed into one. The scheme now consists of 33 codes.

Developmental Phases of Analytic Framework	*Explanation and Description of Resulting Changes to Coding Scheme*
(4) Coding scheme version 4: December 2006 Based on a further round of discussions with an advisor and on emergent data from the open coding of pilot interviews, coding scheme is further refined and reduced.	The coding scheme becomes more streamlined because seven descriptors are eliminated: four from Category 3 ("informed others," "graduates," family/friends," "coursework"), one from Category 4 ("interest in topic"), and two from Category 5 ("academic requirements" and "insufficient knowledge of process"). This version includes 26 codes.
(5) Coding scheme version 4.1: February 2007 The researcher conducted three further interviews, open coded using version 4.1.	Coding grids are drawn up to plot which codes are being utilized and how often. This sheds light on which descriptors are relevant and which are redundant. Three more descriptors are deleted: "writing skills," "tolerance or perseverance," and "status/recognition." The final scheme consists of 23 alphanumeric codes (see Appendix I).
(6) Coding scheme version 5: March 2007 As interviews are read, reread, and open coded, minor modifications are made with regard to certain descriptors. This version now constitutes the final coding scheme developed for this research. In line with qualitative research, the scheme remains flexible. As the researcher proceeded to use this coding scheme, she acknowledged that as new descriptors emerged from the data, they would be added; conversely, if descriptors became superfluous or redundant, they would be omitted from the scheme.	

Appendix K. Sample Research Consent Form

University Letterhead
Department Name
PART 1: Research Description

Principal Researcher: _____

Research Title: _____

You are invited to participate in a research study that explores the Doctoral experience. Your participation in this study requires an interview during which you will be asked questions about your opinions and attitudes relative to your experience in a Doctoral program. The duration of the interview will be approximately 60 minutes. With your permission, the interview will be audio taped and transcribed, the purpose thereof being to capture and maintain an accurate record of the discussion. Your name will not be used at all. On all transcripts and data collected you will be referred to only by way of a pseudonym.

This study will be conducted by the researcher _____, a doctoral candidate at _____University. The interview will be undertaken at a time and location that is mutually suitable.

Risks and Benefits:
This research will hopefully contribute to understanding the Doctoral experience, and so the potential benefit of this study is improvement of Higher Education practice. Participation in this study carries the same amount of risk that individuals will encounter during a usual classroom activity. There is no financial remuneration for your participation in this study.

Data Storage to Protect Confidentiality:
Under no circumstances whatsoever will you be identified by name in the course of this research study, or in any publication thereof. Every effort will be made that all information provided by you will be treated as strictly confidential. All data will be coded and securely stored, and will be used for professional purposes only.

How the Results Will Be Used:
This research study is to be submitted in partial fulfillment of requirements for the degree of Doctor of Education at Teachers College, Columbia University, New York, New York. The results of this study will be published as a dissertation. In addition, information may be used for educational purposes in professional presentation(s) and/or educational publication(s).

PART 2: Participant's Rights

- I have read and discussed the research description with the researcher. I have had the opportunity to ask questions about the purposes and procedures regarding this study.
- My participation in this research is voluntary. I may refuse to participate or withdraw from participation at any time without jeopardy to future medical care, employment, student status, or other entitlements.
- The researcher may withdraw me from the research at her professional discretion.
- If, during the course of the study, significant new information that has been developed becomes available that may relate to my willingness to continue to participate, the investigator will provide this information to me.

- Any information derived from the research that personally identifies me will not be voluntarily released or disclosed without my separate consent, except as specifically required by law.
- If at any time I have any questions regarding the research or my participation, I can contact the researcher, _____ who will answer my questions. The researcher's phone number is (404) 256-4090 Ext 19. I may also contact the researcher's faculty advisor, XX, at (212) 678-3754.
- If at any time I have comments or concerns regarding the conduct of the research, or questions about my rights as a research subject, I should contact ____ University Institutional Review Board. The phone number for the IRB is (212) 678-4105. Alternatively, I can write to the IRB at _____University, 525 W. 120th Street, New York, NY, 10027, Box 151.
- I should receive a copy of the Research Description and this Participant's Rights document.
- Audio taping is part of this research. Only the principal researcher and the members of the research team will have access to written and taped materials. Please check one:

(   ) I consent to be audiotaped.
(   ) I do NOT consent to being audiotaped.

My signature means that I agree to participate in this study.

Participant's signature: _____ Date: ____/____/____

Name: (Please print)_____

Investigator's Verification of Explanation

I, _____ (Researcher), certify that I have carefully explained the purpose and nature of this research to _____ (participant's name). He/she has had the opportunity to discuss it with me in detail. I have answered all his/her questions and he/she provided the affirmative agreement (i.e., assent) to participate in this research.

Investigator's signature: _____ Date: ____/____/____

Appendix L. Sample Survey for Demographic Data

Thank you for agreeing to participate in this study! Please complete the survey below and return it in the attached self-addressed, stamped envelope.

Please note that the information collected in this questionnaire is completely confidential and will only be used for the purposes of this research study.

Demographic Data Sheet

1. My gender is: _____ Female _____ Male

2. My age is: _____ 23–30 _____ 31–40 _____ 41–50 _____ 50+

3. My race/ethnicity is:
   a. _____ White
   b. _____ African American
   c. _____ Asian
   d. _____ Hispanic
   e. _____ Native American

4. Occupation: _____

5. University/Program: _____

6. Discipline/area of research: _____

7. Years in doctoral program to date: _____

8. Your purpose in enrolling in a doctoral program:

   _____

   _____

   _____

   _____

Thank you for completing this questionnaire! Your time and participation are very much appreciated, and will contribute to a growing knowledge base on experiences surrounding a doctoral dissertation.

Appendix M. Critical Incident Instrument/Form

Critical Incident

In reflecting on the time that you have been enrolled in your doctoral program, please recall one particular occasion while working on your dissertation that you felt stymied or ill prepared:

In 1–2 short paragraphs, please describe that experience:

- What were you trying to achieve?
- What were you thinking you should/could do to move forward?
- How, if at all, did you overcome this impasse in your work?

Thanks so much!! Your perceptions are very helpful to us in trying to understand the "dissertation experience."

Appendix N. Template for Document Summary Form*

(*Adapted from Miles & Huberman, 1994, pp. 54–55)

Name or Type of Document: _____

Document No.: _____

Date Received: _____

Date of Document: _____

Event or Contact with which Document Is Associated:

_____

☐ Descriptive
☐ Evaluative
☐ Other _____

Page #	Key Words/Concepts	Comments: Relationship to Research Questions

Brief Summary of Contents:

_____

_____

Significance or Purpose of Document:

_____

_____

Is There Anything Contradictory About Document?
☐ Yes
☐ No

Salient Questions/Issues to Consider:

_____

_____

Additional Comments/Reflections/Issues:

_____

_____

_____

Appendix O. Template for Participant Summary Form*

(*Adapted from Miles & Huberman, 1994, "Contact Summary Form," pp. 52–54)

Participant Name: _____

Type of Contact: Contact Date: _____
(Check where appropriate)
                                                   Today's Date: _____

☐ Face to Face
☐ Phone
☐ Videoconference

Summary of Information for Each Research Question:

Research Question 1

Research Question 2

Research Question 3

Research Question 4

Research Question 5

Additional Information Needed:

_____

_____

Questions, Concerns, Implications, Issues Still to be Addressed:

_____

_____

Appendix P. Sample Segment of Coded Interview Transcript

Participant: FH
Date: May 12, 2006

LB: When there were no more formal classes to attend and you had to begin your research, how did you know what to do and how to do it?

FH: [The coursework helped somewhat. You might have an inkling of what a dissertation represents. But the sheer magnitude of it—it is mind-boggling really in terms of research. And nothing prepares you for that.] **FORM 1** Knowing what I know now, I probably would not have gone into it at all in the first place! (laughs).

LB: Going into the program, what were some of the things you thought were important to know to successfully conduct and write your dissertation?

FH: At the beginning, 20 years ago, I thought I knew what I needed to do. I mean, the field was a lot less technical. It seemed to me that it was a lot less structured. But even then, I wasn't really clear. [The truth is that I feel that people get engaged in dissertation work without being really absolutely clear as to what it would be taking in terms of research, in terms of the support we were going to get, in terms of the type of writing we were going to have to do, the time frame as to how long it was going to take.] **KSA 2** [I was never able to have a direct enlightened conversation. I got all the brochures, and I was trying to plan things for myself. I had to research this myself. I checked with many schools.] **INFORM 2**

LB: How did you get the information you needed?

FH: [What was most helpful to me was the Internet. It makes information so accessible. Today that's a major advantage.] **INFORM 2** [What helped me also was my single-mindedness. I relied on myself mostly. I just persevered and persevered.] **FAC 4**

LB: After you completed the coursework, how did you know what you needed to do to conduct the research and complete the dissertation?

FH: I was working at the time. And I didn't see much of my advisor, didn't hear from them at all. And I was not really very proactive in looking them up or calling them. I have to admit that. That time was very difficult because I was working and traveling and then I had a child. I had no time for my studies at all, so I abandoned it [the doctorate]. By the time I started my dissertation, I was really exhausted. Without great focus of what I was going to be doing with my degree, I lost motivation and drive.

LB: How did you go about finding out how to do what was needed?

FH: [Nobody was really clear. The really annoying thing from my perspective is that nobody is really there to give you strict guidelines. This is a very difficult process, a very lengthy one. And there are so many things that are so vague.] **IMPED 1/IMPED 2**

LB: Being at the point you are now, in what ways have your perceptions of what is needed to complete a dissertation changed?

FH: [Let me just tell you one thing. Help is absolutely not forthcoming from advisors. There is very little counseling about the work that will be required, the commitment, and the expectations from every level. And mostly, I feel the worst part of it is how you are left to figure it all out for yourself. Most of the time, the feeling is one of loneliness. Hanging out in the wind—it was overwhelming.] **IMPED 1**

LB: What do you think are the important personal characteristics needed to carry out this kind of work?

FH: Personal characteristics, um, well, I think it's perseverance and patience, and basically a very independent spirit—someone who really pretty much knows what they want to do and doesn't feel disheartened by lack of support and caring.

LB: How do these personal characteristics describe you?

FH: I'm someone who prides myself on really being able to dig out information, pursue it, and try to get some kind of sense what it would mean. [And I was very discouraged about how many phone calls I put in . . . and how many e-mails I sent to various heads of departments, and various instructors. . . . I couldn't believe how little support was forthcoming. That's the downside of the academic world. And I found that so discouraging.] **IMPED 1/IMPED 2**

LB: If you were to advise someone entering a doctoral program on what they needed to do or know, what would you tell them?

FH: You need to build up a relationship with somebody over a number of years. And you need that person to follow through with you. I would say that you have to be prepared—I mean [I think we all have a lot of good ideas about what we want to write about. But I think you have to be aware that the process is a lot more structured than one might think.] **IMPED 3**

Appendix Q. Survey Finding: Motivation for Enrollment in Doctoral Program

	Name	Extrinic Factors		Intrinsic Factors		
		Credentials	Marketability	Personal Fulfillment	Take on Challenge	Desire for Continuous Learning
1	Mollie		X	X		
2	Hank	X				
3	Morris				X	X
4	Debbie		X			X
5	Doris			X		
6	Anthony	X				
7	Anne	X				
8	B. J.	X				
9	Angela		X	X	X	
10	Jane	X				
11	Brad		X	X		
12	Dexter		X			
13	Frank		X	X	X	
14	Sal	X				
15	Shana			X		
16	Lin	X		X		
17	Carin		X			
18	Fay	X				
19	Connie	X				
20	Julia		X	X		
TOTAL	20	9 (45%)	8 (40%)	8 (40%)	3 (15%)	2 (10%)

Appendix R. Data Summary Table: Finding 1

	Name	Coursework Prepared Students For Dissertation Process		
	Name	*Prepared*	*Somewhat Prepared*	*Unprepared*
1	Mollie			X
2	Hank			X
3	Morris			X
4	Debbie			X
5	Doris			X
6	Anthony			X
7	Anne			X
8	B. J.			X
9	Angela			X
10	Jane			X
11	Brad			X
12	Dexter			X
13	Frank			X
14	Sal			X
15	Shana			X
16	Lin		X	
17	Carin			X
18	Fay			X
19	Connie			X
20	Julia			X
TOTAL			1 (5%)	19 (95%)

Appendix S. Data Summary Table: Finding 2

	Name	What They Needed To Learn		
		Knowledge About Content	Understand the Process	Need to Be Assertive
1	Mollie	X CI	X	
2	Hank	X		
3	Morris	X CI		
4	Debbie		X	
5	Doris		X	
6	Anthony	X		
7	Anne		X	
8	B. J.	X		
9	Angela	X	X	X
10	Jane		X	
11	Brad	X	X	
12	Dexter	X		
13	Frank	X	X	
14	Sal	X	X	
15	Shana	X CI		
16	Lin		X	X
17	Carin		X	
18	Fay	X		
19	Connie	X		
20	Julia		X	
TOTAL		13 (65%)	12 (60%)	2 (10%)

*CI denotes data obtained from critical incident.

Appendix T. Data Summary Table: Finding 3

	Name	*How They Learned What They Needed*					
		Dialogue With Colleagues	*Self-Directed Reading/ Research*	*Post-Coursework Seminars*	*Advisor*	*Coursework*	*Outside Expert Advice*
1	Mollie	X		X	X		
2	Hank	X					
3	Morris	X	X				
4	Debbie	X					
5	Doris	X					
6	Anthony	X	X				
7	Anne	X					
8	B. J.	X					
9	Angela		X				
10	Jane	X			X		X
11	Brad	X	X				
12	Dexter			X			
13	Frank	X					
14	Sal			X	X		
15	Shana	X					
16	Lin	X				X	
17	Carin		X				
18	Fay		X	X	X		
19	Connie	X		X			
20	Julia	X					
TOTAL	20	15 (75%)	6 (30%)	5 (25%)	4 (20%)	1 (5%)	1 (5%)

Appendix U. Data Summary Table: Finding 4

	Name	Facilitators			
		Personal Attributes	Colleagues	Other Faculty	Advisor
1	Mollie	X			
2	Hank	X			
3	Morris	X			
4	Debbie	X		X	
5	Doris	X		X	
6	Anthony	X	X		
7	Anne	X	X		
8	B. J.		X		
9	Angela	X			
10	Jane		X		X
11	Brad		X		
12	Dexter	X			
13	Frank		X		
14	Sal	X			
15	Shana	X		X	
16	Lin	X			
17	Carin	X	X		
18	Fay	X			X
19	Connie	X			
20	Julia		X		
TOTAL	20	15 (75%)	8 (40%)	3 (15%)	2 (10%)

Appendix V. Data Summary Table: Finding 5

	Name		*Impediments*					
	Name	*Advisor*	*Professional/ Work Demands*	*Personal/ Family Issues*	*Other Faculty/ Admin*	*Financial*	*Lack of Confidence in Ability*	*Rigid Process*
1	Mollie			X		X	X	
2	Hank	X	X		X CI			
3	Morris							X CI
4	Debbie	X		X				
5	Doris	X	X			X	X	X
6	Anthony	X	X					
7	Anne	X			X		X	
8	B. J.	X						
9	Angela		X	X	X			
10	Jane		X		X			
11	Brad	X		X		X		
12	Dexter	X	X					
13	Frank	X	X					
14	Sal		X			X		X
15	Shana	X					X	
16	Lin	X	X					
17	Carin	X		X		X		
18	Fay				X		X	
19	Connie	X	X					
20	Julia	X		X	X			
TOTAL		14 (70%)	10 (50%)	6 (30%)	6 (30%)	5 (25%)	5 (25%)	3 (15%)

*CI denotes data obtained from critical incident.

Appendix W. Photo of Flip Charts on Wall

Photo by Phillip Volpe. Reprinted with permission.

Appendix X. Sample Roadmap of Findings

Finding 1

The overwhelming majority (19 of 20 [95%]) of the participants indicated that the coursework did not prepare them to conduct research and write their dissertations.

- Coursework overall didn't sufficiently prepare students to conduct research.
- Disjuncture between the research courses and the practical realities of the research process.

Finding 2

All 20 participants (100%) expressed the need to know the *content* and understand the *process* involved in conducting research and writing their dissertations.

Knowledge of content (11 [55%])

- Difficulty in selection of researchable problem (3 [15%])
- Difficulty in developing and completing proposal (4 [20%])

Understanding of process (12 [60%])

- Challenges involved in conducting research at various stages of the process (5 [25%])

Need to be assertive (2 [20%])

Finding 3

The majority (15 of 20 [75%]) of participants attempted to learn what they needed to know by reaching out in dialogue with colleagues, rather than through more formal means.

- Reaching out to other students and colleagues (10 [50%])
- Self-directed learning; researching and reading (6 [30%])
- Post-coursework dissertation seminars (5 [25%])
- Advisors (4 [20%])
- Coursework (1 [5%])
- Outside expert help (1 [5%])

Finding 4

The majority of participants (15 of 20 [75%]) indicated that they relied on themselves to facilitate their progress. More than half of these same participants (8 of 20 [40%]) also said colleagues were instrumental in helping them as well.

- Personal characteristics: self-reliance, persistence, faith in self (15 [75%])
- Reached for colleagues (8 [40%])
- Help from other faculty members (3 [15%]) and advisor (2 [10%])

Finding 5

The majority of participants (14 of 20 [70%]) cited lack of good, timely, and consistent advisement as a major barrier standing in the way of their progress.

Structural impediments

- Advisement (14 [70%])
- Lack of faculty and administrative support (5 [25%])
- Rigidity of the process itself (3 [15%])

Personal impediments

- Professional work demands (10 [50%])
- Personal and family issues (6 [30%])
- Financial constraints (5 [25%])
- Lack of confidence in ability (5 [25%])

Appendix Y. Sample Interpretation Outline Tool

Analytic Category 1: Coursework did not prepare students for the dissertation process
It is conceivable that the coursework is not the primary reason that students are not progressing. Why? What are other possibilities? There are two major underlying themes:

➢ **Program design**
➢ **Why??**
  - The primary purpose of higher education is to foster critical thinking by exposing students to philosophical and theoretical concepts. The focus, therefore, is not to prepare students to be practitioners, but rather to develop students as academic scholars.
  - Aside from the research skills, writing skills are not easily taught. Coursework cannot be expected to fully prepare one for a project as intense and complex as a dissertation.
  - Unlike quantitative research, qualitative research is not as structured, systematic, and procedural. Students have no prior experience with this type of work. It is unfamiliar to them. As such, coursework cannot fully prepare students for the experience of *doing* it. Students learn by *doing*—that is, through experience.
  - Design of the doctoral program. Programs don't provide a supportive environment.
  - The academic institution in general and doctoral programs in particular have an expectation that students working on a terminal degree will most likely be highly self-directed. This expectation is often unspoken. Is this expectation realistic? The expectation among many doctoral students is that, as part of their educational experience, they will be prepared to carry out research and write a dissertation.
  - Unprepared may mean that students are *unsocialized* as to the scope and meaning of a dissertation. This is about the traditional institution of a doctoral dissertation and all the expectations that go along with it, including the political aspects involved with faculty, the university system/institutional protocol (ambiguities, nuances, rules, regulations), working with committee members (who often have differing requirements), and so on. Students often do not have a grasp of the policies and procedures involved. It is unfamiliar to them, hence the general feeling of "unpreparedness."
  - BUT: We must acknowledge that some programs do a much better job at preparing their students than others. This is not reflected in this study's sample.

➢ **Personal factors**
➢ **Why??**
  - Personal idiosynchrancies can come into play, including such things as motivation, commitment, academic ability, and other psychological and personal factors and inadequacies. It may be that some students are not sufficiently motivated to do the rigorous work, others are not confident in their own ability, and still others simply do not possess the requisite skills to conduct research and write the dissertation.
  - BUT: Some students do succeed. So what are the factors that lead to success?

Links to literature on higher education/doctoral programs, and adult learning theory (Self-directed learning; Experiential learning; Informal learning)

Analytic Category 2: *What* students needed to learn and *how* they acquired that learning
Students acknowledged that to do the dissertation they needed knowledge of both content and process. Why? Because content and process are intertwined.

What Did They Need to Know?

> ➤ **Needed content knowledge**
> ➤ **Why??**
> - It may be that during the coursework they were focused on other course demands. That is, they were not ready to learn about research because they had not yet begun really thinking about their dissertations. Therefore, the work was not yet "relevant."
> - When they did start paying attention to dissertation work, they didn't know how to go about conducting research.

> ➤ **Needed process knowledge**
> ➤ **Why??**
> - When they later embarked on dissertation work, it was completely unfamiliar. They have never carried out a project like this before and did not understand the rigor involved.
> - They were not getting the necessary support in the process.
> - They didn't have the confidence that they would get the help they needed from advisors or post-coursework seminars.
> - Motivation is dissipating. Students have spent many years at this point and, despite all good intentions, are not sufficiently motivated to get the dissertation done. Both extrinsic and intrinsic factors come into play. Which are more compelling???

Coursework seemingly wasn't preparing them adequately, so they sought knowledge elsewhere.

How Did They Get The Knowledge They Needed?

> ➤ **Largely through informal learning**
> ➤ **Why??**
> - Reliance on self. Reading and conducting literature searches. Why?
>   We draw on personal strengths when all else fails.
>   Preference to finding things out on their own. Adults want to be independent.
> - Reliance on colleagues. Why?
>   Draw on strengths of others "in the same boat" both for support and know-how.
>   Learning with colleagues is less threatening than approaching "experts."
>   Literature shows that adults tend to learn best through dialogue, reflection, and collaboration, rather than in isolation.
> - Informal learning is not surprising. Why?
>   Literature shows that adults tend to learn informally in unstructured ways.
> ➤ **Sometimes through formal learning**
> ➤ **Why??**
> - Received some help in post-coursework seminars.
> - Seminars are not always successful. Why?
>   Lack of accountability. Not enough structure, therefore lack of commitment.
>   Students not involved in planning and setting objectives, therefore disconnected.

Links to literature on adult learning as it relates to cognitive development (Knowles' Principles of Adult Learning; Informal Learning Theory) and theories of motivation (Houle, Wlodkowski).

(Continued)

Appendix Y (Continued)

Analytic Category 3: Supports and Barriers Influencing Students' Progress
In the absence of formal help, either through coursework, faculty, or advisement, they had to rely on themselves and their colleagues to try to understand and carry out their research.

Supports:

- Personal attributes. People speak about needing dedication, commitment, determination, tenacity, perseverance, and persistence
- Colleagues
  ◄ Why??

Reasons discussed in analytic Category 2.

Barriers/Impediments to Progress:

  ◄ **Advisement was seen as the biggest impediment.**
  ◄ **Why???**
- Advisor plays a critical role at all stages of the dissertation process
- Advisor is needed for guidance and support
- Students want to be able to seek advice from advisors
- Students can have unrealistic expectations of advisors
- Advisement can indeed be inadequate, thereby not meet the needs of students
- Not all advisors are committed to their students. Some might prefer the European method; that is, students should largely be independent and fend for themselves

Advisement can intentionally or unintentionally be less than suitable; that is, it can be a real impediment to students' progress.
BUT: We must acknowledge that all things are not equal; some advisors do much more to prepare their students than others, and this contrast is not reflected in this study's sample.

  ◄ **Professional work demands and personal life issues are also impediments**
  ◄ **Why??**
- Dissertation work is highly demanding.
- Dissertation work is often in conflict with life demands and other commitments.
- Most of the participants are working adults who are confronted with the challenges and demands of both work and school. Need to understand the challenges holistically within the context of adulthood.
- Look across cases: Does not appear that in this study any demographics play a significant role in explaining the findings one way or another.

The reasons that some students do not progress more quickly and that others abandon the process altogether are most likely the result of a complex set of factors and combinations of factors. In other words, it does not appear to be a function of coursework not preparing students, advisors not providing guidance, students not being able to handle the pressures of daily life, or students not being sufficiently motivated or self-directed. It is most likely due to a combination of these factors.
Link to literature on higher ducation/doctoral programs and adult learning theory.

Appendix Z. Sample Consistency Chart of Findings, Interpretations, and Conclusions

Findings	Interpretations	Conclusions
1. The overwhelming majority of participants indicated that the coursework did not prepare them to conduct research and write their dissertations.	* Coursework cannot fully prepare students for the practicalities involved in conducting research and writing a dissertation. * Doctoral programs do not provide a supportive environment. * There are unrealistic expectations on the part of programs vis-à-vis what students should be able to do. * There are unrealistic expectations on the part of students. * Personal idiosyncracies come into play.	Students who enroll in doctoral programs should not expect that coursework alone will or can fully prepare them to conduct research and write their dissertations. Completion of a dissertation is a journey the student undertakes that is content-specific and, as such, becomes a process of discovery. The primary purpose of coursework is to provide a sound theoretical foundation.
2. All 20 participants expressed the need to know the *content* and to understand the *process* involved in conducting research and writing their dissertations.	* Content and process are intertwined. * During coursework, students are not yet ready for the content knowledge. * Later, when students embark on dissertation work, they don't understand the rigorous process. * Students are unmotivated to carry out the process.	Being grounded in theory alone is insufficient. Students also need practical know-how, and they need to acquire this through more informal means. In the absence of formal preparation, students need to be open to learning informally.
3. The majority of participants attempted to learn what they needed to know by reaching out in dialogue with colleagues and others, rather than through more formal means.	* Adults learn best through dialogue, reflection, and collaboration, and so students struggling through the dissertation process seek out their colleagues. * Learning with colleagues who are in the same boat is comforting and might be less threatening than approaching "experts" to ask for advice.	Dialogue with colleagues in a similar situation can provide a source of support. Dialogue also offers the opportunity for reflection and action. Collaborative opportunities hold the potential for development of new understanding and new learning.

(Continued)

Appendix Z (Continued)

Findings	Interpretations	Conclusions
4. The majority of participants indicated that they relied on themselves to facilitate their progress. More than half of these same participants also said that colleagues were instrumental in helping them.	* Adults generally want to feel in charge. * Adults generally want to be self-reliant. * When students find themselves in a "common" situation, they tend to band together in camaraderie and are empathic toward one another. * Determination is important!!	Most adult students have a preference for directing their own learning. Progress also is largely a function of personal characteristics as well as motivation and drive.
5. The majority of participants cited lack of good, timely, and consistent advisement as a major barrier standing in the way of their progress.	* The advisement that is available does not always meet students' needs. * Students might have unrealistic expectations of their advisors. * Advisement might be intentionally or unintentionally ineffective, and may in fact be a real impediment to students' progress.	To move forward, students need support, feedback, and guidance from advisors. Timely and consistent advisement must be an integral part of the doctoral experience. The experience cannot function optimally as a solitary endeavor.

Appendix AA. Sample Abstract

Abstract

The Qualitative Dissertation Experience:
Issues and Challenges That Impact Successful Completion

Author Name

Research indicates that significant numbers of people in doctoral programs complete all the course requirements yet they do not go on to produce the dissertation. This qualitative case study was designed to explore with a sample of doctoral candidates their perceptions of why they have not managed to complete their dissertations. The rationale for this study emanates from the researcher's desire to uncover ways to encourage and help students complete their dissertations. It was the writers' assumption that increased understanding of the research process and development of the skills needed to conduct research and write a dissertation would reduce the numbers of ABDs and increase the potential for greater numbers of students to attain a doctoral degree.

The purposefully selected sample was composed of 20 doctoral candidates who were drawn from a range of doctoral programs at eight universities across the United States. The primary data-collection method was in-depth interviews. Supportive methods included survey, critical incidents, and a focus group. The data were coded and organized according to the research questions. Analysis and interpretation of findings were organized by way of three analytic categories that were based on the study's conceptual framework: (a) relationship between coursework and students' ability to complete the dissertation, (b) perceptions of *what* students needed to learn and *how* they acquired the learning they needed, and (c) supports and barriers influencing students' progress.

This research revealed that coursework often does not prepare students to conduct research and write their dissertations. Therefore, students attempt to learn what they need to know by being self-reliant and by reaching out in dialogue with colleagues, rather than through more formal means. The lack of good, timely, and consistent advisement is experienced as a major barrier standing in the way of students' progress.

Recommendations are offered for doctoral program administrators and faculty, current and prospective doctoral students, and for further research possibilities. Given that there are multiple factors that affect attrition rates and acknowledging that these vary across universities, the recommendations put forth should be considered for their appropriateness on an individual basis.

Word count: 342 (Permissible is 350)

(Note: Typing to be double spaced)

Appendix BB. Sample Table of Contents

Table of Contents

Abstract

Dedication

Acknowledgments

CHAPTER I: INTRODUCTION
    Overview of Context
    Problem Statement
    Statement of Purpose and Research Questions
    Research Approach
    Researcher's Perspectives
    Researcher's Assumptions
    Rationale and Significance
    Definition of Key Terminology

CHAPTER II: LITERATURE REVIEW
    Overview and Organization
    Section I: Higher Education
        Introduction
        Research on Doctoral Programs
        Synthesis: Research Implications
    Section II: Adult Learning Theory
        Introduction
        Self-Directed Learning
        Experiential Learning
        Informal Learning
        Synthesis: Research Implications
    Chapter Summary and Discussion
        Conceptual Framework

CHAPTER III: METHODOLOGY
    Introduction
    Rationale for Research Approach
        Rationale for Qualitative Research Design
        Rationale for Case Study Methodology
    Sample and Population
    Information Needed
    Overview of Methodology
        Pre-Data Collection: Literature Review
        Data-Collection Phase I: Survey
        Data-Collection Phase II: Interview
        Data-Collection Phase III: Critical Incident
    Methods and Procedures for Data Analysis and Synthesis
        Overview
        Analytic Approach
        Synthesis
    Issues of Trustworthiness

Author Index

Subject Index

Early Praise for **Completing Your Qualitative Dissertation**

"Bloomberg and Volpe wisely, caringly, and thoughtfully share their hard-earned experience and the experiences of many doctoral students' journeys from diverse universities, which are profound. Their wisdom is offered in an easy-to-understand fashion and provides practical advice for doctoral students as they move forward in each and every step of their dissertation journeys. They speak eloquently to broad and intricate principles and nuances of qualitative research and to how to work with qualitative data. This is extremely valuable book and I suggest that you use it in your courses as you work to support your students—and your teaching. I will use it in mine. It is a gift!"

—Dr. Ellie Drago-Severson, *Teachers College, Columbia University*

* * * * * * * * *

"Working in the post-course limbo that is the dissertation stage is the hardest part of the life of a graduate student. Drawing on the experiences of doctoral students across the United States, Linda Dale Bloomberg and Marie Volpe aim to provide a practical and accessible guide to dealing with the obstacles and pitfalls that confront researchers as they struggle with writing a qualitative dissertation."

—Dr. Stephen D. Brookfield, *University of St. Thomas, Minneapolis/St. Paul*

* * * * * * * * * * * *

"Bloomberg and Volpe have written a refreshingly pragmatic, must-read text that is geared toward getting doctoral students back on the fast track to completing their qualitative dissertations. They expertly unveil the shroud of mysticism that surrounds the process of writing a qualitative dissertation by writing in a succinct, straightforward manner, providing concrete examples, and offering ample practical advice and hope. The ideas presented are extraordinarily clear and simple, yet comprehensive in breadth and profound in depth—precisely what's needed to complete a qualitative dissertation."

—Dr. Julia Sloan, *Sloan International Consulting,*
author of *Learning to Think Strategically*

* * * * * * * * *

"The dissertation study can seem, to many people, like the longest, loneliest, and most difficult open book exam that they will ever take. Bloomberg and Volpe give not just a clear roadmap, but a personal account of the journey—both of the research task and of the interpersonal and political processes that must be navigated to complete it. What I like best is that they do not stop with the dissertation document, but help the student think beyond the study to the publications and potential research streams that it may launch. This then is really a mentoring guide for new scholars, not just a great resource for students writing a dissertation."

—Dr. Karen E. Watkins, *College of Education, University of Georgia*

* * * * * * * * * *

"Bloomberg and Volpe's *Completing Your Qualitative Dissertation: A Roadmap From Beginning to End*, is a must read for students committed to the wonderful and rewarding journey that transforms an idea requiring passionate research, into a dissertation that merits scholarly and confident completion. This work is an essential resource, and in it are meaningful lessons for all students serious about qualitative research."

—Dr. John M. Carfora, *Office of the Dean of the Faculty, Amherst College*

* * * * * * * * * *

"This book does so much to de-mystify both the process of conducting qualitative research as well as writing a dissertation. Not only do I wish the book had been available when I was a student, but I wish all of my advisees had been able to have such a rich resource. This book will definitely be required reading and reference for my future students!"

—Dr. Barbara A. Macaulay, *UmassOnline, University of Massachusetts*

* * * * * * * * * * * * * * * *

"The authors display a truly impressive understanding of qualitative dissertation writing as *students* experience the process. There are a number of good books available on the topic of dissertation writing, but this one stands out because it looks at the dissertation writing process so much through students' eyes. It also is especially strong in being suitable as a *teaching* text, as I mentioned earlier. Just as the authors have consistently approached dissertation writing through the lens of student needs, they have done an outstanding job of conceptualizing how to *teach* dissertation writing through this book. I thoroughly enjoyed reading the manuscript and fully expect to use it when it becomes available. Indeed, I wish dearly that I could use it when I teach my dissertation course next quarter."

—Alan Hirvela, *Ohio State University*